anthology for a new era
edited by stephen hayward
design by barnbrook

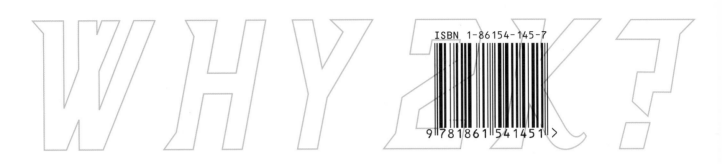

WHY 2K?

ISBN 1-86154-145-7

9 781861 541451 >

1977   1978   1979   1980   1981   1982   1983   1984   1985   1986 1987 1988 1989 1990 1991

STEVE AYLETT / PAUL BAI...
BAYLEY / MARGARET BUSB...
CHATWIN / NIK COHN / NIC...
CRAWFORD / RICHAR...
DOUGLAS / CAROL ANN DUFF...
GRIGSON / ROBERT HARRI...
HOBSBAWM / KAZUO ISHIGU...
JARMAN / VICTOR KIERNAN...
LEFANU / RACHEL LICHTENS...
MEDAWAR / TIMOTHY MO / G...
POWELL / MICHELE ROBERTS...
SAMUEL / MATT SEATO...
SPENCER / CAROLINE SUL...

LEY/J. G. BALLARD/JOHN
Y/SIMON CALLOW/BRUCE
HOLAS CRANE/MICHAEL
D DAWKINS/NORMAN
Y/GERMAINE GREER/JANE
S/SEAMUS HEANEY/ERIC
RO/C. L. R. JAMES/DEREK
/HANIF KUREISHI/SARAH
TEIN/DAVID MARSH/PETER
EORGE ORWELL/ANTHONY
/CLAUDIA RODEN/RAPHAEL
N/LORE SEGAL/COLIN
LIVAN/VIRGINIA WOOLF

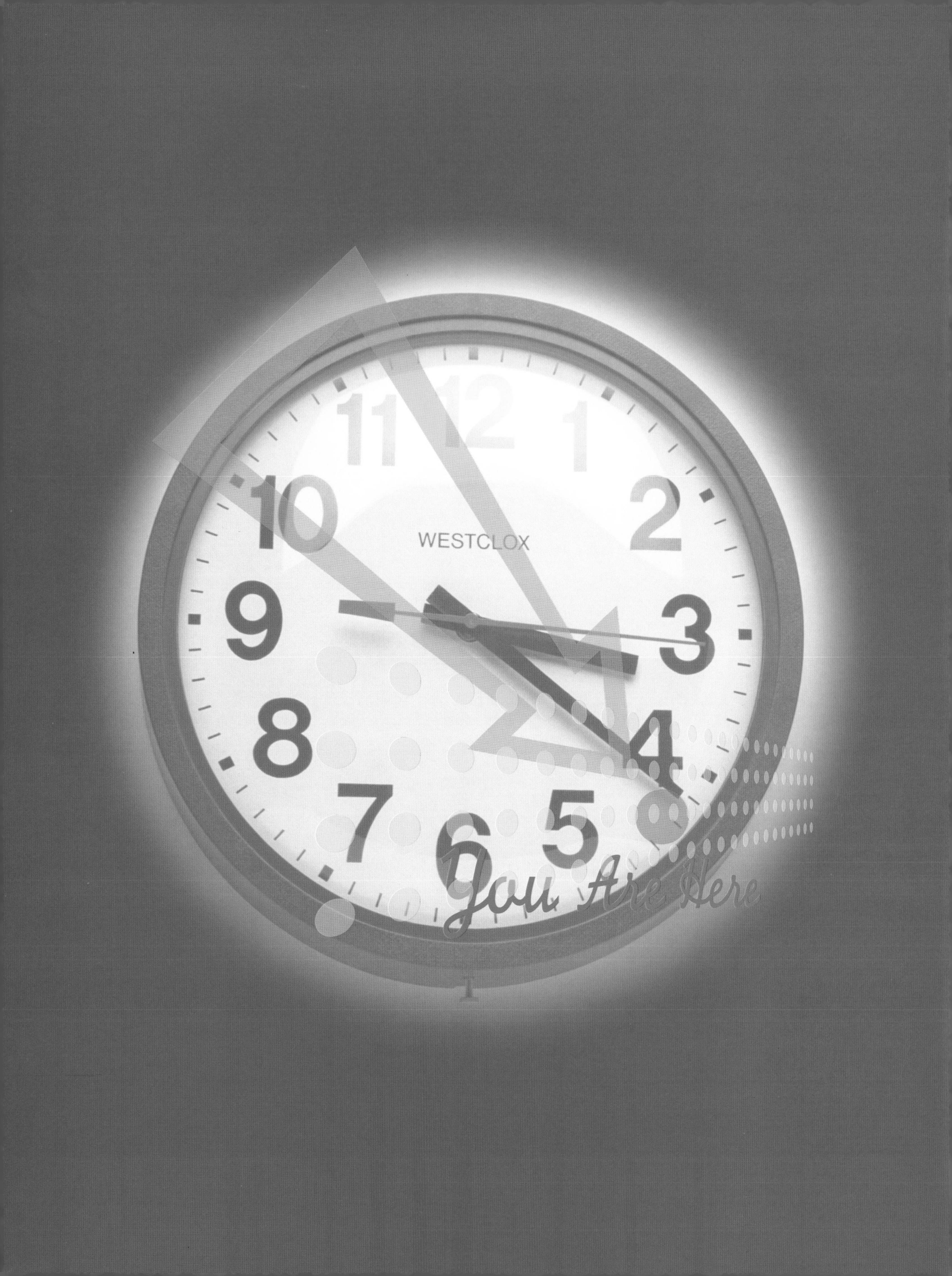
WESTCLOX
You Are Here

You Are Here

You Are Here

You Are Here

You Are Here

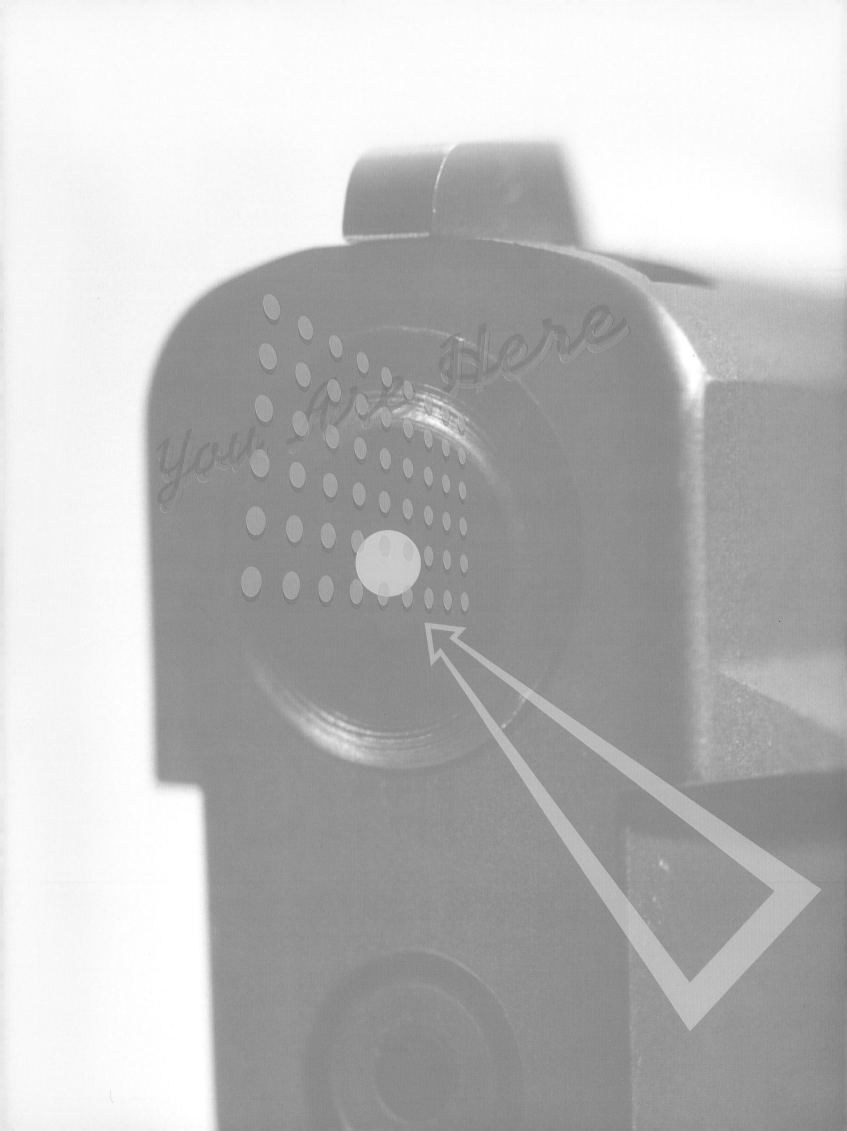

You Are Here

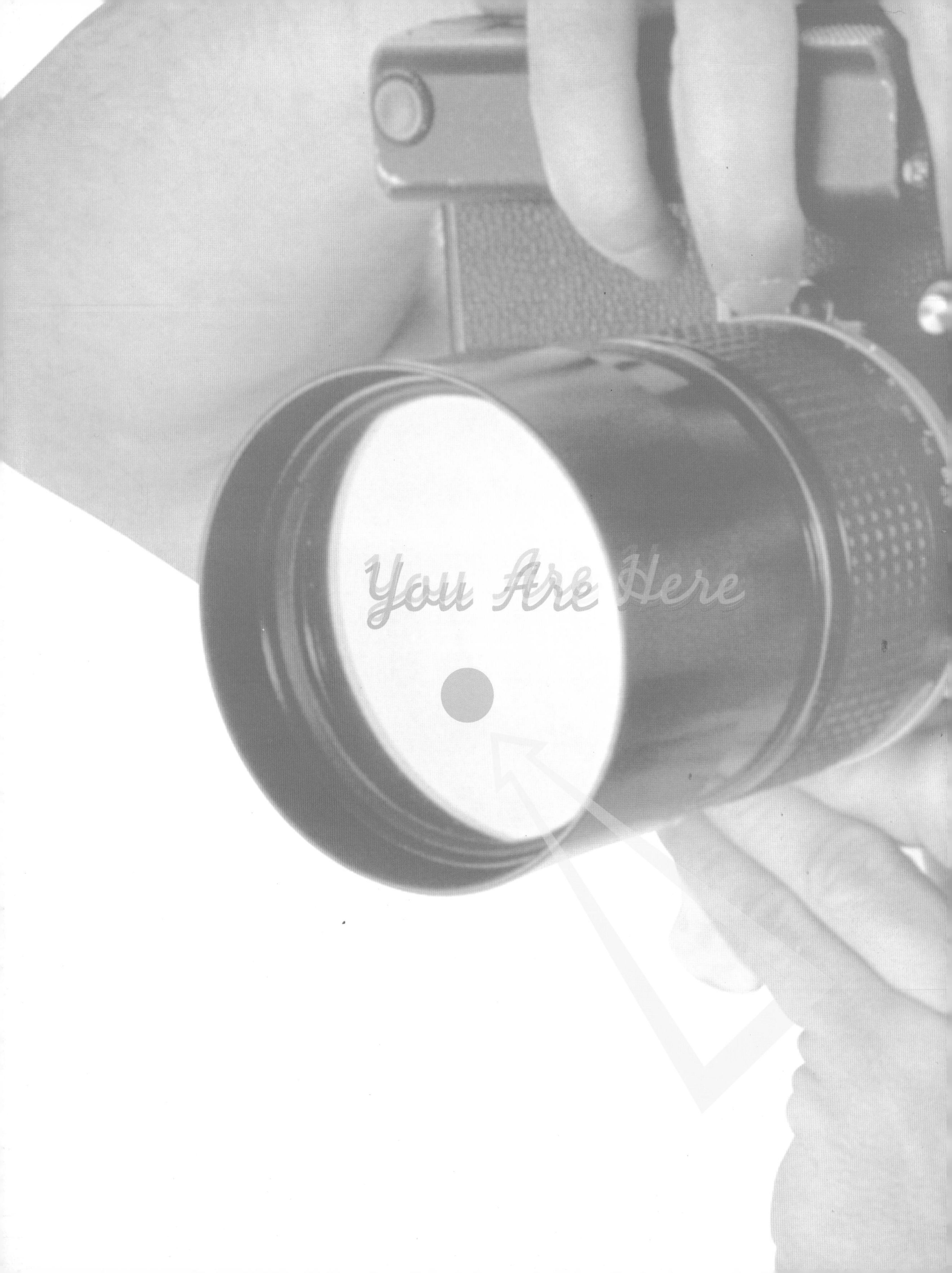
You Are Here

You Are Here

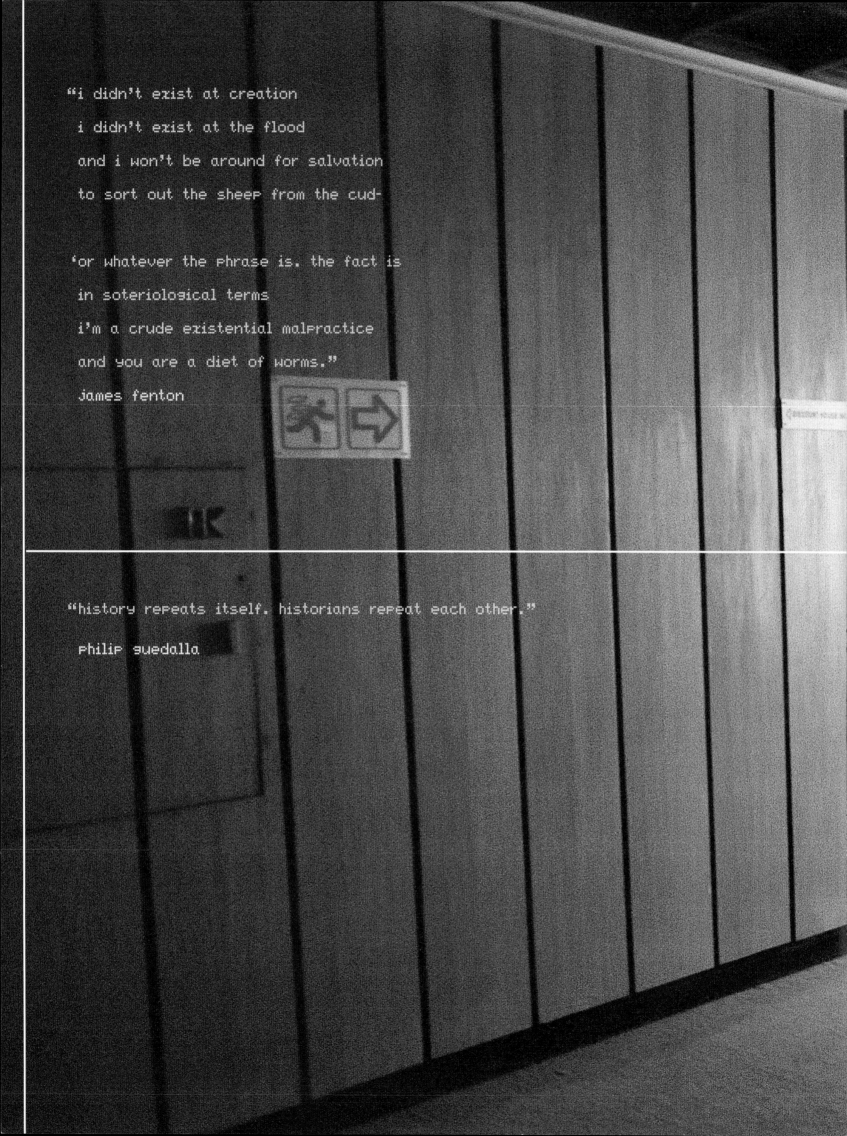

"i didn't exist at creation

i didn't exist at the flood

and i won't be around for salvation

to sort out the sheep from the cud-

'or whatever the phrase is. the fact is

in soteriological terms

i'm a crude existential malpractice

and you are a diet of worms."

james fenton

"history repeats itself. historians repeat each other."

philip guedalla

on the move?

ERIC HOBSBAWM
Overture

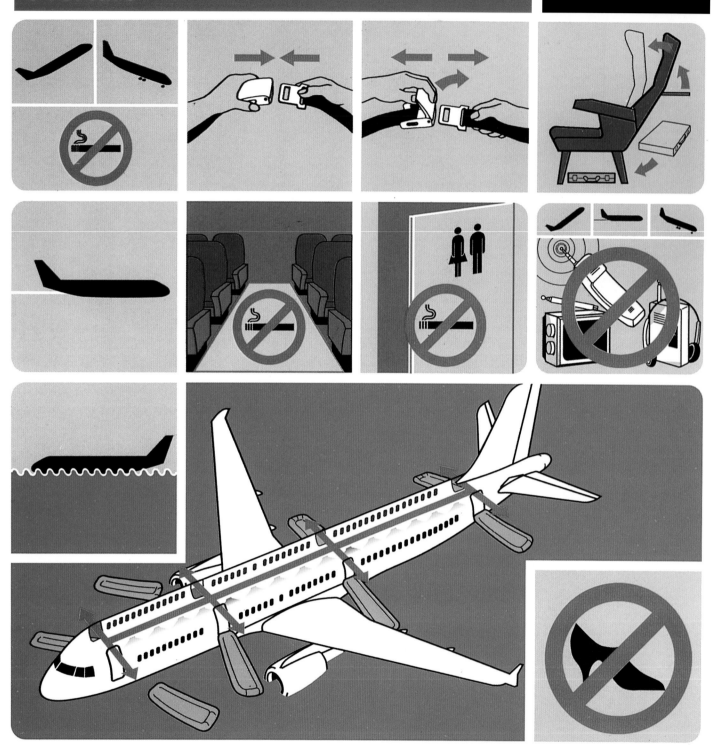

In the summer of 1913 a young lady graduated from secondary school in Vienna, capital of the empire of Austria-Hungary. This was still a fairly unusual achievement for girls in central Europe. ↗

To celebrate the occasion, her parents decided to offer her a journey abroad,

and since it was unthinkable that a respectable young woman of eighteen should be exposed to danger and temptation alone, they looked for a suitable relative. Fortunately, among the various interrelated families which had advanced westwards to prosperity and education from various small towns in Poland and Hungary during the past generations, there was one which had done unusually well. Uncle Albert had built up a chain of stores in the Levant — Constantinople, Smyrna, Aleppo, Alexandria. In the early twentieth century there was plenty of business to be done in the Ottoman Empire and the Middle East, and Austria had long been central Europe's business window on the orient.

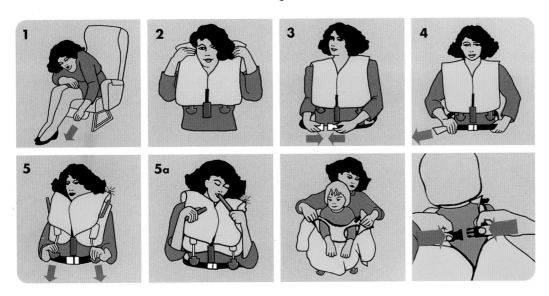

Egypt was both a living museum, suitable for cultural self-improvement, and a sophisticated community of the cosmopolitan European middle class, with whom communication was easily possible by means of the French language, which the young lady and her sisters had perfected at a boarding establishment in the neighbourhood of Brussels. It also, of course, contained the Arabs. Uncle Albert was happy to welcome his young relative, who travelled to Egypt on a steamer of the Lloyd Triestino, from Trieste, which was then the chief port of the Habsburg Empire and also, as it happened, the place of residence of James Joyce. The young lady was the present author's future mother.

Some years earlier a young man had also travelled to Egypt, but from London.

Take-off, Landing and during Surface Movement

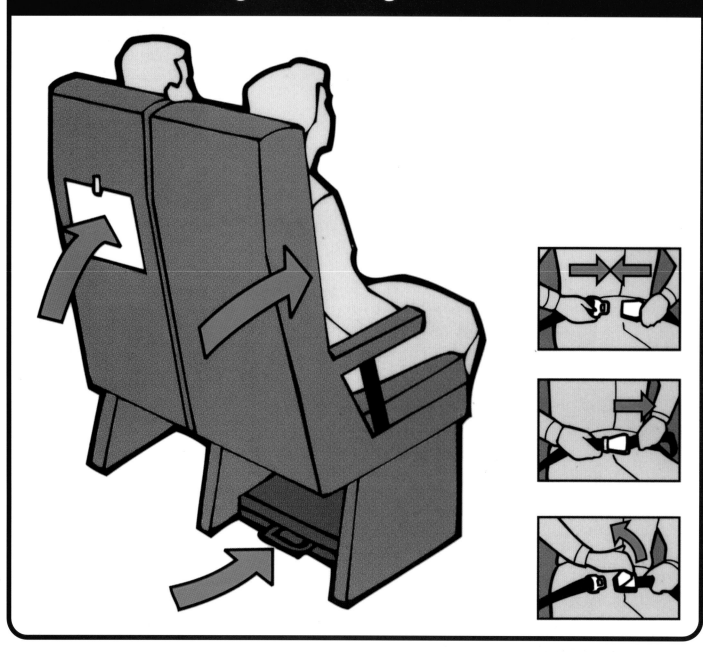

Emergency Oxygen

1 **2** **3** **4**

His family background was considerably more modest.

His father, who had migrated to Britain from Russian Poland in the 1870s, was a cabinet-maker by trade, who earned an insecure living in East London and Manchester, bringing up a daughter of his first marriage and eight children of the second, most of them already born in England, as best he could.

Except for one son, none of them was gifted for business or drawn to it. Only one of the youngest had the chance to acquire much schooling, becoming a mining engineer in South America, which was then an informal part of the British Empire. All, however, were passionate in the pursuit of English language and culture, and anglicized themselves with enthusiasm. One became an actor, another carried on the family trade, one became a primary school teacher, two others joined the expanding public services in the form of the Post Office. As it happened Britain had recently (1882) occupied Egypt, and so one brother found himself representing a small part of the British Empire, namely the Egyptian Post and Telegraph Service, in the Nile delta. He suggested that Egypt would suit yet another of his brothers, whose main qualification for making his way through life would have served him excellently if he had not actually had to earn a living: he was intelligent, agreeable, musical and a fine all-round sportsman as well as a lightweight boxer of championship standard. In fact, he was exactly the sort of Englishman who would find and hold a post in a shipping office far more easily in 'the colonies' than anywhere else.

That young man was the author's future father, who thus met his future wife where the economics and politics of the Age of Empire, not to mention its social history, brought them together – presumably at the Sporting Club on the outskirts of Alexandria,

near which they would establish their first home. It is extremely improbable that such an encounter would have happened in such a place, or would have led to marriage between two such people, in any period of history earlier than the latter part of the nineteenth century.

> What was it that so linked my Aunt Judith with cricket as I, a colonial, experienced it? The answer is in one word: Puritanism; more specifically, restraint, and restraint in a personal sense.
>
> C.L.R. James, Old School-Tie

But that restraint, did we learn it only on the cricket field, in *The Captain* and the *Boy's Own Paper*, in the pervading influence of the university men who taught me, as I once believed? I don't think so. I absorbed it from Judith and from my mother — it was in essence the same code — and I was learning it very early from my *Vanity Fair*. In recent years, as I have re-read Thackeray, I see the things which I did not note in the early days. I took them for granted and they were therefore all the more effective. I used to read and re-read and repeat the famous passage on Waterloo which ended: 'No more firing was heard at Brussels — the pursuit rolled miles away. Darkness came down on the field and city: and Amelia was praying for George, who was lying on his face, dead, with a bullet through his heart.'

I can remember the violent shock which that gave me. To my childhood imaginings George Osborne was the hero, here he was killed and the book I could see had still much more than half to go. I laughed without satiety at Thackeray's constant jokes and sneers and gibes at the aristocracy and at people in high places. Thackeray, not Marx, bears the heaviest responsibility for me.

But the things I did not notice and took for granted were more enduring: the British reticence, the British self-discipline, the stiff lips, upper and lower. When Major Dobbin returns from India, and he and Amelia greet each other, Thackeray asks: Why did Dobbin not speak? Not only Dobbin, it is Thackeray who does not speak. He shies away from the big scene when Rawdon Crawley returns and finds Becky entertaining Lord Steyne. George Osborne writes a cold, stiff letter to his estranged father before going into battle, but he places a kiss on the envelope which Thackeray notes that his father did not see. Rawdon Crawley (whom I have always liked) chokes when he tries to tell Lady Jane how grateful he is for her kindness, he chokes when he discusses with Macmurdo the arrangements for the duel. Rawdon is a semi-illiterate and Jos Sedley is little better. But how much different is the erudite Major Dobbin? His life is one long repression of speech except when he speaks for others.

In Pendennis it is the same. George Warrington returns from Europe and he and Arthur exchange the most casual of greetings. Two Frenchmen, Thackeray says, would have embraced and kissed. George's mind is full of the great things he has seen, he will talk of them at odd times later. When Warrington is grinding out the story of his disastrous early marriage Laura begins to stretch out her hand to him, but restrains herself and manages it later only by a great effort. Henry Esmond, that supreme embodiment of the stiff upper lip, finally unlooses his tongue only when a kingdom has been lost by the lasciviousness of the young King. 'I lay this at your feet and stamp upon it: I draw this sword, and break it and deny you: and had you completed the wrong you had designed us, by heaven I would have driven it through your heart, and no more pardoned you than your father pardoned Monmouth. Frank will do the same, won't you, cousin?'

The last sentence takes us immediately back to normal. This is not the aristocracy of the early eighteenth century. It is the solid British middle class, Puritanism incarnate, of the middle of the nineteenth. If Judith had been a literary person that is the way she would have spoken. The West Indian masses did not care a damn about this. They shouted and stamped and yelled and expressed themselves fully in anger and joy then, as they do to this day, whether they are in Bridgetown or Birmingham. But they knew the code as it applied to sport, they expected us, the educated, the college boys, to maintain it; and if any English touring team or any member of it fell short they were merciless in their condemnation and shook their heads over it for years afterwards. Not only the English masters, but Englishmen in their relation to games in the colonies held tightly to the code as example and as a mark of differentiation.

I was an actor on a stage in which the parts were set in advance. I not only took it to an extreme, I seemed to have been made by nature for nothing else. There were others around me who did not go as far and as completely as I did. There was another cultural current in the island, French and Spanish, which shaped other characters. I have heard from acute observers that in Barbados, an island which has known no other strain but British, the code was unadulterated and even more severe. In his book Cricket Punch Frank Worrell tells that his being suspected of conceit as a youthful cricket prodigy made his life so miserable that he ran away from Barbados as soon as he could. When Worrell played for Barbados as a schoolboy he had to go to school every morning of the match and leave only an hour before play. We were not quite as extreme in Trinidad, but that was the atmosphere in which I grew and made my choices. Read the books of Worrell and Walcott, middle-class boys of secondary education, and see how native to them is the code. In an article welcoming the West Indies team of 1957 E.W. Swanton has written in the Daily Telegraph that in the West Indies the cricket ethic has shaped not only the cricketers but social life as a whole. It is an understatement. There is a whole generation of us, and perhaps two generations, who have been formed by it not only in social attitudes but in our most intimate personal lives, in fact there more than anywhere else. The social attitudes we could to some degree alter if we wished. For the inner self the die was cast. But that is not my theme except incidentally. The coming West Indies novelists will show the clash between the native temperament and environment, and this doctrine from a sterner clime.

The depth psychologists may demur. I can help them. Long before I had begun my immersion into Vanity Fair, when I was so small that I had to be taken to school, I would refuse to leave the school grounds with the older child who brought me in the morning. I would fight and resist in order to watch the big boys playing cricket, and I would do this until my grandmother came for me and dragged me home protesting. I was once knocked down by a hard on-drive, my ear bled for a day or two and I carefully hid it by exemplary and voluntary washings. Later, when reading elementary English history books, I became resentful of the fact that the English always won all, or nearly all, of the battles and read every new history book I could find, searching out and noting the battles they had lost. I would not deny that early influences I could know nothing about had cast me in a certain mould or even that I was born with certain characteristics. That could be. What interests me, and is, I think, of general interest, is that as far back as I can trace my consciousness the original found itself and came to maturity within a system that was the result of centuries of development in another land, was transplanted as a hot-house flower is transplanted and bore some strange fruit.

CARROTS
JANE GRIGSON

WHEN YOU ARE TURNING OVER A BOX OF CARROTS IN THE WINTER, OR BUYING A COLLECTION OF POT HERBS FOR STEW OR STOCK,

it is difficult to realize that carrots were once as exotic as artichokes or Chinese leaf or avocados seemed in the 1960s. Ladies of the Stuart court pinned the young feathery plumage of young carrots to their heads and on their splendid hats. The leaves drooped down from exquisite brooches on sleeves, instead of the more usual feathers. I had always thought that the growing of carrot tops in a small dish of water was part of the nursery curriculum of my lifetime. Here is the famous garden designer J.C. Loudun most solemnly recommending the idea in his enormous and serious *Encyclopaedia of Gardening* of 1827, as 'an elegant chimney ornament' for winter, 'Young and delicate leaves unfold themselves, forming a radiated tuft, of a very handsome appearance, and heightened by contrast with the season of the year.' One may imagine the chimney pieces of grand houses or *cottages ornées*, sprouting with carrot tops set on pretty New Hall saucers.

WHY SO MUCH ENTHUSIASM FOR SO ANTIQUE A VEGETABLE?

Carrots were found in the excavations of Swiss lake villages at Robenhausen. They were eaten, without great enthusiasm, by the Romans, who did not even think they were good for the bowels. Carrots were not, it seems, forced down the infant Nero with the purpose of making his hair curl, or giving him cat's eyes to see in the dark. Perhaps he would have grown up more satisfactorily under such nannyish attentions. Though to be fair to the Romans, they at least dignified vegetables and plants with more serious virtues than nannies were accustomed to do.

THE THING WAS THAT THESE EARLY CARROTS WERE NOT THE BRIGHT ORANGE, EVEN RED ONES WE EAT TODAY.

Ours have come from a purple carrot grown first in Afghanistan at the beginning of the seventh century AD. Seeds of this purple carrot and a yellow mutant came with the Moors to Western Europe, along the coast of North Africa. Like spinach and aubergines, they spread from Spain into Holland, France and finally England. The Dutch seem to have produced the modern bright orange carrot in the Middle Ages. About 1390 they were still strange to many of the French and in particular to the young girl who married the Goodman of Paris: he wrote a book for her on running the house and looking after him (everything from dealing with fleas, to how to welcome him home - slippers by the fire and a welcoming bed in every sense of the word). An important part was the cookery. He has plenty to say about vegetables, but there is only one that he has to explain to her, 'Carrots are red roots sold by the handful in the markets: in each bunch there is a white one.' Nowadays we have long slender carrots, shorter stumpy carrots, even round carrots like ping-pong balls, but to be successful they must be as bright a colour as possible.

AS FAR AS EUROPE IS CONCERNED, CARROTS BECAME A COMMON STANDBY IN THE LAST CENTURY.

Vichy apart, where carrots were once eaten daily in many hotels as part of the cure (for overloaded digestions), we do not seem to have relied on them medicinally. The gentlemen of Teheran in the 1870s took carrots stewed with sugar as an aphrodisiac, to increase both the quality and the quantity of sperm; they were taken for dropsy, too, and if cooked and pickled in vinegar, they were said to reduce a swollen spleen (this comes closer to Vichy). For the wealthy of the Belle Epoque in Paris, oysters and caviare and champagne were regarded as more helpful in matters of love; carrots belonged to bourgeois cookery and the penitential weeks at Vichy.

NONETHELESS COOKS IN FRANCE, ITALY AND ENGLAND WERE PRODUCING EXCELLENT SWEET CARROT CAKES AND TARTS,

in particular an angel's hair charlotte, that would have delighted the weariest Persian with its rich beauty. A pity we have dropped such recipes from our general European repertoire. The nearest we come to such things here is at Christmastime, when shredded carrots are sometimes substituted – for economy – for part of the expensive quantity of dried fruit.

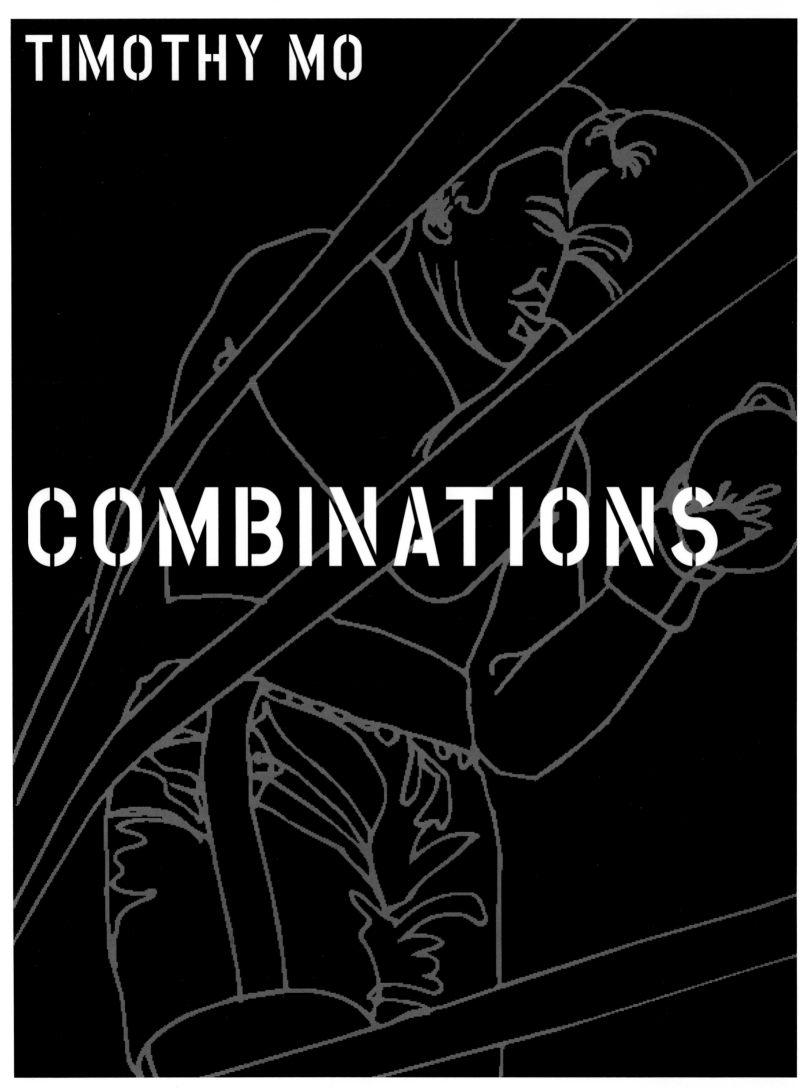

TIMOTHY MO

COMBINATIONS

FOLLOWING THE SENSIBLE PRECEPT OF DR GOEBBELS, WHEN I HEAR THE WORD

'CULTURE'

I REACH FOR MY ESKRIMA STAVES. FROM CHILDHOOD, MY ASSOCIATION OF RACE, OF THE CLASH OF INIMICAL CIVILISATIONS, HAS BEEN WITH THE SEDUCTIVE BECKONINGS OF RIVAL SYSTEMS OF HAND-TO-HAND VIOLENCE THAT WERE AS TECHNICALLY INGENIOUS AS THEY WERE PHILOSOPHICALLY INCOMPATIBLE.

I WAS BORN IN HONG KONG IN 1950 ON RIZAL DAY TO A TWENTY-EIGHT-YEAR-OLD CANTONESE LAWYER AND A TWENTY-TWO-YEAR-OLD YORKSHIRE/WELSHWOMAN WITH FAMILY ORIGINS IN RURAL LABOUR AND DOMESTIC SERVICE (MY GRANDMOTHER SHINING TABLES FOR THE MARQUIS OF ANGLESEY AT AGE TWELVE).

The Chinese side could point to a military mandarin in the pedigree and gold ingots stashed in the chimney. In other words, it was a union where the woman had clearly married beneath herself. The Peak Residence Ordinance, restricting the mist-shrouded heights of the Victoria Peak and Mount Austin (resolutely unmetric and imperial at 2,175ft) to Whites, had been repealed but four years previously. Pug marks of lost tigers could still be seen in the New Territories on paddy that is now the site of light industrial satellite towns, while Old China Hands spoke of lunch as 'tiffin' and, with a strange affection, of 'Camp' - internment under sadistic Korean and Japanese guards on (Lord) Stanley Peninsula. Sikh guards with shotguns protected the already unassailable 15ft high counters of the traditional South China pawnshops of the Western District (our 'Bazaar'), Sikh Bren-gun teams and Vickers crews having won a reputation for suicidal valour in December 1941 in contrast to the prejudiced local perception of the resistance offered by the Middlesex Regiment and the Winnipeg Grenadiers. Similarly, Cantonese bank-guards were perceived by their compatriots as being so cowardly they couldn't be trusted even to discharge their firearms in the air before fleeing from Triad attackers, whereas a pair of turbaned, **tulwa**-wielding temple-guards had made mincemeat of a horde of secret-society robbers in pre-war days. Chinese loan-sharks backed these racial hunches with their capital, or it might be the other way round. Of course, the disadvantage of the **mo lo cha** ('no morals people') was that they got your maid pregnant and spat red juice all over the place. Nowadays, Gurkhas from the battalions disbanded under post-imperial defence budgets supply an equally formidable but unarmed private security corps for the car-parks owned by Jardine Matheson, the quondam opium traders.

But it was Billy Tingle and Robert Louis Stevenson, not the **mo lo cha**, who were my first preceptors in the unarcane but noble arts of Western self-defence. This was the heyday of 1950s Man who put Brylcream or Vaseline on his hair at a time when only two brands of cigarette were available in the Crown Colony, Camel and Lucky Strike. My stepfather, ex-Indian Navy, ex-BOAC, ex-Ben Line, thought I ought to know 'how to look after myself'. The word 'manly' was mentioned without contemporary embarrassment, but not the likely circumstance that I might have occasion to punch a greater number of noses on my way through an English school than a blue-eyed boy with less ambiguous cheekbones.

Billy Tingle was an Australian but, naturally, more English than the English. Mr Tingle was no mere cricket coach or boxing instructor: he was character-builder extraordinary by appointment to the children of the expatriate gentry. And what a name, with its overtones of the TV school comedy **Whacko!** and that other Billy, Bunter. He didn't look unlike a spry, weight-trained, cross-countried version of the Owl of the Remove, down to his wire-frame spectacles. At the time I was enrolled in Tingle's

Athletic Institute at the age of seven, I was slightly shorter than him and by the time I left, pushing ten, I could look him straight in the eye, so I deduce he must have been about 4ft 11ins. Mr Tingle had been flyweight champion of the Queensland goldfields in the early years of the century but his values were pure Victoriana. Recently, I came across a yellowing photograph of us Tingle boys in our red and white caps, sitting glumly before a placard emblazoned TRUTH, LOYALTY, DILIGENCE. I can still hear BT's gravelly voice as he led us in the Institute oath: 'I will conduct myself like a sportsman and a gentleman at all times. I will not abuse my knowledge but use it to protect women and the defenceless. I will respect my opponent and not take unfair advantage of him.'

This was the boxing preamble. Cricket vows were unnecessary as enshrined in the game itself 'keeping a straight bat in life', 'not cricket, old boy'. Mr Tingle's cricket I dreaded: both boring and scary, the ball hard and reminiscent of sutured eyebrows.

But right from the start flurries of fists held no terrors for me. I had an affinity for the gloves, dank with the clammy hands of previous users and prickly with horse-hair as they were. It does have to be said that Mr Tingle's method of teaching boxing was hopelessly outmoded even in 1956. We stood up like guardsmen and were drilled by numbers: one, left lead to the head, two left lead to the body, three double left lead to head, four (you guessed it), double left lead to the body, and so on. That was the Tingle offence in all its rectilinear classicism. Defence consisted of: one, block, two, parry, three (distinctly as a last resort), duck. We all ended up with the same Corinthian style as Mr Tingle, probably not dissimilar to that of the great eighteenth-century Jewish champion, Daniel Mendoza. Some three decades previously Gene Tunney and Joe Louis had developed modern boxing but Mr Tingle reserved the same scorn for the up-jab, the left hook, combination punching, and a bob-and-weave defence as admirals of the battleship era had for the aircraft carrier. In its way it was a splendid disdain.

However, the spirit of Western boxing could not be denied. Unlike classical Asian systems of unarmed combat, from earliest days pugilism was geared for an eventual real confrontation and free sparring was a vital part of the training. No oriental style laid such an emphasis on the individual and the practical. From the days of Mendoza and those other great bareknucklers, the Gas Man and Hen(ry) Pearce (the Game Chicken), from the time of Byron and the Fancy and their dabblings with the 'mufflers' on, during the heyday of the great school of arms at the cavernous Fives Court in St Martin's Lane (boxing, small- and back-sword, single-stick, cudgels, and rackets – with rackets clearly the most dangerous, many a retired champion losing an eye to the evil little ball), the essence of boxing instruction was that the academic lessons should be put to a moment of proof, if not truth.

AT THE AGE OF EIGHT I HAD MY FIRST FIGHT, OR 'CONTEST' AS MR TINGLE INSISTED WE CALL IT. THIS WAS AGAINST ONE ANTHONY MAINE IN A RAISED RING PITCHED IN THE CENTRE OF THE CRICKET GROUND WHERE AT THE HEIGHT OF THE CULTURAL REVOLUTION TEN YEARS LATER SOMEONE WOULD HIT A SIX STRAIGHT THROUGH THE WINDOWS OF THE COMMUNIST BANK OF CHINA. THE BLUE CORNER WAS RESERVED FOR THE USUAL TINGLE BOYS FROM THOSE BASTIONS OF RACIAL SUPREMACY, THE PEAK SCHOOL AND QUARRY BAY, THE RED FOR CHINESE FOUNDLINGS FROM A LESS DISTINGUISHED INSTITUTION WHERE MR TINGLE COACHED FOR FREE.

TO MY EXTREME CHAGRIN, I WAS HANDED NOT A BLUE BUT A RED SASH.

WITHOUT EXCEPTION ALL TWENTY-ODD CHINESE BOYS WHO HAD PRECEDED ME FROM THE CORNER HAD LOST, PUTTING ME IN CHILDE ROLAND'S BOOTS ON THE LONELY WALK TO THE RING. ENGLISH SERGEANTS FROM THE GARRISON SECONDED BOTH CORNERS. JOVIAL FELLOWS IN THE MOULD OF KIPLING'S LEAROYD, ORTHERIS AND MULVANEY, THEY DIDN'T SPEAK TO ME WHEN I ARRIVED OR DURING THE INTERVAL BETWEEN THE OPENING AND SECOND ROUNDS, BUT SPONGED MY FACE DOWN, HELD THE BOTTLE AND SPITTOON FOR ME AND PULLED MY SHORTS AWAY FROM MY ABDOMEN SO I COULD BREATHE MORE EASILY.

RECUPERATING BETWEEN ROUNDS TWO AND THREE, I ASKED, 'HOW AM I DOING?'

IF A DOG OR A CAT HAD SPOKEN TO THEM IN ENGLISH, THEY COULD HARDLY HAVE LOOKED MORE FLABBERGASTED. A BURST OF URGENT INSTRUCTIONS FOLLOWED: STICK OUT THE LEFT, KEEP YOUR GUARD UP, ALL THE CLICHÉS OF THE BRITISH AMATEUR CORNER. AS MR TINGLE'S CONTEMPORARIES WOULD HAVE PUT IT, I SUCCEEDED IN 'TAPPING THE CLARET' FROM MASTER MAINE'S NOSE IN THE THIRD, AND I THINK THE SERGEANTS TWO WERE MORE PLEASED THAN I WAS WHEN AFTER THE CARDS HAD BEEN COLLECTED I HAD MY HAND RAISED BY MR TINGLE. THE SBO IN THE COLONY, A NAVAL COMMODORE, PRESENTED ME WITH AN ELECTRO-PLATED NICKEL SILVER CUP WHICH THE SOUTH-WEST MONSOON CORRODED BEFORE THE AUTUMN.

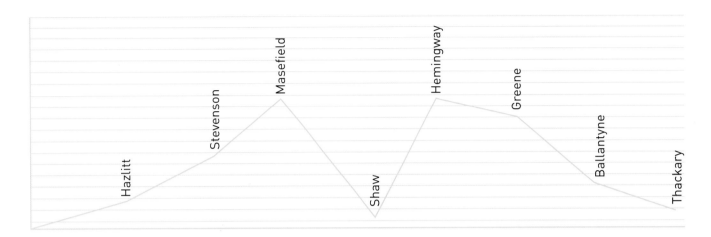

Mr Tingle's stern code was underpinned by a romantic literary culture which I embraced with an even greater enthusiasm. All this time I was devouring the work of Robert Louis Stevenson, **Kidnapped** first, and second **Treasure Island**, and, much too early, **Island Nights Entertainments**. Graham Greene, in **A Sort of Life**, rates Stevenson highly as a master of the language of descriptive action. I agree 99 per cent. The scene in the cramped round-house of the brig **Covenant** is still vivid in my mind: that violent tableau where the dandyish little Jacobite Alan Breck, mindful of the disadvantages of a long blade in such a situation, runs through half a dozen men in as many seconds, then with a bad, blazing exultation cries out to the narrator; David Balfour, 'Oh, man, am I no' a bonny fighter!' The tubercular Stevenson's description in **The Beach of Falesá** of the blood from a fatally stabbed man gushing over the hands of his assailant 'hot as tea' is a brilliant entry from the quotidian into the exotic. Earlier, the same assailant, Wiltshire, 'gave him first the one and then the other so that I could hear his head rattle and crack and he went down straight'. (Which I instantly recognised as the only combination in the Tingle repertoire, the left-right or one-two.) And when Wiltshire says to his victim, 'Speak up, and don't be malingering there, or I'll take my feet to you,' I get the authentic whiff of Scottish street violence going abroad - as it still does - in the robes of mandarin irony. Stitch that, Jimmy, says the modern lout as his head-butt goes in. Yet don't we hear in Wiltshire's words a consciousness of the infraction of the Tingle code?

Where I believe Stevenson, and Greene, fall short is as comprehenders of action. Greene states as an axiom for authors that action must be described as sparely, e.g. high verb content and low adjectival quotient per mandatorily simple sentence. This is all very well for creating an effect in the untutored reader's mind but is not adequate for **analysing** what actually happened. There is a grammar of combat, a syntax of movement, which the human body has to obey in all fighting systems, just as there are less iron rules governing language and communication.

Unfortunately the literary skill of the writer is not at all related to her or his comprehension of the action they are realising. Hazlitt's **On Going to the Fight**, for instance, is

the perfect example of the literary intellectual waffling stylishly about something he has no knowledge of whatsoever. **Cashel Byron's Profession**, GBS's contribution to the genre, is quite feeble and Thackeray, one of my very favourite novelists, is also distinctly unreliable on a fist-fight, whereas the comparatively mediocre R M Ballantyne (better known for **Coral Island**) excels in **Martin Rattler** where in the first few pages the eponymous schoolboy narrator jams a rising kick with a counter-kick of his own: this the sophisticated measure only a prince among street-fighters could employ (although it's also part of the approach work of the classic short-range style of Chinese boxing, Wing Chun). 'Where did you learn that?' someone asks young Martin. 'I only ever saw that used at Eton.' No comment.

I would put John Masefield on a par with Hemingway as a first-rate writer who knew what he was watching. I read **Sard Harker**, his only novel, aged ten, so the pastiche Conradian time-jump which begins it was lost on me, but the boxing match which follows struck me as perfect then as it does now: the unpaired cluster of tatty gloves thrown into the ring in some back-of-beyond Latin American port, the lanky young blacks scrambling for them and boxing with great speed and skill before the main event, a clandestinely fixed match between an evil-aspected white man ('the muscle had all gone to brothel with his soul,' says Masefield of the fixer) and a magnificently built Carib. 'He's well-ribbed,' Harker's captain observes of the white man and then memorably adds, 'If we have to meet, may it be moonlight and may I be first.' What a line!

I don't believe I'm being partisan, but I also find Americans, with the exceptions of Hemingway and James Jones, notably poor on fisticuffs. Jack London was hugely overrated in this area.

I disparage the Americans but I embraced Yankee culture wholeheartedly at my English-language school, Quarry Bay. All the more so after my short-lived Chinese classical education at the Convent of the Precious Blood, an institution run by ferocious Cantonese nuns who thought RC meant Rigid Confucianism. I called it Bloody Blood, influenced, I think, by tales of Japanese atrocities in **Camp on Blood Island**.

I was the dunce of the calligraphy class who managed the characters for one, two and three, but baulked at four. I wore the same tall white dunce's cap Cultural Revolution victims would wear to their executions. I got put in the corner with sticking-plaster over my mouth for asking questions. I got hit in the face ten times, very, very lightly, but still ten times.

Unfortunately, Billy Tingle had yet to drill me in his one, two, three defensive routine. (Twenty years later, I was interested to read in the local paper that a teacher had just got the sack for striking one child in the face three hundred times.) The nuns instructed my amahs to feed me just white rice, without soya sauce. In fact, it was fish fingers and chips at home.

With all my heart, I detested these attempts to brainwash me out of such individualism as I already cherished, but the real problem, as I reflect on it now, was to find myself, endowed through genes and upbringing with a precocious conceptual intelligence, adrift within an ideographic literary culture. I had no gift at all for Chinese characters, those complex and beautiful constructs of spatial metaphor and pictorial allusion, both external and internal, to the closed universe of the system. Just as I have no musical inclination or mathematical acumen (I was to fail Elementary Mathematics O-level eight times), so I lack all artistic ability in appreciation of proportion or perspective, or the extension of line. Virtually all Chinese literate in their own characters have elegant Western handwriting in the same effortless way the Dutch speak almost accentless English from lesson one. I have the handwriting of a child of five, sundered by potent but ill-understood psychopathic drives. Had I remained within the Chinese pedagogic system I would never have been an intellectual, still less one with artistic aspirations. God knows what I would have been, but certainly a lot richer than I am.

Once dropped into the alphabetic information flow, I was the ugly duckling taking to water. I found an immediate reassurance in the logic and coherence of the system, in the way the mere twenty-six letters could be taken apart and bolted together like a Meccano set over and over again into limitless meanings. Even words utterly alien and perhaps unsuitable in a childish vocabulary could be stuttered out phonetically, like summoning a genie from thin air, and their adult power exploited. 'Zounds, ten thousand curses upon you,' I said to my new teacher, the New Zealander Mrs Penman, and got a laugh, rather than the death of a thousand cuts. One could read a journal and later ascertain the meaning of 'rape', 'heuristic' and 'counter-productive', or often enough work it out from context - on empirical OED lines, did one but realise it, in the spirit of Marco Polo's explorations - whereas Chinese children have no notion at all how an unknown character might be pronounced and once taught the sound and its pitch have to remember it by parroting it every time the ideograph is displayed to them. Some time later they might be spoon-fed its meaning by the benevolent teacher.

Some say reading Chinese is like viewing a vast, darkened plain from a mountain-top through flashes of lightning, association and allusion piling in fast and thick in a way alphabetic languages cannot match. This I can accept and the Sino-Arabic convention of opening a book from the back (to the Occidental eye) and reading the lines from right to left should disconcert no one. What I have never adjusted to is the maddening circular logic of traditional Chinese dialectic (only those who've faced it can understand the full depth of exasperation) and the notion that somehow a middle position between opinions is always the correct one, however absurd it actually is (the centre being crucial to the Chinese intellectual and moral position, even figuring as a compass direction and the name of the country itself, the Middle Kingdom).

By the time I had spent a year at Bloody Blood, I'd learned to hate both my teachers and my classmates. Taunting and ostracism were the weapons both young and old employed to break recalcitrant spirits, to make them obedient to instructors and parents and, in due course, government, frightened to be different from all the other sniggering conformists. It was the quintessence of small-mindedness - in its extreme form, the petty spite of solemnly sending an executed man's family the bill of five cents for the bullet which terminated his existence - while both Tingle and RLS with all their ingenuousness, their romanticism, were large-minded spirits.

I've always smiled inwardly when people complain about Western 'racism'. The vilest racists in the world, without guilt or compunction, are drawn from the ranks of the Japanese and the Chinese, those people who can read each other's script with mutual transparency. Ask any African who studied in Peking.

WHAT I LEARNED EARLY WAS THIS:

THOSE CRAVEN SOULS WHO LIKE TO MAKE LIFE MISERABLE FOR THOSE WHO ARE DIFFERENT, WHETHER BLUE MAO-SUITED MOB OR BOVVER-BOOTED GREEN JACKETS, DO NOT HAVE NOBLE INSTINCTS TO WORK ON. THEY ARE BEST MET WITH AN UTTERLY INAPPROPRIATE DEGREE OF RETALIATORY VIOLENCE; IF YOU, OR YOURS, LOSE YOU ARE FAR LESS LIKELY TO BE PICKED ON AGAIN BECAUSE YOU ARE CRAZY AND DANGEROUS. LET ME ILLUSTRATE: BANGLADESHIS ARE EASY PREY; SIKHS, WITH THE BLADE THEIR RELIGION ENJOINS THEM TO CARRY, ARE NOT.

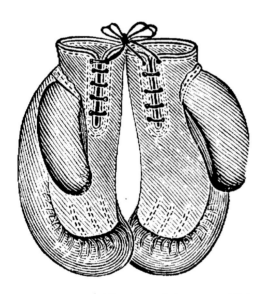

After I was taken to a child psychiatrist for dreaming about the nuns hanging from trees (the shrink thought I meant by executioner's knots), I was removed to the international Quarry Bay School. I dived into American junk culture with a vengeance. We devoured Blackhawk comics (the black-uniformed Olaf, Heinz, Chop-Chop and their comrades as cosmopolitan a bunch as we); we played softball, watched the 77th Bengal Lancers on black and white TV, Kipling in the argot of the waggon-train: 'Hey, guys, the adjutant says to go get chow.' We aped the accents of the American boys, couldn't understand why the Brit parents had hysterics at the school play when the Bishop of Hereford asked Robin Hood in the accents of Galveston: 'Say, good my fellow, who is the leader of your rascally bee-aa-nd?'

For me it was a blessed middle-ground between Confucius and Kipling, because I knew I didn't belong within our third-rate Raj (it being on the whole a historical fact that those not blue-blooded or talented enough for the ICS went to Hong Kong). The most harrowing film I saw in those years didn't feature violence or the supernatural; it was **Bhowani Junction** from John Masters' novel, starring Ava Gardner as the young Anglo-Indian, Victoria Jones. Indian friends have subsequently assured me that Masters' portrait of the Eurasians (ran the railways, called the Indians 'wogs') was by and large fair. The film left me with a dread of the aimless confusion of train stations which has never departed my adult psyche, a dismay which connects loss of identity with the darkness of tunnels, flaring torches and the possibility of missing one's platform change for the express to clarity. The Bhowani Eurasian's hatred of native culture could never have been offensive to the indigene even at the height of empire: it was merely pitiable. How sad, how full of pathos, this self-mutilation.

Unfortunately, it was all too common a phenomenon in the Dutch, British and French possessions, though far less pronounced with the Portuguese in Macao and Timor. One of the problems was the gender direction of most marriages then. Forty years ago 90 per cent of mixed unions involved a Western male marrying a native female, much like modern marriages between Westerner and Filipina with their huge disparities in age and income. For a Chinese man to have the audacity to take an English wife was virtually unheard of, even for Chinese males coming from those affluent classes where instead of sport a man's recreation was taken in the horizontal plane. So most Eurasians looked white on paper when they wrote their names - Higginbottom, Carruthers - but my surname revealed me: baldly monosyllabic, clearly Chinese.

This didn't suit quite everyone. I was with some sleight of hand registered for school in my stepfather's British surname, though my passport and birth certificate still bore my real name until, aged eighteen, I was able to register myself at Oxford under the correct title.

SO, AGED TEN, I ARRIVED IN THE UK POSING AS A LITTLE ENGLISHMAN, WITH THE CLASSICAL DUKES-UP STYLE OF CORINTHIAN TOM.

| Margaret Busby | Memorial to a Migrant | GJC, 1869-1940 | Roseau, Dominica, Windward Islands — Sekondi, Gold Coast, West Africa |

| Two hundred miles along the western coast | duty becomes a pilgrimage of sorts: |

| We scramble up through warrior leaves and words, | tearing green branches with a fresh dismay | directed by ancestral memories | to where a restless spirit finds its ease. | But when at last we come upon the place |

where breath and bone lie still beneath the grass | pour no libation to appease his ghost, | knowing he was a man to reckon with; | for even now the special-import stone | has cracked to safety from the next tomb's thieves. |

| And all the lands he saw and seas he crossed |

| are measured in these untamed yards of earth. |

| Aiming to seize a space back from the wild | to reinstate a cultivated past, | with shards of glass we try to clear the weeds. | Yet when they win a stubborn victory, |

two thousand seasons late for birth and blood, | we turn in silent prayer down the hill, | steps speeding as we veer towards the road | each with a red hibiscus in her hair. |

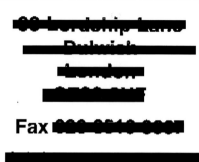

Fax ███████████████

████████████████████

JUST INSTRUCTED

ACORN ESTATE AGENTS ARE PROUD TO OFFER FOR SALE THIS WELL MAINTAINED ONE BEDROOM VICTORIAN GARDEN FLAT SITUATED ON A QUIET RESIDENTIAL ROAD. THE PROPERTY COMPRISES OF 15' LOUNGE, SPACIOUS KITCHEN/DINER, DOUBLE BEDROOM. THREE PIECE BATHROOM SUITE AND 30'(APPROX) PRIVATE REAR GARDEN. THE PROPERTY ALSO BOASTS FULL GAS CENTRAL HEATING (UNCHECKED), STRIPPED WOODEN FLOORING AND A SPACIOUS CELLAR. TO AVOID CERTAIN DISAPPOINTMENT CALL AND VIEW TODAY.

* VICTORIAN *   * GARDEN FLAT *   * CELLAR *

* DOUBLE BEDROOM *   * STRIPPED WOODEN FLOORING *

* SPACIOUS LOUNGE *   * QUIET RESIDENTIAL ROAD *

* CLOSE TO ZONE 2 B.R. *   * PRIVATE GARDEN *   * WELL MAINTAINED *

PRICE........£80,000........LEASEHOLD

Also at: ██

Our ref: 31/JM/89   Prop Ref: 0-96140

ENTRANCE: Communal door opening to hallway, own front door leading to;

LOUNGE APPROX. 15'3 X 14'9:   Sash bay window to front, stripped wood flooring, radiator, power points, picture rail, original coving.

KITCHEN/DINER APPROX. 13'1 X 10'8:   Stripped wooden flooring, sash window to side, fitted wall and base units, stainless steel sink and drainer, extractor fan, power points, boiler, door leading to bathroom.

BEDROOM 1. APPROX. 14' X 12'9:   Sash window to rear, stripped wood flooring, radiator, power points, phone point, original coving.

BATHROOM APPROX. 10'8 X 7'2:   Window to rear, panel enclosed bath, pedestal wash hand basin, lino flooring, splash back tiles, radiator, door leading to;

SEPARATE WC :   Low level W C, lino flooring, splash back tiles, window to side.

REAR GARDEN APPROX. 30' X 10':   Patio area, lawn, insulated shed approx. 12' x 8' currently used as a workshop.

LEASE (VENDOR INFORMS US):   To be advised.

MAINTENANCE (VENDOR INFORMS US):   To be advised.

GROUND RENT (VENDOR INFORMS US):   To be advised.

AGENTS NOTE: Acorn as our Vendors Agents have endeavoured to check the accuracy of these sales particulars, but however can offer no guarantee, we therefore must advise that any prospective purchaser employ their own independent experts to verify the statements contained herein. All measurements are approximate and should not be relied upon. No equipment, utilities, circuits or fittings have been tested.

VIEWING: BY APPOINTMENT WITH ACORN ESTATE AGENCY ONLY

WE'VE FOUND THE SITE THROUGH A FRIEND WHO DOUBLES AS A SOCIAL WORKER. A LIAISON BETWEEN FRAGGLE ROCK AND THE OUTER WORLD, SHE HAS WARNED US TO EXPECT A CHILLY WELCOME. 'THEY DON'T TRUST STRANGERS,' SHE SAYS. SO HERE I STAND, UP TO MY HOCKS IN SPIT AND SLURRY, WHILE GEORGE WEIGHS ME UP, THEN OPENS HIS MOUTH AND DOES NOT SHUT IT AGAIN.

So much for English reserve. Leading me through the puddles to his van, George keeps talking a blue streak. His living space, steamy with wet heat, is crammed with mattresses and fat cushions. George squats cross-legged on the bed, I hunker on the floor, other travellers drift in and out. Some look battered, others merely drenched, but the atmosphere is comradely; they seem joined in a common cause. 'An endangered species, that's us. They keep trying to stamp us out but we won't oblige,' George remarks. 'We're professional survivors.'

'Who's they?'

'Government, the police, the Southern Intelligence Unit in Devizes, they all want us gone, and why? Because we don't live by rules, and rules are all they have, without rules they'd have no control.'

This speech sounds ominously pat. Reaching under his mattress, he starts to pull out documents; newspaper cuttings, legal papers, correspondence. He waves them at me to demonstrate his point, and at that point is always the same: travellers are victims.

Why do they get so much grief? 'We're seen as a threat, right? We don't fit, so we must be wiped out. And many of us have been, too. Busted, banged up in jails, dispersed. Ten years ago, we felt like an army, but how many's still left today? Five thousand? But you'd think we were a horde. A human plague, right? Drug fiends, rapists, scum. And what's our crime, once you get past the scapegoating? We don't know our place, that's all.'

In George's case, this is largely because he's never had a place to know. Born in Lincoln, he grew up without family or structure. 'I was in care homes, detention, Borstal – the full Comply or Die programme.' He was always taught that he was a freak, a total no-hoper. Then he went to a free festival and found out he wasn't alone. 'Suddenly I saw that we were a tribe. Freaks like me, right? We could have a life, after all.'

It was the start of the eighties, glory days for dissent. The movement that had kicked off with Flower Power, back in the late sixties, had spread and deepened its roots. For most, it was still a summer sport, a chance to grab some cheap drugs and cheaper sex, work up a tan and blow off a few rebel clichés. But there was also a core group, in for the long haul. 'People like me, we had nothing to go back to. The road was all there was. So we made it our home.'

Travellers came from all kinds of backgrounds then. They might be old hippies or punks or New Age mystics or anarchists or junkies, but their differences weren't important. 'We all shared the same spirit, we all believed. The world was going to change.' George marched and chanted with the Anti-Nazi League, played in a punk band, toured the country with Circus Normal. In winter, he scraped by. And in summer, when the festival season rolled round, he felt a free man.

THE KEY GATHERING. OF COURSE, WAS STONEHENGE, THE ANNUAL FREE FESTIVAL TO CELEBRATE THE SOLSTICE, AND CELEBRATE THE CELEBRANTS. 'YOU'D MEET THE SAME PEOPLE EACH YEAR, IT WAS LIKE ONE HUGE FAMILY. A MASS OF MUSIC AND LIGHT, AS FAR AS YOU COULD SEE. PEOPLE, JUST PEOPLE, THAT'S WHAT IT WAS. HUMANITY, FEELING GOOD'. BUT ALL THAT HAD CHANGED ON 1 JUNE 1985; THE NIGHT OF THE BEANFIELD.

EXACTLY WHAT HAPPENED DEPENDS ON WHO YOU'RE TALKING TO. THE CONSENSUS, THOUGH, IS THAT A LOOSE COALITION OF POWERS – LOCAL LANDOWNERS, THE POLICE, THE COUNTY COUNCIL – GOT TOGETHER AND DECIDED THAT

they didn't want any more of these dirty, hairy, drug-addled people messing up Stonehenge and its surrounds.

THE NATIONAL TRUST AND ENGLISH HERITAGE TOOK OUT INJUNCTIONS AGAINST THE COMING FESTIVAL. THEN THE LAW WENT INTO ACTION.

Each year a ramshackle regiment of brightly-painted vans and buses, trucks, London taxis, fire engines and old bangers, grandly titled the Peace Convoy, made a ceremonial approach to the festival site. In 1985, the procession numbered some 150 vehicles. Close to a village called Shipton Billinger, they were met by the police. There were 1,363 officers on hand. The road was blocked off with mounds of gravel and the convoy trapped, but the travellers broke through a fence and took refuge in a beanfield. There followed some hours of stalemate, with the police ordering the fugitives to come out and be arrested, and the fugitives refusing to budge. Finally, the police attacked. Using riot gear, shields and truncheons, they stormed the vehicles, smashed in windows, broke teeth and noses and heads. TV camera crews followed them, recording the bloodshed, but the police were undeterred. 'I'm not here to bargain,' said Assistant Chief Constable Grundy, the Operational Commander. 420 arrests were made.

'That did our heads in. We never got over it,' says George. Squatting in his next of documents, he waves one arm jaggedly, disjointedly, like a maimed bird. 'One day we felt unstoppable, the next we were dog turds, right?'

The terrible thing about the Beanfield was that it couldn't happen, and yet it did. Growing up English and white, you took certain limits for granted. If you rattled their chains, the police might snap at you, even rough you up a little. That's how the game was played. A bit of aggro to ginger things up; a pleasant fizz of paranoia. But not this. Not these science-fiction terminators with their batons and flying boots. That wasn't a bit of bother, it was terror. 'People thought they were going to die.'

The road was never easy again. Confidence drained away, and travellers went on the defensive. If they tried to stop the authorities moved them on; if they protested, the riot gear and attack dogs came out.

The Criminal Justice Act and the Public Order Bill had tightened the screws still further. Anyone with a choice had given up, got off the road. 'We're down to the hardcore now.' A few battered dissenters like George himself, assorted alcoholics and junkies, a scattering of petty criminals. 'They've whittled us to the bone.'

The Children's Transport
by Lore Segal

'I have to pack her enough food to last till they get to England,' my mother said. 'How can I pack enough food to keep two days?' Her face was red. All that day my mother's face looked thick and hot, as if she had a fever, but she moved about as on an ordinary day and her voice sounded ordinary, she even joked. She said we were going to pretend it was the first day of the month. Before my father had lost his job, the first of the month had been payday and the day I was allowed to choose my own favorite supper, against a promise that there would be no fussing about food during the rest of the month. But today my mother had no imagination, I said I didn't want anything. 'I don't mean for now, I mean to take with you,' said my mother. She was wanting me to need something that she could give me. I searched around in my mind, wanting to oblige her. '*Knackwurst*?' I said, though I could not at the moment remember exactly what kind of sausage that was.

'*Knackwurst*,' said my mother. 'You like that? I'll go down this minute and get you one.' But at that moment the doorbell rang.

All day the room was full of people coming to say good-by, friends of the family, and aunts and uncles and cousins. Everyone brought me bonbons, candied fruit, dates, sour sweets, and chocolates we called cat's tongues, and homemade cookies, and *Sacher torte*. Even my Tante Grete came, though she was angry with my parents because I had been smuggled onto the transport and her twins were to be left behind.

My father tried to explain. 'This is just an experimental transport, don't you see. They don't even know if they can get across the German border, and Lore only got on because Kurt's cousin happens to work on the Committee and did us a favor. I could hardly ask her for more.'

'Naturally. How could you be expected to ask for help to save someone else's children?' Tante Grete said. She had a long and bitter face. 'But maybe Lore can ask people once she gets to England. She can tell about her cousins Ilse and Erica, who had to stay behind in Vienna while she got away. Maybe she can find a sponsor for them.'

I stood in the corner of my circle of relatives, nodding solemnly. I said I would write letters to everybody and I would tell the *[...]* about everything that was happening and would get sponsors for my parents and my grandparents and for everybody.

When Tante Grete left the apartment, it was after seven and my nervous father said we should be going, but my mother cried out, she had forgotten to get the *Knackwurst*. 'I'm going to run down,' she said, and already she had flung her coat about her, but my father blocked her way.

'Are you an idiot? Do you want her to miss her train?'

'She wants a *Knackwurst*,' my mother cried.

'Do you know what time it is? Suppose you get arrested while you're out?'

I had never before seen my parents standing shouting into each other's faces. I kept saying, 'I don't really want any *Knackwurst*,' but they took no notice of me.

My mother came back with her triumphant, beaming, sad red face. Nothing had happened – no one had even seen her. She had got a whole sausage and had made the man give her an extra paper bag. She called me to come and look where she was putting it in my rucksack, between my sandwiches and the cake.

'Let's go, for God's sake,' said my father.

We went over the Stefanie Bridge on foot. I walked between my parents. Each

held a hand. My father talked to my mother about going to the Chinese Consulate in the morning.

The assembly point was a huge empty lot behind the railway station in the outskirts of Vienna. Along a wire fence, members of the Committee stood holding long poles bearing placards; flashlights lit the numbers painted on them. Someone came over to me and checked my papers and made me stand with the group of children collecting around the placard that read '150-199.' He hung a cardboard label with the number

152

strung on a shoelace around my neck, and tied corresponding numbers to my suitcase and rucksack.

I remember that I clowned and talked a good deal. I remember feeling, this is me going to England. My parents stood with the other parents, on the right, at the edge of the darkness. I have no clear recollection of my father's being there – perhaps his head was too high and out of the circle of the lights. I do remember his greatcoat standing next to my mother's black pony fur, but every time I looked toward them it was my mother's tiny face, crumpled and feverish inside her fox collar, that I saw smiling steadily toward me.

We were arranged in a long column four deep, according to numbers. The rucksack was strapped to my back. There was a confusion of kissing parents – my father bending down, my mother's face burning against mine. Before I could get a proper grip on my suitcase, the line set in motion so that the suitcase kept slipping from my hand and bumping against my legs. Panic-stricken, I looked to the right, but my mother was there, walking beside me. She took the suitcase, keeping at my side, and she was smiling so that it seemed a gay thing, like a joke we were having together. Someone from the Committee, checking the line, took the suitcase from my mother, checked it with the number around my neck, and gave it to me to carry. 'Go on, move,' the children behind me said. We were passing through great doors. I looked to my right; my mother's face was nowhere to be seen. I dragged and shoved the heavy suitcase across the station floor and bumped it down a flight of stairs and along a platform where the train stood waiting.

There was a young woman in charge inside our carriage. She was slight and soft-spoken. She walked the corridors outside the compartments and put her head in and told us to settle down. We asked her when we were going to leave. She said, 'Very soon.'

It was after midnight when the train left the station. There was only room enough for four of the eight girls in the compartment to stretch out on the seats. I was the smallest one. I remember that I had the place by the window and I kept trying to bend my neck into the corner and at the same time shield my eyes with an arm, a hand, or in the crook of an elbow against the electric bulb in the corridor. The chattering of the children subsided little by little until there was no sound except the noise of the train. I have no notion that I went to sleep, except that I was awakened by a flashlight shining into my face. In its light, behind it and lit like a negative, was a girl's face. She said it was time for someone else to lie down in my place.

The girl on the suitcase asked me if I wanted to go to the lavatory and wash my face. I wandered down the corridor, peering into every compartment door to see people sleeping. In the lavatory there was a glass sphere over the washbowl. If you turned it upside down, green liquid soap squirted out. If you stepped on the pedal that flushed the toilet, a hole opened and you could look through it at the ground tearing away underneath.

By the time I got back to my compartment, everyone was up. The children were eating breakfast out of their paper bags. I didn't feel like *Knackwurst* for breakfast and it was too much trouble to eat a sandwich, so I had candied pear and three cat's tongues and a piece of *Sacher Torte*. A big girl said we had left Austria during the night and were actually in Germany. I looked out, wanting to hate, but there was nothing out of the window but cows and fields. I said maybe we were still in Austria. The big girls said it was so Germany, and it puzzled me.

As the morning advanced, the noise swelled. In the next compartment, a tall, vivacious girl had organized a game. I went in and found a place to sit, and after a bit I organized the small girl sitting beside me into playing ticktacktoe on the outside of her paper food bag. Just as we were getting interested, the morning was over and we had to go to our own compartments to each lunch.

The train had become deadly hot. A trance fell. We ate silently. I had bitten into the sausage and found I couldn't bear the taste, and I thought I would eat it for supper. The sandwiches had become too dry to eat, so I had some dates and cat's tongues and a piece of cake and then I sat and sucked some candy. I noticed again the noise of the train, which had been quite drowned out in the commotion of the morning, and I fell asleep.

I started up as the train rode into a station and stopped. The big girl said this was the border and now the Nazis would decide what to do with us. She told us to sit as quiet as we could. There was much walking about outside. We saw uniforms under the lights on the platform. They entered the train in front. I held myself so still that my head vibrated on my neck and my knees cramped. Half an hour, an hour. We knew when they were in our carriage which seemed to settle under their added weight. They were coming towards us down the corridor, stopping at each compartment door. Then one of them stood in our doorway. His uniform had many buttons. We saw the young woman who was in charge of our carriage behind his shoulder. The Nazi signed to one of the children to come with him, and she followed him out. The young woman turned back to tell us not to worry – they were taking one child from each carriage to check papers and look for contraband.

When the little girl returned, she sat down in her place and we all stared at her. We did not ask her what had happened and she never told us. The carriage rocked; the Nazis had got off. Doors slammed. The train moved. Someone shouted, 'We're out!' Then everyone was pressing into the corridor. Everyone was shouting and laughing, I was laughing. The doors between carriages opened and children came spilling in. Where there had been only girls there was suddenly a boy - two - three boys. Dozens of boys. They pulled hats out of the recesses of their clothing, like conjurers, and the hats unfolded and set on their heads were seen to be the hats of forbidden Scout uniforms. The boys turned back the lapels of their jackets and there were rows of badges – the Zionist blue-and-white, Scout buttons, the *Kruckenkreuz* of Austria – and it was such

Rudolf Laub
(b. 1929, perished)
Lines, Cubes...
Pencil, 140 x 90mm
Jewish Museum, Prague
Inv. No. 131996

a gay thing and it was so loud and warm. I wished I had a badge or a button to turn out. I wished I knew the songs that they were singing and I sang them anyway. 'Wah, wah, la la,' I sang. Someone squeezed my head; I held someone around the waist and someone held me; we were singing.

The train stopped in a few minutes, we were in Holland. The station was brightly lit and full of people. They handed us paper cups of hot tea through the windows, red polished apples, chocolate bars, and candy, and that was my supper. When the train started up once more, a hundred children from our transport who were staying in Holland (the advancing German Occupation was to trap them there within two years) stood ranged on the platform — the smallest, who were four years old, in front, the big ones in the back. They were waving. We waved, standing at the open windows, and all along the train we shouted 'God bless Queen Wilhelmina' in chorus.

Inside the train the party went on, but I could not stay awake. Someone shook me. 'We're getting off soon,' they said. I heard them, but I could not wake up. Someone strapped my rucksack onto my back again and put the suitcase in my hand. I was lifted down from the train and stood on my feet in the cold black night, shivering.

Inside the ship, I lay between white sheets in a narrow bed, wide awake. I had a neat cabin to myself. I had folded my dress and stockings with fanatical tidiness and brushed my teeth to appease my absent mother. I prayed God to keep me from getting seasick and my parents from getting arrested, and I lay down and woke next morning on the English side of the Channel.

We waited all morning to be processed. We waited in the large, overheated crimson smoking room. For breakfast we finished what was in our lunch bags. I had to throw my sandwiches in the wastepaper basket; they were so dry they curled — but when I came to the *Knackwurst*, which was beginning to have a strange smell about it, I remembered my grandmother always said that there was always time to throw things out. I put the sausage back in the bag.

Newspapermen had come aboard. All morning they walked among us flashing bulbs, taking pictures. I tried to attract their attention. I played with my lunch bag. 'Little Refugee Looking for Crumbs.' Not one of them noticed. I tried looking homesick, eyes raised ceilingward as if I were dreaming. They paid no attention.

My number was called late in the morning. I was taken to a room with a long table. Half a dozen English ladies sat around it, with stacks of paper before them. One of the papers had my name on it. It even had my photograph pinned to it. I was pleased. I enjoyed being handed from one lady to the next. They asked me questions. They smiled tenderly at me and said I was finished and could go.

I stood on land that I presumed was England; the ground felt ordinary under my feet, and wet. A workman was piling logs. I stood and watched him. I don't know if it was a man or woman who came and took my hand and led me into a shed so huge and vaulted it dwarfed the three or four children who were at the other end and swallowed the sound of their walking. I was told to find my luggage. I walked among the rows of luggage, the floor was covered with it from end to end. It seemed utterly improbable that I should come across my own things. After a while, I sat down on the nearest suitcase and cried.

Some grown-up came and took my hand, and led me to my belongings (following the numbers until we came to 152), and showed me the way to the waiting room. It was full of children and very warm. The photographers were there taking pictures. I pulled my suitcase a little away from the wall and sat on it, looking dreamy. I think I fell asleep.

At the wharf we waited for hours. There was another railway carriage, a new station, other platforms where we stood in columns four deep, photographers taking pictures. At the end of the day, we arrived at Dovercourt. There was a fleet of double-decker buses waiting to take us from the station to a workers' summer camp where we would stay while the Committee looked for foster homes. I began to take notice again. I had never seen double-decker buses before. This at last must be something English. I remember asking if I might ride on top. I sat on top and in front, and was the first to see, through the dull gray winter dusk, the camp, like a neat miniature town on the edge of the ocean.

The camp consisted of a couple of hundred identical one-room wooden cottages built along straight intersecting paths. To the right, at the bottom of every path, we could see the flat black ocean stretching toward the horizon over which we had come. Back of us was England.

Our little cottage had little curtained windows that gave onto a miniature veranda. We thought it was sweet. We squealed, choosing our beds. The counselor, a thin girl of fourteen or fifteen, held her nose and asked what the horrid smell in here was. 'Whew!' said all the little girls. 'What a horrible smell! What can it be?'

I knew it was my sausage, and was badly frightened. Like a pickpocket whose escape has been cut off, I mingled with the crowd. I held my nose, looked ostentatiously in corners, and helped curse the dirty, idiotic,

Novák J. X. 13 hod.

Metzl Georg
Heim I
1. Abt.   13 Jahre

disgusting person who was responsible for stinking up the place.

'All right, everybody!' said the counselor. 'Let's go, then.'

I told her I didn't feel very well and did not want any supper. I would stay in the cottage and go to bed. As soon as the others were gone, I fetched the brown paper bag out of my rucksack and looked the cottage over for some place, some corner where a sausage could be hidden so as not to smell. I kept thinking that I would presently find such a special niche for it. Meanwhile it was cold in the unheated cottage. I took off my shoes and got under the blanket. I got up again. I thought of starting a letter to ask someone to be a sponsor for my parents, but instead I went and knelt at the bottom of the bed with my elbows on the window sill and looked out. In the direction of the assembly hall the sky glowed with light. I wished I had gone along with the others. I was thinking of putting my shoes back on and going to look for my roommates, when I heard them coming along the path and I remembered my sausage. Now it seemed what I needed was a long stretch of time to take care of it – and here were feet already on the veranda steps. The door opened. I was lying between the sheets, breathing hard, having just in time skidded the *Knackwurst* into the corner under my bed.

The children did not let me forget it. The counselor said, 'Someone must have made in her bed!' I hummed a song to show I did not feel myself meant in the least, and one of the little girls asked me if I had a stomach-ache, to be making such a horrible noise.

During the night the temperature dropped; the memorable, bitter winter of 1938 had set in on England's east coast. By morning, the water in the sink in our cottage was a solid block of ice. We could not wash our faces, and we set out guiltlessly for breakfast with unbrushed teeth and our mothers not even betrayed.

Outside, the vicious cold wind from the ocean knocked the breath out of us. We bucked it with lowered heads. The hall had been constructed for summer use. At our first breakfast, we watched the snow that had seeped between the glass squares of the roof and the iron framework fall in delicate drifts through the indoor air. It sugared our hair and shoulders and settled briefly on the hot porridge, salt kippers, and other wrong, strange foods. It was rumored that one of the girls had had her toes frozen off. We were fascinated. It seemed right that the weather should be as unnatural as our circumstances.

My mind during that first breakfast was on my sausage. I had to do away with the sausage without doing away with it. It was difficult to focus on the problem; I kept forgetting to think about it, yet, all the time, the place where the sausage lay on the floor against the wall, under the bed, remained the center of my guilt, a sore spot in my mind.

I ate in nervous haste. I meant to get to the cottage before the others came back, but when the meal was done we all had to sit and listen to the camp leader make announcements through his megaphone. He told us the camp regulations, that we were to write letters to our parents, that we must stay in hall because some English ladies from the Committee were coming to choose children to go and live with families in different parts of England.

I went and stood with some children watching workmen install two extra stoves. They were big black stoves with fat black L-shaped chimneys that carried the smoke out through the roof. When the stoves were lit, they created rings of intense heat in which we stood all morning jostling for places, for the warmth made no inroad on the general chill.

I looked for the camp leader and saw him standing with a group of ladies in fur coats. He was bowing and bobbing his head to the ladies. He walked them all round the hall. They stopped and talked to some of the children. I stalked the party with my eyes. I would ask them about getting a sponsor for my parents and the twins. They were moving toward me. I felt flushed; it came to me that I did not know the words to say to them. A cloud of confusion blocked the ladies from my sight, though I knew when they were in front of me and when they had passed. I saw them going out to inspect the kitchens. The camp leader held the door for them.

Before I knew what I had decided, I was walking out of the hall into the freezing air, going around the outside of the building toward the kitchens. It had stopped snowing. A door opened and a man in a long white apron came out with a steaming bucket, which he emptied into a trash can. He waved to me and went back in and shut the door. The trash can went on steaming.

For a moment there, I saw what to do with my sausage. The idea of throwing into the trash can what my mother had gone especially to buy me, because I had lied that I wanted it, brought on such a fierce pain in my chest where I had always understood my heart to be that I stood still in surprise. I was shocked that I could be hurting so. I started walking toward the cottage, weeping with pain and outrage at the pain. I had a clear notion of myself crying, in my thickly padded coat and mittens that were attached to one another by a ribbon threaded through the sleeves and across the back. I noticed that I had stopped hurting, I suspected that

I was somehow not crying properly, was perhaps only pretending, and I stopped, except for the sobbing, which went on for a while.

When I came to the cottage, I walked around to the back, having decided that I would bury the sausage. I found a piece of wood and scraped away the top layer of snow, but, underneath, the earth was frozen and unyielding. I scraped and hacked at it with my heel. Tufts of muddy iced grass came loose. I stood looking around me. The wind had dropped and the air froze silently. And then I saw something; I saw where, in the middle of a semi-circle of snow that must in summer have been a flower bed in a grassplot behind the cottage, there grew a meagre rosebush with a single bright red rosebud wearing a clump of freshly fallen snow, like a cap askew. This struck me profoundly. I was a symbolist in those days, and roses and the like were just my speed. It excited me. I would write it in a letter to Onkel Hans and Tante Trude in London, saying that the Jews in Austria were like roses left over in the winter of the Nazi Occupation. I would write that they were dying of the cold. How beautifully it all fell into place! How true and sad! They would say, 'And she is only ten years old!' I ran around the cottage and up the veranda steps. I emptied my rucksack onto the blanket, looking for pen, paper, and my father's list of addresses with a rapidity that matched the rate at which my metaphor was growing and branching. I was going to say, 'If good people like you don't pluck the roses quickly, the Nazis will come and cut them down.' I hopped onto the edge of the bed, and, hampered by coat and gloves, with freezing ears, plunged with a kind of greedy glee into my writing.

The counselor's thin face appeared behind the cold glass of the window. She opened the door and came in. Everyone was sitting down to lunch, she said, and they had sent her to look for me. I recognized the authentic voice of the exasperated grownup. I wanted to get her to like me. I kept chatting. I walked to the dining hall beside her, telling how I was writing to some people in London who were going to get a visa for my parents.

To my surprise, she began to talk to me. She said people were saying that there were new persecutions going on in Vienna, that all food shops were closed to Jews, that Jews weren't allowed to go into the streets day or night and were being fetched out of their apartments and taken away in cartloads. She said she was frightened because of her mother. I told her not to worry; there were so many Jews, they probably wouldn't even get to her mother.

After lunch I went and sat on a bench by the wall. Outside, the dusk of an English winter day, which starts imperceptibly almost immediately after lunch, was settling over the camp, and it looked cold. I sat with my mittened hands inside my pockets, sinking every moment more deeply into my coat. My head kept nagging me to go and write another sponsor letter; it might be this letter I might be writing this instant that would save my parents. The lights came on in the hall, but still I sat. I tried to frighten myself into activity by imagining that the Nazis had come to the flat to arrest my father, but I didn't believe it. I tried to imagine my father and mother put into carts, but found I did not really care. Alarmed, I tried imagining my mother taken away and dead; I imagined myself dead and buried in the ground, but still I couldn't care anything about it. My body felt, for the first time in days, wonderfully warm inside my coat.

In the evening there was an entertainment. We sat in rows. The camp leader got up on the stage and taught us to sing songs in English: 'Ten Green Bottles,' 'Rule Britannia,' and 'Boomps-a-Daisy.' Then he introduced a muscle man. The muscle man threw off his cape and he had nothing on underneath except a little pair of plum-coloured satin trunks. He looked bare and pink standing all by himself on the stage, but he didn't seem to feel the cold. He flexed his biceps for us. He could flap his diaphragm left side and right side separately, and wiggle each toe in turn. His head was small and perfectly round, like a walnut. Afterward, the camp leader went up to thank him. He said the muscle man was sorry that he could not speak German but that he had come all the way from London to entertain us. The muscle man stood smiling with great sweetness, but I knew he didn't even know that I was there.

In bed that night, our counselor told us that a new transport of Jewish children from Germany was expected in camp. I understood from her that this was to be regarded as a calamity, because German Jews talked like Germans and thought they knew everything better than everybody else and would ruin the whole camp. I was surprised. At home I had learned that it was the Polish Jews who always thought they knew everything and were noisy and pushy in public and ruined everything for the *real*, the Austrian, Jews.

That night I woke in a thumping panic from a dream that a crowd of people had discovered my sausage. When I had calmed a little, I leaned out into the dark and felt under the bed. There was the paper bag. I brought it out and stealthily squeezed it well down into my rucksack, and I thought the crackling and rustling of the paper must be echoing from one end to the other of the sleeping camp.

of room in my memory. I cannot keep the subsequent days separate in my mind or remember how many there were. There was some attempt to keep us occupied. I remember English lessons going on in various corners of the hall. I remember a drawing competition that I either won or thought I ought to have won – I don't recall which.

One evening the youngest of my roommates and I were sent to go to bed and found four large boys in our cottage. They were heaving our belongings over the veranda railing into the snow. The little girl and I watched, holding the spokes, our eyes on a level with the big boys' feet. They wore long wool socks and short pants, and, in between, their knees were knobbly. I thought they were lovely. I admired the energetic, devil-may-care way they told us the cottage was theirs and we should go and find out where we belonged. Then they went in and shut the door. 'That's those Germans,' said the little girl and began to cry, but I felt suddenly extraordinarily happy to think of the boys inside the familiar walls of our cottage; I had a sense of the camp and the cottages full of boys and girls – Austrians, Germans, and even Poles – and I hated the little girl beside me who had sat down on her suitcase and has howling dismally. She was interfering with my loving everybody.

I don't know how long we sat outside the cottage. Eventually, some person came walking by and found us sitting on our suitcases in the snow. The little girl was still wailing in a bored sort of way. This person asked us what had happened and was quite upset and took us along to the office, and the muddle was discovered. It seemed that we were part of the original Austrian

camp, but not until the next day. And so it turned out that the Germans really had ruined everything. The little girl and I were put into a narrow room with bunk beds for the night. We cursed the Germans with heated indignation and excited ourselves. We talked far into the night. We told each other things and we became quite intimate.

About the second camp I remember only that it was not a proper camp like our first camp. The assembly hall was made of brick; the cottages, instead of being wooden, were made of stucco. It was all wrong and strange, and before the newness of it could pass away I moved again.

One evening I was sitting by one of the stoves, writing a letter to my parents, when two English ladies came up to me. One of them carried a pad of paper, and she said, 'How about this one?' and the other lady said, 'All right.' They smiled at me. They asked my name and age and I told them. They said I spoke English very nicely. I beamed. They asked me if I was Orthodox. I said yes. They were pleased. They said then would I like to come and live with a lovely Orthodox family in Liverpool. I said yes enthusiastically, and we all three beamed at one another. I asked the ladies if they would find a sponsor for my parents, and watched them exchange glances. One lady patted my head and said we would see. I said and could they get a sponsor for my grandparents and for my cousins Erica and Ilse, who had not been able to come on the children's transport like me. The ladies' smiles became strained. They said we would talk about it later.

I finished my letter to my parents, saying that I was going to go and live with this lovely Orthodox family in Liverpool and

would they please write and tell me what did 'Orthodox' mean.

There were cars waiting early the next morning to take twenty little girls to the railway station. All day we traveled north. All day it snowed. I looked out of the corridor window until I was tired, and then I went along to the lavatory and messed with the soap. When I judged I had been away a reasonable time, I came back. I stopped stock-still in the doorway of my compartment. My rucksack stood on my seat; the brown paper bag had been taken out and torn open, and my guilty sausage lay exposed to the light. It was ugly and shrivelled, with one end nibbled off. The thing had lost the fierce and aggressive stench of active decay and had about it now the suffocating smell of mold; it thickened the air of the compartment. One of the English ladies was standing looking at it, her nose crinkled. The seven children were sitting looking at me, and I died there on the spot, drowned in shame. The waters closed over my head and through the thumping and roaring in my ears I heard one of the little girls say, 'And it isn't even kosher.' The English lady said, 'You can throw it away in the station when we change trains.' Dead and drowned under their eyes, I walked to my seat, I packed up the sausage; I took the rucksack off the seat and sat down. After a while, I noticed that the other girls were no longer staring at me and that the lady, when she looked in to see how we were doing, smiled pleasantly.

In the station there was a large trash can and I dropped my sausage in. I stood and roared with grief. Through my noise and my tears I saw the foolish children standing around, and heard one of the English ladies saying, 'Come on, now. Are you all right?' They both looked upset and frightened. 'Will you be all right?' they asked.

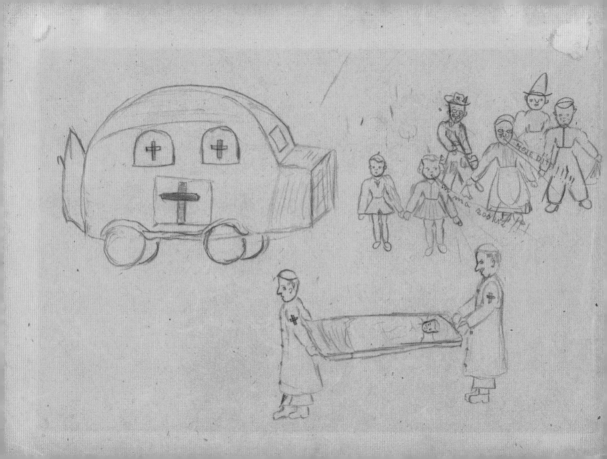

"the evolution of the human race will not be accomplished in the ten thousand years of tame animals, but in the million years of wild animals, because man is and will always be a wild animal."

charles darwin

"how inappropriate to call this planet earth when it is clearly ocean."

arthur c. clarke

"[journalists are] more attentive to the minute hand of history than to the hour hand."

sir desmond maccarthy

down to earth:

Pollen Grains
+
Magic Bullets

Richard Dawkins

I was driving through the English countryside with my daughter Juliet, then aged six, and she pointed out some flowers by the wayside.
I asked her what she thought wildflowers were for. She gave a rather thoughtful answer. 'Two things,' she said. 'To make the world pretty, and to help the bees make honey for us.'
I was touched by this and sorry I had to tell her that it wasn't true.

My little girl's answer was not too different from the one that most adults, throughout history, would have given. It has long been widely believed that brute creation is here for our benefit.

The first chapter of Genesis is explicit. Man has 'dominion' over all living things, and the animals and plants are there for our delight and our use. As the historian Sir Keith Thomas documents in his *Man and the Natural World*, this attitude pervaded medieval Christendom and it persists to this day. In the nineteenth century, the Reverend William Kirby thought that the louse was an indispensable incentive to cleanliness. Savage beasts, according to the Elizabethan bishop James Pilkington, fostered human courage and provided useful training for war. Horseflies, for an eighteenth-century writer, were created so 'that men should exercise their wits and industry to guard themselves against them'. Lobsters were furnished with hard shells so that, before eating them, we could benefit from the improving exercise of cracking their claws. Another pious medieval writer thought that weeds were there to benefit us: it is good for our spirit to have to work hard pulling them up.

As a creation, man is far superior to the animals.

Animals have been thought privileged to share in our punishment for Adam's sin. Keith Thomas quotes a seventeenth-century bishop on the point: 'Whatsoever change for the worse is come upon them is not their punishment, but a part of ours.' This must, one feels, be a great consolation to them. Henry More, in 1653, believed that cattle and sheep had only been given life in the first place so as to keep their meat fresh 'till we shall have need to eat them'. The logical conclusion to this seventeenth-century train of thought is that animals are actually eager to be eaten.

The pheasant, partridge and the lark
Flew to thy house, as to the Ark.
The willing ox of himself came
Home to the slaughter, with the lamb;
And every beast did thither bring
Himself to be an offering.

Douglas Adams developed this conceit to a futuristically bizarre conclusion in *The Restaurant at the End of the Universe*, part of the brilliant *Hitchhiker's Guide to the Galaxy* saga. As the hero and his friends sit down in the restaurant, a large quadruped obsequiously approaches their table and in pleasant, cultivated tones offers itself as the dish of the day. It explains that its kind has been bred to want to be eaten and with the ability to say so clearly and unambiguously: 'Something off the shoulder, perhaps? ... Braised in a white wine sauce? ... Or the rump is very good ... I've been exercising it and eating plenty of grain, so there's lots of good meat there.' Arthur Dent, the least galactically sophisticated of the diners, is horrified but the rest of the party order large steaks all round and the gentle creature gratefully trots off to the kitchen to shoot itself (humanely, it adds, with a reassuring wink at Arthur).

Douglas Adams's story is avowed comedy but, to the best of my belief, the following discussion of the banana, quoted verbatim from a modern tract kindly sent by one of my many creationist correspondents, is intended seriously.

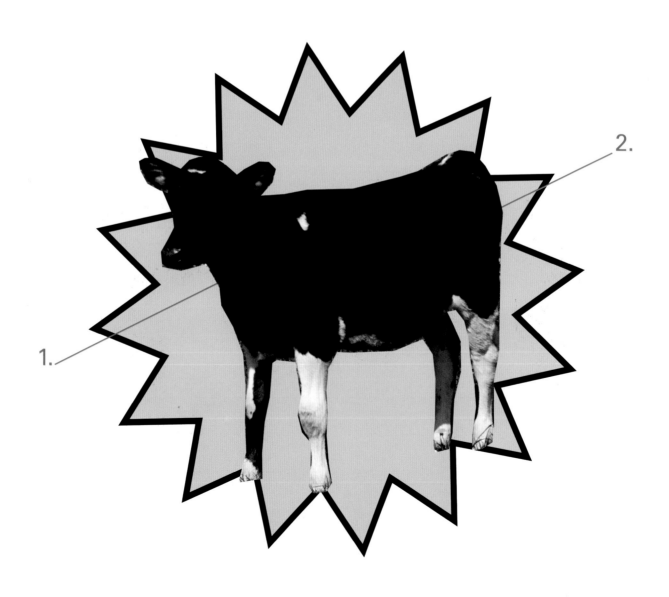

Note that the banana:

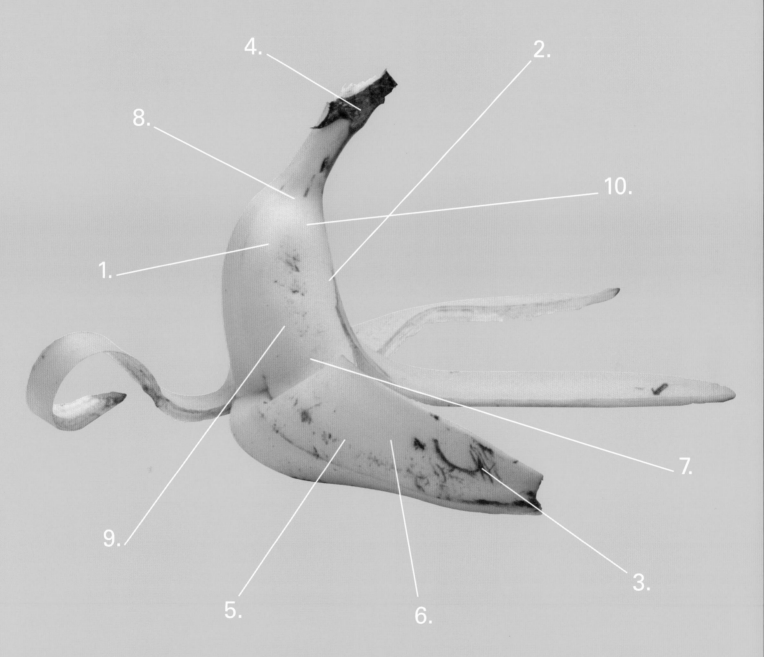

1. Is shaped for human hand
2. Has non-slip surface
3. Has outward indicators of inward contents:
Green – too early; Yellow – just right; Black – too late
4. Has a tab for removal of wrapper
5. Is perforated on wrapper

6. Biodegradable wrapper
7. Is shaped for mouth
8. Has a point at top for ease of entry
9. Is pleasing to taste buds
10. Is curved towards the face to make eating process easy.

The attitude that living things are placed here for our benefit still dominates our culture, even where its underpinnings have disappeared.

We now need, for purposes of scientific understanding, to find a less human-centred view of the natural world for any purpose – and there is a respectable figure of speech by which they can – it surely is not for the benefit of humans. We must learn to see things through non-human eyes. In the case of the flowers with which we began our discussion, it is at least marginally more sensible to see them through the eyes of bees and other creatures that pollinate them.

The whole life of bees revolves around the colourful, scented, nectar-dripping world of flowers. I am not just talking about honey-bees, for there are thousands of different species of bee and they all depend utterly on flowers. Their larvae are fed on pollen, while the exclusive fuel for their adult flight-motors is nectar which is also entirely provided for them by flowers. When I say 'provided for them'

I mean it in slightly more than an idle sense. Pollen, unlike nectar, is not provided **purely** for them, because the plants make pollen mainly for their own purposes. The bees are welcome to eat some of the pollen because they provide such a valuable service in carrying pollen because from one flower to another. But nectar is a more extreme case. It doesn't have any other **raison d'être** than to feed bees. Nectar is manufactured, in large quantities, purely for bribing bees and other pollinators. The bees work hard for their nectar reward. To make one pound of clover honey, bees have to visit about ten million blossoms.

'Flowers,' the bees might say, 'are there to provide us bees with pollen and nectar.' Even the bees haven't got it quite right. But they are a lot more right than we humans are if we think that flowers are there for our benefit.

We might even say that flowers, at least the bright and showy ones, are bright and showy because they have been 'cultivated' by bees, butterflies, humming-birds and other pollinators.

MY EARLIEST MEMORIES

ARE OF THE OLD LAWN-MOWER WITH WHICH WE LABOURED TO CUT THE GRASS.

I am so glad there are no lawns in Dungeness. The worst lawns, and for that matter the ugliest gardens, are along the coast in Bexhill – in Close and Crescent. These are the 'gardens' that would give Gertrude Jekyll a heart attack or turn her in her grave.

LAWNS, IT SEEMS TO ME

barren and often threadbare – the enemy of a good garden. For the same trouble as mowing, you could have a year's vegetables: runner beans, cauliflowers and cabbages, mixed with pinks and peonies, shirley poppies and delphiniums;

WOULDN'T THAT BEAUTIFY THE LAND AND SAVE US FROM THE GARDEN TERRORISM THAT PREVAILS?

ARE AGAINST NATURE,

When I came to Dungeness in the mid-eighties, I had no thought of building a garden. It looked impossible: shingle with no soil supported by a sparse vegetation. Outside the front door a bed had been built – a rockery of broken bricks and concrete: it fitted in well. One day, walking on the beach at low tide, I noticed a magnificent flint. I brought it back and pulled out one of the bricks. Soon I had replaced all the rubble with flints. They were hard to find, but after a storm a few more would appear. The bed looked great, like dragon's teeth – white and grey.

My journey to the sea each morning had purpose. I decided to stop there; after all, the bleakness of Prospect Cottage was what had made me fall in love with it. At the back I planted a dog rose. Then I found a curious piece of driftwood and used this, and one of the necklaces of holey stones that I hung on the wall, to stake the rose.

THE GARDEN HAD BEGUN.

I SAW IT AS A THERAPY and a pharmacopoeia. I collected more driftwood and stones and put them in. I dug small holes – almost impossible, as the shingle rolled back so that two spadefuls became one – and filled them with manure from the farm up the road. THE PLANTS WERE JUST PLONKED IN AND LEFT TO TAKE THEIR CHANCES IN THE WINDS OF DUNGENESS. The easterlies are the worst; they bring salt spray which burns everything. The westerlies only give a battering. WE HAVE THE STRONGEST SUNLIGHT, THE LOWEST RAINFALL, AND TWO LESS WEEKS OF FROST THAN THE REST OF THE UK. Dungeness is set apart, at 'the fifth quarter', the end of the globe; it is the largest shingle formation, with Cape Canaveral, IN THE WORLD.

SEA KALE, CRAMBE MARITIMA, IS THE NESS'S MOST DISTINGUISHED PLANT.

There are more of them here than anywhere in England
– they come up between the boats. Crambe are edible,
but a radiologist told me that they accumulate radioactivity
from the nuclear power station more than any other plant.

They die away completely in winter, just a bud on the corky
stem. In March they start to sprout – the first sign of spring.
The leaves are an inky purple which looks fine in the ochre
pink pebbles, but they rapidly lose the purple and become
a glaucous blue-green.

Then buds appear; by May these turn into sprays of white flowers with little yellow centres
– they have a heavy, honey scent which blows across the Ness. The flowers then turn into
seeds – which look like a thousand peas. They lose their green and become the colour
of bone. At this stage they are at their most beautiful – sprays of pale ochre, several
thousand seeds on each plant. The autumn winds return, the leaves rot at the base, dry
out and blow away; by November the Crambe has completely disappeared.

Year after year they come back – some of the plants must
be fifty years old. In the humus that collects around them
other plants spring up, but the Crambes hold sway.
Caterpillars give up on them – they are too tough; a snail
or two might bite a hole, but on the whole they are left
alone. They look their best in sunlight after rain as the
leaves are designed to catch the rain and feed it to the
centre of the plant; the beads of water glittering on the
plant are an ecstasy.

They survive in this terrain because they have roots at
least twenty feet long – I discovered this after a storm
washed the shingle away, exposing them.

MY GARDEN IS ECOLOGICALLY SOUND, THOUGH WORK OF ANY KIND DISRUPTS THE EXISTING TERRAIN.

Dungeness is an SSSI (Site of Special Scientific Interest), so there are restrictions on what plants can be grown – though to extend this to the fishermen's gardens seems a little hard.

In any case, so many weeds are spectacular flowers: the white campion, mallow, rest-harrow and scabious look wonderful. Introducing these local flowers into the garden makes a little wilderness at the heart of paradise. And there can be no complaints about my flint garden – it spoilt nothing. It was built over the drive of the old cottage.

The dog roses are the joy of the copse by the lakes. Once, when I was transplanting a small seedling to the garden, I was assaulted by an ecological puritan from Canterbury.

DO YOU REALIZE YOU COULD BE DOING DAMAGE?
YES, I SAID.
WELL WHY ARE YOU PLANTING THAT ROSE?
IT'S A DUNGENESS PLANT. IF THE WORLD STOPPED
STILL AND HUMANITY CEASED, WHO COULD TELL IF
IT HAD BEEN PLANTED BY ME OR BY A BIRD?
HE DROVE OFF.

THE NUCLEAR POWER STATION IS A
WONDERMENT. AT NIGHT IT LOOKS LIKE
A GREAT LINER OR A SMALL MANHATTAN
ABLAZE WITH A THOUSAND LIGHTS OF
DIFFERENT COLOURS. A MYSTERIOUS
SHADOW SURROUNDS IT THAT MAKES
IT POSSIBLE FOR THE STARS STILL
TO GLOW IN A CLEAR SUMMER SKY.

I SOLVED THE ROSE PROBLEM:
THE PLANTS I PUT IN NEVER GREW
THEY REMAIN JUST A FOOT HIGH.

But then, when Brian built my extension, it threw up a lot of shingle and I built a bank beyond the white rugosa. Immediately, the roses improved because the bank caught a leeward damp. **I'VE PLANTED ALL OF THEM ALONGSIDE THE DRAINPIPES AND THEY ARE AS GREEN AND HEALTHY AS CAN BE.**

There are three shingle mounds, all very carefully placed. The first was here when I came; it has a dog rose growing on it and a new broom at its side, as well as vetch, and what I call clover – grass pompoms that dance in the wind.

The dry grasses also do this and seem to catch fire in the setting sun.

Michèle Roberts
The Earth Moves

In my garden, here in the **bocage**

In my garden, here in the bocage

mayennais, I grow veg. for **potage**

mayennais, I grow veg. for potage

also herbs such as chives, parsley, sage.

also herbs such as chives, parsley, sage.

At night, promiscuous moles rampage

At night, promiscuous moles rampage

from bed to bed, and rummage

from bed to bed, and rummage

through rosemary, thyme and lovage.

through rosemary, thyme and lovage.

Bursting through borders they put me in a rage

Bursting through borders they put me in a rage

next day, when I survey the damage

next day, when I survey the damage

done to mint, tarragon and borage:

done to mint, tarragon and borage:

all my neat plots messed up. Like vast blots on a page

all my neat plots messed up. Like vast blots on a page

these erupting earthworks revive the adage:

these erupting earthworks revive the adage:

the unconscious is always with us. So I'll engage

the unconscious is always with us. So I'll engage

to free my subversive Inner Mole. I shall no longer wage

to free my subversive Inner Mole. I shall no longer wage

war on the Mole Within. Out of my cage

war on the Mole Within. Out of my cage

I'll tunnel towards the New Molennium Age.

I'll tunnel towards the New Molennium Age.

'THEY ARE OTHER NATIONS'

COLIN SPENCER

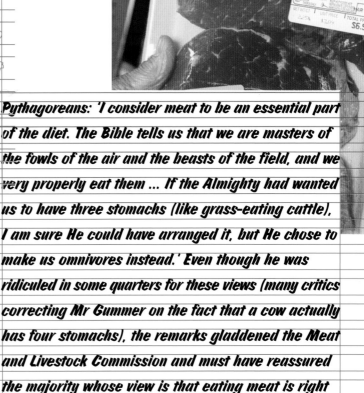

The precise beginnings of the vegetarian ethic are lost in the priestly cults of Ancient Egypt, but through the Orphic movement vegetarianism became one of the influences upon Pythagoras, who gave his name to the diet. After his death a clear thread can be traced from antiquity to present times. In the East, in India and China, as part of Hinduism and Buddhism, vegetarianism has flourished and numbers millions of converts. In the West the story has been one of persecution, suppression and ridicule. From the days of imperial Rome, when both Ovid and Seneca were equivocal in their vegetarianism, lying about their true preferences, to the Gnostic heretics, some of whom worshipped the creator as female and extended kindness and peace to all living things, to the most hated Christian heresy of all, Manicheanism and its progeny, the Bogomils and the Cathars, abstention from meat was seen as a sign of the devil's works, a clear rebellion against the word of God as revealed in Biblical text. Persecution began once Pauline Christianity started to colonise Europe, and wherever it spread vegetarianism was reviled.

In a very significant way the abstainers from animal flesh still are reviled, ridiculed and considered dangerous outsiders in our society - at least by one Cabinet Minister. The statements expressed by the Right Honourable John Gummer in a speech at the International Meat Trade Association on 1 May 1990 might have been said, word for word, any time in the last two thousand years by those who persecuted the

Pythagoreans: 'I consider meat to be an essential part of the diet. The Bible tells us that we are masters of the fowls of the air and the beasts of the field, and we very properly eat them ... If the Almighty had wanted us to have three stomachs (like grass-eating cattle), I am sure He could have arranged it, but He chose to make us omnivores instead.' Even though he was ridiculed in some quarters for these views (many critics correcting Mr Gummer on the fact that a cow actually has four stomachs), the remarks gladdened the Meat and Livestock Commission and must have reassured the majority whose view is that eating meat is right and proper whatever anybody says. Later, in January 1992, Mr Gummer went on to launch Food Sense, a campaign against women who abstain from meat because it could damage their health.

Never before in history has humankind produced such vast quantities of milk and meat, so that these foods have become part of the daily staple diet in the developed world. However much the dairy and meat lobbies strive to produce low-fat milk and leaner meat, the excess saturated fat has to go somewhere and almost certainly ends up elsewhere in our diet. In fact, subsidies are given to hospitals and schools that use saturated-fat products. Cooks at such establishments are encouraged to use more cream, butter, cheese and milk in their catering. Through such policies governments do not show the care due to vulnerable areas of our society, the very young and the infirm and elderly, and knowingly jeopardise their health. Governments are in league with the dairy and meat industries: though with one hand they dispense health advice on changing the diet from one high in sugars and fats, and low in fibre and unrefined carbohydrates, to one very low in fats and sugars and high in grains, legumes, fruits and vegetables, with the other hand they dig deep into Treasury coffers to propagate the present system of over-production in milk and meat.

Recently in the USA the Department of Agriculture offered the same healthy advice, but livestock-producers complained and the agency retracted its statement. In Britain, when the Vegetarian Society placed an advertisement in the press, under the heading 'Putting meat on your plate takes the food from theirs', saying that famine in the developing world is caused partly by grain being imported by developed nations to feed livestock, both the National Farmers Union and the Meat and Livestock Commission complained to the Committee of Advertising Practice (CAP). The Vegetarian Society substantiated every point in the advertising, showing that the UK imports each year from the developing nations £46 million worth of grain grown on land that could be better used to grow food for their own peoples, but the CAP decided the advertisement was misleading, that the image of famine was unacceptable and that the Society had oversimplified the issues.

Government subsidies need to be taken away from the meat and the dairy industries and transferred to fish, fruit and vegetable farming. Further, farmers should be helped not only to change from livestock farming, but to grow a greater diversity of vegetable produce. Many hundreds of types of vegetables and fruits have been lost to us because growers have been encouraged by commerce to concentrate on a very few kinds, from an ever-narrowing range of species. This needs to be reversed.

What, then, could change the policy of governments? They are slow to act, as we have recently seen in the case of holes in the ozone layer – even when there is a direct threat of disaster to our planet, governments tend to procrastinate. Many people consider that the feeding and slaughter of eleven billion fowls and four billion livestock each year are a growing environmental problem which needs immediate consideration. Livestock should be restored to its historical role as a boon to the environment and to enrich agriculture, or in their sheer numbers they will, in their slurry and carcase waste, overwhelm humankind and the earth we live with from insuperable ecological problems. But to do this, to cut down the numbers of livestock, will require dietary changes among the world's meat-eaters. As we have seen, this appears to be happening on a small scale in the UK and the USA. But this reduction is far outweighed by the rise in meat consumption in China, Hungary, the former Czechoslovakia and the Arab world. For, to the majority of nations, meat-eating is still irrevocably entwined with status and wealth, and it is these concepts, as well as Christian tenets of belief, that underpin the desire for meat.

It may be that the desire for meat is also a sensual, even an atavistic one - the texture of cooked muscle is unique and cannot be replicated by vegetables and may give a deep and mysterious satisfaction, stirring a race memory of a time when meat was the prize of arduous hunting. Such responses to food should not be underestimated, but they are also habitual. A change in diet away from meat can soon eradicate such a response and replace it with horror at the burnt corpse lying on the table. If we want to save ourselves, our children and their future, and this planet that we live on, we must alter our diet radically and rethink our concepts of the living world and the respect and consideration that is ultimately due to it.

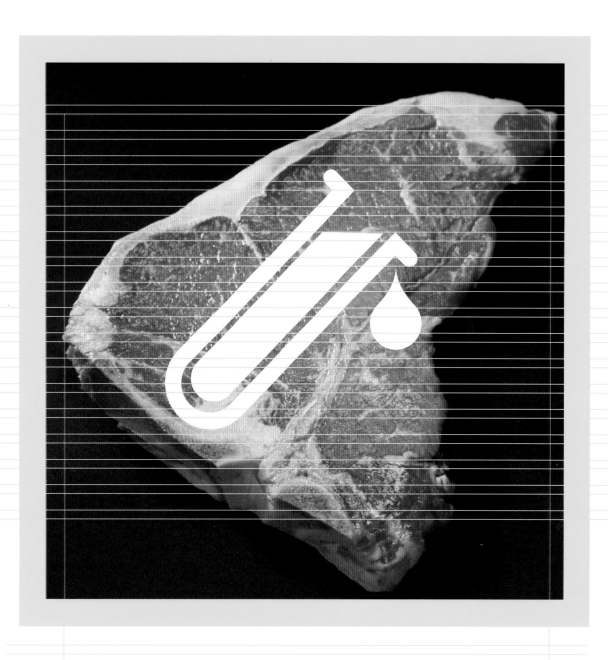

INGREDIENTS:

While the vegetarian lobby today is perhaps not so overtly ridiculed as it once was, vegetarians are still tainted with the image of the morally earnest and the downright cranky. (How many TV sit-coms get a laugh out of having a dig at the veggies? It is as prevalent as it was in Attic comedy in 300 BC.) But the issues that vegetarianism includes are profound and all-embracing, and this invites the scorn of the nervous and insecure. Today the diet has powerful millennial associations of salvation. For the believers it is the diet which will save the planet, halt the greenhouse effect, feed the Third World, banish malnutrition. It is the diet which heals the self, in both mind and body, halts the killer heart attack and the insidious growth of cancer. It is the diet which can feed the whole of the earth's population even if it doubles within the next forty years. It is the diet which Gaia approves of and, if the human race are her infants, it is the only one by which she will suckle her brood. Whether all this is true or not, these notions are passionately believed in by great numbers of people, many of them distinguished and articulate. And the number of adherents is swelling daily. Several facts are indisputable: as omnivores, human beings can easily survive and sustain themselves in full vigour on a diet without animal flesh; what is more, such a diet is on the whole healthier; and such a diet, without cruelty or unnecessary killing, is more humane.

The American naturalist Henry Beston, in his account of a year in the life of the Great Beach of Cape Cod, The Outermost House, first published in 1928, put his finger on it when he said: 'We need another and a wiser and perhaps a more mystical concept of animals.' He rejected the fact that the animal was measured against man and patronised for its incompleteness. Animals have extended senses that we have lost and they hear voices to which we are deaf. Beston says: 'They are not brethren; they are not underlings; they are other nations, caught with ourselves in the net of life and time, fellow prisoners of the splendour and travail of the earth.'

Think on that, then turn to a broiler shed of seven-week-old chickens: twenty thousand of them, about to be slaughtered, with legs so deformed and brittle they snap when the stockman picks them up; with the equivalent of bed sores suppurating on their thighs where they have inevitably rested on urine-sodden litter. All this for a cheap chicken dinner? Think on what Beston has said and turn to a calf crammed in a wooden crate for eight months unable to move, fed on a rich liquid diet of pig's blood, chocolate and dried milk, deficient in iron so that its flesh will be white to please the gourmet. Look at the dairy cow who should give only five litres of milk a day to her calf but under intensive milking gives anything from 25 to 40 litres a day and after six or seven years is a broken creature, old long before her years, who goes to slaughter to make mince for burgers.

Our common humanity tells us that this is no way to treat animals, so eminently worthy of our respect and kindness. But worldwide, the exploitation of animals is a flourishing industry that grows more diabolic every day.

"life is a matter of passing the time enjoyably.
there may be other things in life, but i've been
too busy passing my time enjoyably to think very
deeply about them."
peter cook

"'you' your joys and your sorrows, your memories and ambitions, your sense of
personal identity and free will, are in fact no more than the behaviour of a vast
assembly of nerve cells and their associated molecules."
francis crick

"civilization gets the historians it deserves."
roy porter

test tubes:

Robert Harris

Bletchley Park

In the aftern00n the cryptanaly5t5 were 5p1it int0 team5.

Turing wa5 a55igned t0 w0rk with Puk0w5ki, rede5igning the 'b0mbe', the giant decrypt0r which the great Marian Rejew5ki 0f the P01i5h Cipher Bureau had bui1t in 1938 t0 attack Enigma. Jerich0 wa5 5ent t0 the 5tab1e b10ck behind the man5i0n t0 ana1y5e encrypted German radi0 traffic.

Jericho's work was pleasantly academic. Three or four times a day, a motorcycle dispatch-rider would clatter into the courtyard at the back of the big house bearing a pouch of intercepted German cryptograms. Jericho sorted them by frequency and call sign and marked them up on charts in coloured crayons - red for the Luftwaffe, green for the German Army - until gradually, from the unintelligible babble, shapes emerged. Stations in a radio net allowed to talk freely to one another made, when plotted on the stable wall, a crisscross pattern within a circle. Nets in which the only line of communication was two-way, between a headquarters and its out-stations, resembled stars. Circle-nets and star-nets. Kreis und Stern.

This idyll lasted eight months, until the German offensive in May 1940. Up to then, there had been scarcely enough material for the cryptanalysts to make a serious attack on Enigma. But as the Wehrmacht swept through Holland, Belgium, France, the babble of wireless traffic became a roar. From three or four motorcycle pouches of material, the volume increased to thirty or forty; to a hundred; to two hundred.

It wa5 1ate One mOrning abOut a week after thi5 had
5tarted that JerichO fe1t a tOuch On hi5 e1bOw and
turned tO find Turing, 5mi1ing.

'There'5 5OmeOne I want yOu tO meet, TOm.'

'I'm rather bu5y at pre5ent, A1an, tO be hOne5t.'

'Her name'5 Agne5. I rea11y think yOu Ought tO 5ee her.'

JerichO a1mO5t argued. A year 1ater he wOu1d have
argued, but at that time he wa5 5ti11 tOO much in
awe Of Turing nOt tO dO a5 he wa5 tO1d. He tugged hi5
jacket Off the back Of hi5 chair and wa1ked Out,
5hrugging it On, intO the May 5un5hine.

By this time the Park had already started to be transformed. Most of the trees at the side of the lake had been chopped down to make way for a series of large wooden huts. The maze had been uprooted and replaced by a low brick building, outside which a small crowd of cryptanalysts had gathered. There was a sound coming from within it, of a sort Jericho had never heard before, a humming and a clattering, something between a loom and a printing press. He followed Turing through the door. Inside, the noise was deafening, reverberating off the whitewashed walls and the corrugated iron ceiling. A brigadier, an air commodore, two men in overalls and a frightened-looking Wren with her fingers in her ears were standing round the edge of the room staring at a large machine full of revolving drums. A blue flash of electricity arced across the top. There was a fizz and a crackle, a smell of hot oil and overheated metal.

'It's the redesigned Polish bombe,' said Turing. 'I thought I'd call her Agnes.' He rested his long, pale fingers tenderly on the metal frame. There was a bang and he snatched them away again. 'I do hope she works all right …'

The bombe was heavy – Jericho guessed it must weigh more than half a ton – and even though it was mounted on castors it still took all his strength, combined with the engineer's, to drag it away from the wall. Jericho pulled while the engineer went behind it and put his shoulder to the frame to heave. It came away at last with a screech and the Wrens moved in to strip it.

The decryptor was a monster, like something out of an H. G. Wells fantasy of the future: a black metal cabinet, eight feet wide and six feet tall, with scores of five-inch-diameter drum wheels set into the front. The back was hinged and opened up to show a bulging mass of coloured cables and the dull gleam of metal drums. In the place where it had stood on the concrete floor there was a large puddle of oil.

Jericho wiped his hands on a rag and retreated to watch from a corner. Elsewhere in the hut a score of other bombes were churning away on other Enigma keys and the noise and the heat were how he imagined a ship's engine room might be. One Wren went round to the back of the cabinet and began di5c0nnecting and rep1ugging the cab1e5. The 0ther m0ved a10ng the fr0nt, pu11ing 0ut each drum in turn and checking it. Whenever 5he f0und a fau1t in the wiring 5he w0u1d hand the drum t0 the engineer wh0 w0u1d 5tr0ke the tiny bru5h wire5 back int0 p1ace with a pair 0f tweezer5. The c0ntact bru5he5 were a1way5 fraying, ju5t a5 the be1t which c0nnected the mechani5m t0 the big e1ectric m0t0r had a tendency t0 5tretch and 51ip whenever there wa5 a heavy 10ad. And the engineer5 had never quite g0t the earthing right, 50 that the cabinet5 had a tendency t0 give 0ff p0werfu1 e1ectric 5h0ck5.

Jerich0 th0ught it wa5 the w0r5t j0b 0f a11. A pig 0f a j0b. Eight h0ur5 a day, 5ix day5 a week, c00ped up in thi5 wind0w1e55, deafening ce11. He turned away t0 100k at hi5 watch. He didn' t want them t0 5ee hi5 impatience. It wa5 near1y ha1f pa5t e1even.

It 100k5 a5 if B1etch1ey Park i5 the 5ing1e greate5t achievement 0f

Britain during 1939-45, perhap5 during thi5 century a5 a wh01e.'

Ge0rge 5teiner

Of all the changes which have taken place in moving from the baseline, unsophisticated foods of nature to what we eat today, the European manipulation of our domestic animals has been one of the most illustrative.

It is a striking example because the change has been so large and because its new end product has been simulated in so many different ways which today we accept without question.

There is no doubt that today's domestic animals are different from their wild counterparts. Once man began to breed animals selectively and determine what they ate in order to favour this or that useful characteristic, he also began to introduce unintended changes. Juliet Clutton-Brock has some interesting comments to make on this in her book **Domesticated Animals from Early Times**. She points out that domestication 'causes an imbalance in the rate of growth of different parts of the organism' so that the adult animal is shaped differently from its wild counterparts:

Within a very few generations of breeding in captivity, the facial region of the skull and the jaws becomes shortened, this being common in many species but is most apparent in early domestic dogs. At first there is no corresponding reduction in size of the cheek teeth which are genetically much more stable than the bones of the skull. This causes a crowding or compaction of the pre-molars and molars, a character that is used to distinguish the remains of the earliest domestic dogs from those of wild wolves.

The sound-case of the ear drum (known as the timpanic bolla) is much smaller in a dog's skull than in a wolf's; the same thing can be seen by comparing the skull of any domestic species with the corresponding wild one. The timpanic bolla of a sheep's skull seems like a vestigial relic when compared with that of a wild species of similar size. This sense organ seems to become smaller in domestic animals relative to their overall size, and one of the most significant changes is that their relative brain size also shrinks. The reduction is substantial, around 30 per cent.

This loss in brain and sensory capacity is additional testimony for the idea that body size can increase while at the same time relative brain size can diminish. Furthermore, it is tempting to make a connection between this loss of brain capacity and another change which is perhaps the most significant of all in its effect on the humans who eat domesticated animals. It is so unexpected that, when first discovered, it took years of argument and a series of scientific papers to convince the sceptics. The story starts with a buffalo shot in Africa. The animal looked well fleshed and fat and was shot for that reason to provide meat.

When the buffalo was skinned, the most striking feature was the lean nature of the meat: there was virtually no fat to be seen. There was no question of the animal being short of food: it provided mountains of red meat. The picture many people have of wild animals living precariously near the edge of starvation is wide of the mark; this particular buffalo had spent its life in the most lush part of Uganda where tropical heat and ample water produce grass in abundance. These riverine areas of East Africa have an enormous primary productivity, up to 60 tons of plant life per acre in a year. Certainly the buffalo was not lean because it was short of food.

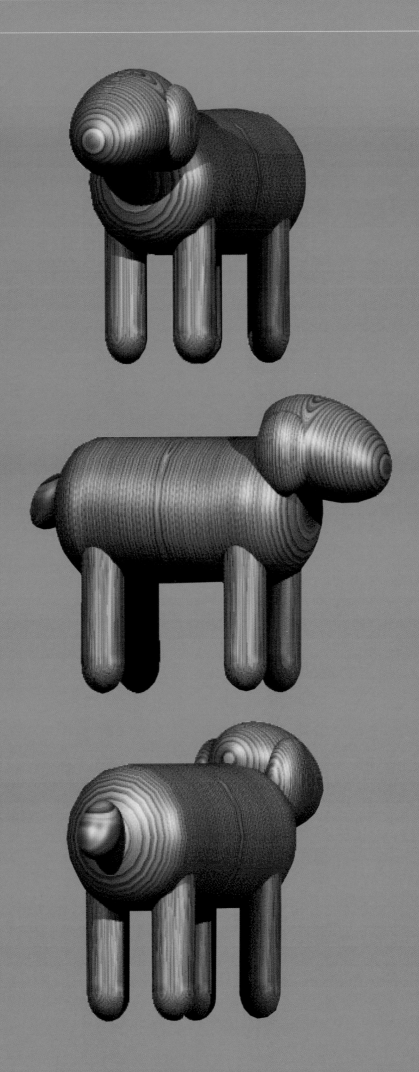

A second unexpected difference became apparent when the buffalo meat was analysed to see if its fatty acids were any different from English beef. Animal fats were assume to be the rigid saturated type, such as is found in domesticated 'fatstock' and used to make candles. This 'fact' has led several government committees to recommend eating less meat to reduce heart disease on the assumption that meat fat was the same saturated fat.

However this assumption turned out to be incorrect. Instead of finding the buffalo meat full of the saturated fatty acids as expected, it was rich in the essential polyunsaturated fatty acids. Meat samples collected from other buffaloes and wild herbivores were all, without exception, rich in essential polyunsaturated fatty acids; the very opposite of the accepted view of meat as a saturated food to be avoided.

Up to this time it had been generally believed that the essential structural lipids were destroyed in the stomachs of ruminant animals. Buffaloes are ruminants so the idea that buffalo fat contained a high proportion of essential, polyunsaturated lipids was automatically greeted with disbelief. A piece of the buffalo meat was then given to the laboratory of the government chemist, where it was subjected to their analytical techniques. They confirmed and published the fact that it was indeed rich in linoleic and alpha-linolenic acids, the two parent essential fatty acids used in structural lipids.

When the article dealing with this appeared in the **Lancet** in 1968, it attracted much criticism. The analytical methods had to be wrong. Some ten scientific papers later, at least some acknowledged that the data was correct. The reason for the confusion was the use of the term 'animal fat'. As described previously, there are two types of fat in the body, storage; and structural. The storage fat is in a sense the rubbish dump reserved for burning as fuel. The structural fat is tailored to the requirement of cellular function and is therefore built with

essential polyunsaturated fatty acids – and quite different in nature to the depot fats.

If an animal is overfed and denied exercise it simply gets fat. If the process is continued long enough, it loses muscle and depot fats infiltrate the retreating muscle fibres, giving the 'marbled' appearance characteristic of modern intensively fed animals. This infiltrating fat is, like the rest of the storage fat of ruminants, saturated fat. Analysis of meat from this type of animal shows its fat to be largely saturated.

By contrast, under natural or free-living circumstances this cannot happen. The animal eats the right kind of food in amounts appropriate to its growth and exercise and the requirements for the different seasons. Hence analysis of its meat shows it to be characterised by the type of fatty acids involved in cell function and structure; that is, it is rich in the essential fatty acids.

Here in the buffalo meat was plain evidence that throughout man's evolution the animals he ate would have had a low fat content, and what fat they had contained a high proportion of essential structural lipid – quite different to 'marbled' beef. The fat in the domestic animal was the opposite: importantly, it is the kind of fat that experimenters had linked with heart disease. Man had unwittingly changed his animals in a direction now known to increase the risk of heart disease.

What went wrong to produce such an unhealthy result? The answer emerges when the history of the development of modern meat animals is examined: in summary, they have been changes by alterations in the conditions under with the animals themselves were made to live.

The natural foodstuff of the ancestor to our domestic cattle was soft bushy, leafy material, the lower branches of trees, sedges, herbs and grasses. This made it ideally suitable for operating in the forest openings and encouragement of the

numbers of these species would undoubtedly have led to a wider and more extensive use of materials. Paintings of cattle done in the seventeenth, eighteenth and nineteenth centuries show them in very much this kind of environment. The vegetation is clearly mixed with trees, bushes and grasses and contrasts starkly with the present use of open fields and electric fences. Darwin provides incidental confirmation of this situation when he discusses the evolution of the long neck. He asks the reader to look at a field of cattle where he will see the lower branches of the trees have been 'planed to an exact height' where the heads of the cattle can reach.

Before the enclosures of the seventeenth century, cattle had mostly been herded in open grass, bushland and forest. When people began to contain them in fields, these were at first fairly simple affairs. They were not cleared and they did not have special grasses growing in them. Even so, the variety of food that the animals could select for themselves was drastically reduced. They ate the hedgerows, but the human response to that was to replace the succulent bushes with thorns. Enclosing an animal in a field meant simply that man now decided what the animal should eat.

The next move was intensification. A paradox in animal management arose fairly soon after the enclosures were created. When the number of animals in a field was increased, instead of doing worse as the food supply was shared out, they did better. The explanation of this paradox is simple. If grass is allowed to grow up unchecked, it produces tall stems with the seed heads at the top. The stems are rich in fibre but not in energy. Intensifying the number of animals on a field therefore increased the energy of the animal's food throughout the growing season. The simultaneous reduction in the amount of exercise reduced muscle development and led to more fat deposition. This tactic reached its zenith in the more modern use of stalls in which to keep and feed the animals. Added to all this was the clever idea of castration, again to make the males quiet and to gain weight faster: but the weight was largely fat – saturated, storage fat. When people later became technically competent enough to manufacture feeds for animals, they modelled the energy balance not on the autumn but on the high-energy spring grass. Hence the development of 'high-energy' feeds which were heralded with the advertising claim that they put on weight much faster than before.

Many know from experience that when anyone puts on weight rapidly what he or she puts on is storage fat, and the same is true of animals. The high-energy grasses made the production of fat carcasses easy and profitable. The process was pushed a long step further by the introduction of high-energy winter feeds. In **As You Like It** Shakespeare's shepherd remarks how his sheep grow fat in the spring and lean in the winter, and these seasonal variations are a necessary part of biology.

Modern farming methods force animals to grow steadily fatter all the year long. They live on a perpetual spring diet.

This high-energy diet combined well with another development. When the animals were sold in the market, the heavier they were the better the price. So they then chose those that put on weight fastest for breeding with the aim of producing big, round well-covered animals. They fell into the trap of selecting genetically for the fat animal.

The combination of all these tactics culminated in the prize-winning beast at the Smithfield Show a few years ago. The butcher who bought it, hoping to win credit for his company by selling this highly acclaimed carcass, found instead that the meat was unsaleable: it was so fat that even in England no one wanted to eat it, or so the story goes.

Mr Gordon Williams farmed animals in the hills above the Wye valley in Wales for most of his life until he retired in 1971. His farmhouse has a bread oven in the kitchen wall and he described how they cooked large amounts of meat for the villagers who helped cut the hay in the autumn. They also used the bread oven to make candles out of the white storage fat from their sheep and cattle to light the house during the winter. Electricity did not reach his farm until the late 1940s.

There are two interesting points which emerge from Mr Williams's story. First, the amount of exercise involved in getting to and from work, in work itself or even cutting enough wood to keep the family warm in winter would have burnt up many calories which today are conserved because we drive by car or bus and have central heating, cooking fuel, electric light and hot water on tap. The second point is that without electricity the house had to be lit by candles. Without Kuwaiti, Texan or North Sea oil, those candles were made from the white storage fat of beef and sheep. Beeswax provided an additional material for making candles, but there were obviously only a few of these and they were most used in churches. Today candles are made from paraffin wax obtained from the oil companies.

Initially storage fat would have been an important form of energy, for people had to work hard and the winter months would have added an extra demand in energy expenditure. However the fat was not only used for food, but also made these candles and boot and saddle polish. Today, with our sedentary lifestyle, the high fat carcass is an anachronism. These commodities are made from fossil oils and the fat now goes into the manufacture of pies, sausages, pastries, cooking fats, margarines, ice-cream, biscuits, cakes, convenience foods, TV dinners, quick-chill meals, snack foods, crisps and even bread.

What is the size of the fat production problem? In the UK the present meat consumption is about 3.9 million tons per year. The energy contained in its storage fat represents about 1.097 times 10 to the power of 14 Joules a day, or enough to keep an oil-fired 1200 Megawatt station in operation for a year. Translated into candle power, the present animal production in the UK provides enough white storage fat for all families to throw away their electric light bulbs. We now eat the candles.

Science and the Sanctity of Life
Peter Medawar

I do not intend to deny that the advance of science may sometimes have consequences that endanger, if not life itself, then the quality of life or our self-respect as human beings (for it is in this wider sense that I think 'sanctity' should be construed). Nor shall I waste time by defending science as a whole or scientists generally against a charge of inner or essential malevolence. The Wicked Scientist is not to be taken seriously: Dr Strangelove, Dr Moreau, Dr Moriarty, Dr Mabuse, Dr Frankenstein (an honorary degree, this) and the rest of them are puppets of Gothic fiction. Scientists, on the whole, are amiable and well-meaning creatures. There must be very few wicked scientists. There are, however, plenty of wicked philosophers, wicked priests and wicked politicians.

One of the gravest charges ever made against science is that biology has now put it into our power to corrupt both the body and the mind of man. By scientific means (the charge runs) we can now breed different kinds and different races – different 'makes', almost – of human beings, degrading some, making aristocrats of others, adapting others still to special purposes: treating them in fact like dogs, for this is how we **have** treated dogs. Or again: science now makes it possible to dominate and control the thought of human beings - to improve them, perhaps, if that should be our purpose, but more often to enslave or to corrupt with evil teaching.

But these things have always been possible. At any time in the past five thousand years it would have been within our power to embark on a programme of selecting and culling human beings and raising breeds as different from one another as toy poodles and Pekinese are from St Bernards and Great Danes. In a genetic sense the empirical arts of the breeder are as easily applicable to human beings as to horses – more easily applicable, in fact, for human beings are high **evolvable** animals, a property they owe partly to an open and uncomplicated breeding system, which allows them a glorious range of inborn diversity and therefore a tremendous evolutionary potential; and partly to their lack of physical specialisations (in the sense in which ant-eaters and woodpeckers and indeed dogs are specialised), a property which gives human beings a sort of amateur status among animals. And it has always been possible to pervert or corrupt human beings by coercion, propaganda or evil indoctrination. Science has not yet improved these methods, nor have scientists used them. They have, however, been used to great effect by politicians, philosophers and priests.

The mischief that science may do grows just as often out of trying to do good - as, for example, improving the yield of soil is intended to do good - as out of actions intended to be destructive. The reason is simple enough: however hard we try, we do not and sometimes cannot foresee all the distant consequences of scientific innovation. No one clearly foresaw that the widespread use of antibiotics might bring about an evolution of organisms resistant to their action. No one could have predicted that X-irradiation was a possible cause of cancer. No one could have foreseen the speed and scale with which advances in medicine and public health would create a problem of over-population that threatens to undo much of what medical science has worked for. (Thirty years ago the talk was all of how the people of the Western world were reproducing themselves too slowly to make good the wastage of mortality; we heard tell of a 'Twilight of Parenthood' and wondered rather fearfully where it all would end.) But somehow or other we shall get round all these problems, for every one of them is soluble, even the population problem, and even though its solution is obstructed above all else by the bigotry of some of our fellow men.

I choose from medicine and medical biology one or two concrete examples of how advances in science threaten or seem to threaten the sanctity of human life. Many of these threats, of course, are in no sense distinctively medical, though they are often loosely classified as such. They are merely medical contexts for far more pervasive dangers. One of them is our increasing state of dependence on medical services and the medical industries. What would become of the diabetic if the supplies of insulin dried up, or of the victims of Addison's disease deprived of synthetic steroids? Questions of this kind might be asked of every service that society provides. In a complex society we all sustain and depend upon each other – for transport, communications, food, goods, shelter, protection and a hundred other things. The medical industries will not break down all by themselves, and if they do break down it will be only one episode of a far greater disaster.

The same goes for the economic burden imposed by illness in any community that takes some collective responsibility for

0011–8532/90 0.00 + .

the health of its citizens. All shared burdens have a cost which is to a greater or lesser degree shared between us: education, pensions, social welfare, legal aid and every other social service, including government.

We are getting nearer what is distinctively medical when we ask ourselves about the economics, logistics and morality of keeping people alive by medical intervention and medical devices. At present it is the cost and complexity of the operation, and the shortage of machines and organs, that denies a kidney graft or an artificial kidney to anyone in need of it. The limiting factors are thus still economic and logistic. But what about the morality of keeping people alive by these heroic medical contrivances? I do not think it is possible to give any answer that is universally valid or that, if it were valid, would remain so for more than a very few years. Medical contrivances extend all the way from pills and plasters and bottles of tonic to complex mechanical prostheses, which will one day include mechanical hearts. At what point shall we say we are wantonly interfering with nature and prolonging life beyond what is proper and humane?

In practice the answer we give is founded not upon abstract moralising but upon a certain natural sense of the fitness of things, a feeling that is shared by most kind and reasonable people even if we cannot define it in philosophically defensible or legally accountable terms. It is only at international conferences that we tend to adopt the conviction that people behave like idiots unless acting upon clear and well-turned instructions to behave sensibly. There is in fact no general formula or smooth form of words we can appeal to when in perplexity.

Moreover, our sense of what is fit and proper is not something fixed, as if it were inborn and instinctual. It changes as our experience grows, as our understanding depends and as we enlarge our grasp of possibilities – just as living religions and laws change, and social structures and family relationships.

I feel that our sense of what is right and just is already beginning to be offended by the idea of taking great exertions to keep alive grossly deformed or monstrous newborn children, particularly if their deformities of body or mind arise from major defects of the genetic apparatus. There are in fact scientific reasons for changing an opinion that might have seemed just and reasonable a hundred years ago.

Everybody takes it for granted, because it is so obviously true, that a married couple will have children of very different kinds and constitutions on different occasions. But the traditional opinion, by which most of us are still unconsciously guided, is that the child conceived on any one occasion is the unique and necessary product of that occasion: **that** child would have been conceived, we tend to think, or no child at all. This interpretation is quite false, but human dignity and security clamour for it. A child sometimes wonderingly acknowledges that he would never have been born at all if his mother and father had not chanced to meet and fall in love and marry. He does not realise that, instead of conceiving him, his parents might have conceived any one of a hundred thousand other children, all unlike each other and unlike himself. Only over the past one hundred years has it come to be realised that the child conceived on any one occasion belongs to a vast cohort of Possible Children, any one of whom might have been conceived and born if a different spermatozoon had chanced to fertilise the mother's egg cell – and the egg cell itself is only one of very many. It is a matter of luck then, a sort of genetic lottery. And sometimes it is cruelly bad luck – some terrible genetic conjunction, perhaps, which once in ten or twenty thousand times will bring together a matching pair of damaging recessive genes. Such a misfortune, being the outcome of a random process, is considered in isolation, completely and essentially pointless. It is not even strictly true to say that a particular inborn abnormality must have lain within the genetic potentiality of the parents, for the malignant gene may have arisen **de novo** by mutation. The whole process is unhallowed – is, in the older sense of that word, profane.[1]

I am saying that if we feel ourselves under a moral obligation to take every possible exertion to keep a monstrous embryo or new born child alive **because** it is in some sense the naturally

[1] *An eminent theologian once said to me that I was making altogether too much fuss about this kind of mischance. It was, he said, all in the nature of things and already comprehended within our way of thinking; it was not different in principle from being accidentally struck on the head by a falling roof tile. But I think there is an important difference of principle. In the process by which a chromosome is allotted to one germ cell rather than another, and in the union of germ cells, luck is of the very essence. The random element is an integral, indeed a defining, characteristic of Mendelian inheritance. All I am saying is that it is difficult to wear a pious expression when the fall of the dice produces a child that is structurally or biochemically crippled from birth or conception.*

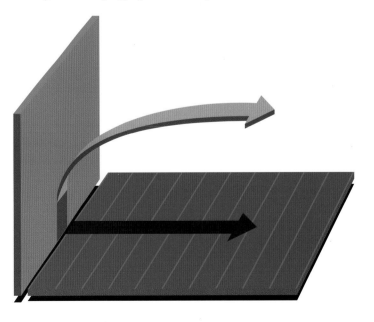

Figure 1.

0011–8532/90 0.00 + .

intended – and therefore the unique and privileged – product of its parents' union at the moment of its conception, then we are making an elementary and cruel blunder: for it is **luck** that determines which one child is in fact conceived out of the cohort of Possible Children that might have been conceived by those two parents on that occasion. I am not using the word 'luck' of conception as such, nor of the processes of embryonic and foetal growth, nor indeed in any sense that derogates from the wonder and awe in which we hold processes of great complexity and natural beauty which we do not fully understand; I am simply using it in its proper sense and proper place.[2]

This train of thought leads me directly to eugenics – 'the science', to quote its founder, Francis Galton, 'which deals with all the influences that improve the inborn qualities of a race; also with those that develop them to the utmost advantage'. Because the upper and lower boundaries of an individual's capability and performance are set by his genetic make-up, it is clear that if eugenic policies were to be ill-founded or mistakenly applied they could offer a most terrible threat to the sanctity and dignity of human life. This threat I shall now examine.

Eugenics is traditionally subdivided into positive and negative eugenics. Positive eugenics has to do with attempts to improve human beings by genetic policies, particularly policies founded upon selective or directed breeding. Negative eugenics has the lesser ambition of attempting to eradicate as many as possible of our inborn imperfections. The distinction is useful and pragmatically valid for the following reasons. Defects of the genetic constitution (such as those which manifest themselves as Down's syndrome ('mongolism'), haemophilia, galactosaemia, phenylketonuria and a hundred other hereditary abnormalities) have a much simpler genetic basis than desirable characteristics like beauty, high physical performance, intelligence or fertility. This is almost self-evident. All geneticists believe that 'fitness' in its most general sense depends on a nicely balanced co-ordination and interaction of genetic factors, itself the product of laborious and long-drawn out evolutionary adjustment. It is inconceivable, indeed self-contradictory, that an animal should evolve into the possession of some complex pattern of interaction between genes that made it inefficient, undesirable, or unfit – that is, **less** well adapted to the prevailing circumstances. Likewise, a motor car will run badly for any one of a multitude of particular and special reasons, but runs well because of the harmonious mechanical interactions made possible by a sound and economically viable design.

Negative eugenics is a more manageable and understandable enterprise than positive eugenics. Nevertheless, many well-meaning people believe that, with the knowledge and skills already available to us, and within the framework of a society that upholds the rights of individuals, it is possible in principle to raise a superior kind of human being by a controlled or 'recommended' scheme of mating and by regulating the number of children each couple should be allowed or encouraged to have. If stockbreeders can do it, the argument runs, why

[2] There are, perhaps, weighty legal and social reasons why even tragically deformed children should be kept alive (for who is to decide? and where do we draw the line?), but these are outside my terms of reference.

should not we? – for who can deny that domesticated animals have been improved by deliberate human intervention?

I think this argument is unsound for a lesser and for a more important reason.

Firstly, domesticated animals have not been 'improved' in the sense in which we should use that word of human beings. They have not enjoyed an all-round improvement, for some special characteristics or faculties have been so far as possible 'fixed' without special regard to and sometimes at the expense of others. Tameness and docility are most easily achieved at the expense of intelligence, but that does not matter if what we are interested in is, say, the quality and yield of wool.

Secondly, the ambition of the stockbreeder in the past, though he did not realise it, was twofold: not merely to achieve a predictably uniform product by artificial selection, but also to establish an internal genetic uniformity (homozygosity) in respect of the characters under selection, to make sure that the stock would 'breed true' – for it would be a disaster if characters selected over many generations were to be irrecoverably mixed up in a hybrid progeny. The older stockbreeder believed that uniformity and breeding true were characteristics that necessarily went together, whereas we now know that they can be separately achieved. And he expected his product to fulfil two quite distinct functions which we now know to be separable, and often better separated: on the one hand, to be in themselves the favoured stock and the top performers – the super-sheep or super-mice – and, on the other hand, to be the parents of the next generation of that stock. It is rather as if Rolls-Royces, in addition to being an end-product of manufacture, had to be so designed as to give rise to Rolls-Royce progeny.

It is just as well these older views are mistaken, for with naturally outbreeding populations such as our own, genetic uniformity, arrived at and maintained by selective inbreeding, is a highly artificial state of affairs with many inherent and ineradicable disadvantages.

Stockbreeders, under genetic guidance, are now therefore inclining more and more towards a policy of deliberate and nicely calculated cross-breeding. In the simplest case, two partially inbred and internally uniform stocks are raised and perpetuated to provide two uniform lineages of parents, but the eugenic goal, the marketable end-product or high performer, is the progeny of a cross between members of the two parental stocks. Being of hybrid make-up, the progeny do not breed true, and are not in fact bred from; they can be likened to a manufactured end-product: but they can be uniformly reproduced at will by crossing the two parental stocks. Many more sophisticated regimens of cross-breeding have been adopted or attempted, but the innovation of principle is the same. Firstly, the end-products are all like each other and are faithfully reproducible, but are not bred from because they do not breed true: the organisms that represent the eugenic goal have been relieved of the responsibility of reproducing themselves. And secondly, the end-products, though uniform in the sense of being like each other, are to a large extent hybrid – heterozygous as opposed to homozygous – in genetic composition.

The practices of stockbreeders can therefore no longer be used to support the argument that a policy of positive eugenics is applicable in principle to human beings in a society respecting

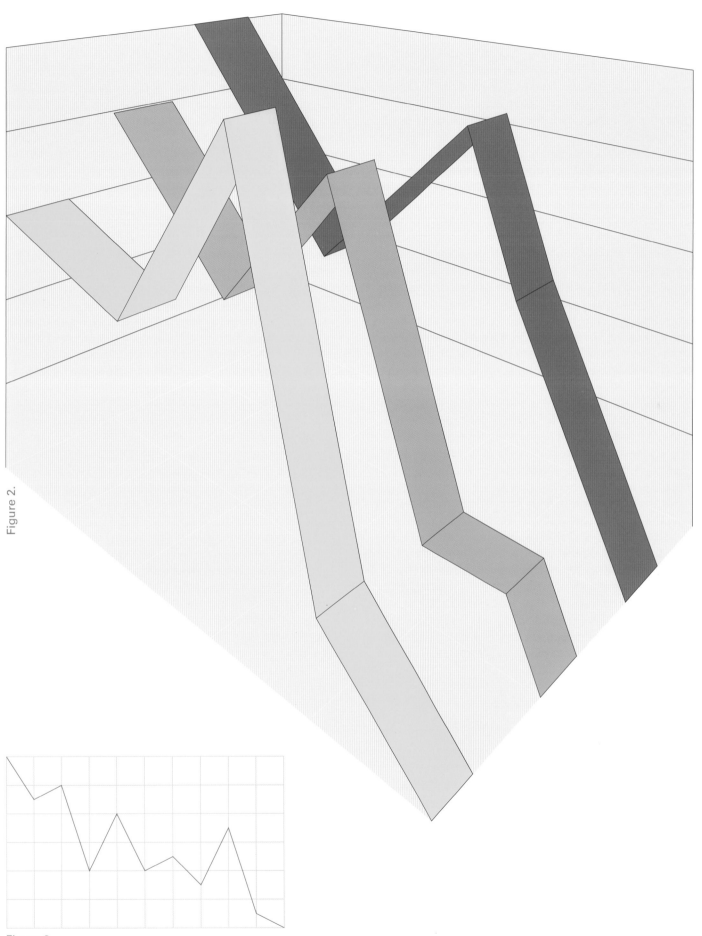

Figure 2.

Figure 3.

0011–8532/90 0.00 + .

the rights of individuals. The genetical manufacture of supermen by a policy of cross-breeding between two or more parental stocks is unacceptable today, and the idea that it might one day become acceptable is unacceptable also.

A deep fallacy does in fact eat into the theoretical foundations of positive eugenics and that older conception of stockbreeding out of which it grew. The fallacy was to suppose that the **product** of evolution, that is the outcome of an episode of evolutionary change, was a new and improved genetic formula (genotype) which conferred a higher degree of adaptedness on the individuals that possessed it. This improved formula, representing a new and more successful solution of the problems of remaining alive in a hostile environment, was thought to be shared by nearly all members of the newly evolved population, and to be stable except in so far as further evolution might cause it to change again. Moreover, the population would have to be predominantly homozygous in respect of the genetic factors entering into the new formula, for otherwise the individuals possessing it would not breed true to type, and everything natural selection had won would be squandered in succeeding generations.

Most geneticists think this view mistaken. It is **populations** that evolve, not the lineages and pedigrees of old-fashioned evolutionary 'family trees', and the end-product of an evolutionary episode is not a new genetic formula enjoyed by a group of similar individuals, but a new spectrum of genotypes, a new pattern of genetic inequality, definable only in terms of the population as a whole. Naturally outbreeding populations are not genetically uniform, even to a first approximation. They are persistently and obstinately diverse in respect of nearly all constitutive characters which have been studied deeply enough to say for certain whether they are uniform or not. It is the **population** that breeds true, not its individual members. The progeny of a given population are themselves a population within the same pattern of genetic make-up as their parents – except in so far as evolutionary or selective forces may have altered it. Nor should we think of uniformity as a desirable state of affairs which **we** can achieve even if nature, unaided, cannot. It is inherently undesirable, for a great many reasons.

The goal of positive eugenics, in its older form, cannot be achieved, and I feel that eugenic policy must be confined (paraphrasing Karl Popper) to **piecemeal genetic engineering**.

That is just what negative eugenics amounts to; and now, rather than deal in generalities, I should like to consider a concrete eugenic problem and discuss the morality of one of its possible solutions.

Some 'inborn' defects – some defects that are the direct consequence of an individual's genetic make-up as it was fixed at the moment of conception – are said to be of **recessive** determination. By a recessive defect is meant one that is caused by, to put it crudely, a 'bad' gene that must be present in **both** the gametes that unite to form a fertilised egg, that is, in both spermatozoon and egg cell, not just in one or the other. If the bad gene **is** present in only one of the gametes, the individual that grows out of its fusion with the other is said to be a **carrier** (technically, a heterozygote).

Recessive defects are individually rather rare – their frequency is of the order of 10^{-4} (one in ten thousand) – but collectively they are most important. Among them are, for example, phenylketonuria, a congenital inability to handle a certain dietary constituent, the amino acid phenylalanine, a constituent of many proteins; galactosaemia, another inborn biochemical deficiency, the victims of which cannot cope metabolically with galactose, an immediate derivative of milk sugar; and, more common than either, fibrocystic disease of the pancreas, believed to be the symptom of a generalised disorder of mucus-secreting cells. All three are caused by particular genetic defects; but their secondary consequences are manifold and deep-seated. The phenylketonuric baby is on the way to becoming an imbecile. The victim of galactosaemia may become blind through cataract and be mentally retarded.

Contrary to popular superstition, many congenital ailments can be prevented or, if not prevented, cured. But in this context prevention and cure have very special meanings.

The phenylketonuric or galactosaemic child may be protected from the consequences of his genetic lesion by keeping him on a diet free from phenylalanine in the one case or lactose in the other. This is a most unnatural proceeding, and much easier said than done, but I take it no one would be prepared to argue that it was an unwarrantable interference with the workings of providence. It is not a cure in the usual medical sense because it neither removes nor repairs the underlying congenital deficiency. What it does is to create around the patient a special little

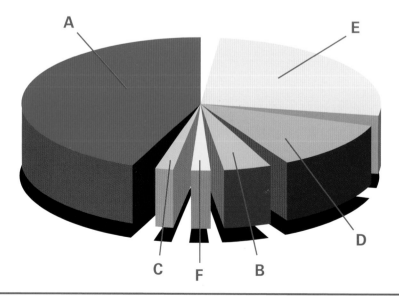

Figure 4.

0011–8532/90 0.00 + .

world, a microcosm free from phenylalanine or galactose as the case may be, in which the genetic deficiency cannot express itself outwardly.

Now consider the underlying morality of prevention. We can prevent phenylketonuria by preventing the genetic conjunction responsible for it in the first instance, that is, by preventing the coming together of an egg cell and a sperm each carrying that same one harmful recessive gene. All but a very small proportion of overt phenylketonurics are the children of parents who are both carriers – carriers, you remember, being the people who inherited the gene from one only of the two gametes that fused at their conception. Carriers greatly outnumber the overtly afflicted. When two carriers of the same gene marry and bear children, one-quarter of their children (on the average) will be normal, one-quarter will be afflicted and one-half will be carriers like themselves. We shall accomplish our purpose, therefore, if, having identified the carriers (another thing easier said than done, but it **can** be done, and in an increasing number of recessive disorders), we try to discourage them **from marrying each other** by pointing out the likely consequences if they do so. The arithmetic of this is not very alarming. In a typical recessive disease, about one marriage in every five or ten thousand would be discouraged or warned against, and each disappointed party would have between fifty and a hundred other mates to choose from.

If this policy were to be carried out, the overt incidence of a disease like phenylketonuria, in which carriers can be identified, would fall almost to zero between one generation and the next.

Nevertheless the first reaction to such a proposal may be one of outrage. Here is medical officiousness planning yet another insult to human dignity, yet another deprivation of the rights of man. First it was vaccination and then fluoride; if people are not to be allowed to marry whom they please, why not make a clean job of it and overthrow the Crown or the United States Constitution?

But reflect for a moment. What is being suggested is that a certain small proportion of marriages should be discouraged for genetic reasons, to help us do our best to avoid bringing into the world children who are biochemically crippled. In all cultures marriages are already prohibited for genetic reasons – the prohibition, for example, of certain types of inbreeding (the exact degree varies from one culture or religion to another). Thus the prohibition of marriage has an immemorial authority behind it. As to the violation of human dignity entailed by performing tests on engaged couples that are no more complex or offensive than blood tests, let me say only this: if anyone thinks or has ever thought that religion, wealth or colour are matters that may properly be taken into account when deciding whether or not a certain marriage is a suitable one, then let him not dare to suggest that the genetic welfare of human beings should not be given equal weight.

I think that engaged couples should themselves decide, and I am pretty certain that they would be guided by the thought of the welfare of their future children. When it came to be learned, some twenty years ago, that marriages between Rhesus-positive men and Rhesus-negative women might lead to the birth of children afflicted by haemolytic diseases, a number of young couples are said to have ended their engagements – needlessly, in most cases, because the dangers were overestimated through not being understood. But that is evidence enough that young people marrying today are not likely to take a stand upon some hypothetical right to give birth to defective children, if, by taking thought, they can do otherwise.

The problems I have been discussing illustrate very clearly the way in which scientific evidence bears upon decisions that are not, of course, in themselves scientific. If the termination of a pregnancy is now in question, scientific evidence may tell us that the chances of a defective birth are 100 per cent, 50 per cent, 25 per cent, or perhaps unascertainable. The evidence is highly relevant to the decision, but the decision itself is not a scientific one, and I see no reason why scientists as such should be specially well qualified to make it. The contribution of science is to have enlarged beyond all former bounds the evidence we must take account of before forming our opinions. Today's opinions may not be the same as yesterday's, because they are based on fuller or better evidence. We should quite often have occasion to say, 'I used to think that once, but now I have come to hold a rather different opinion.' People who never say as much are either ineffectual or dangerous.

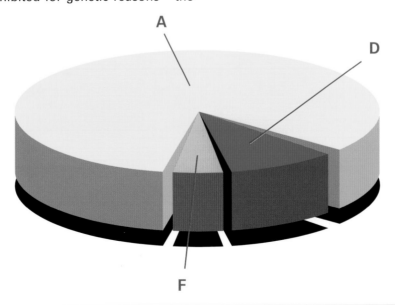

Figure 5.

0011–8532/90 0.00 + .

"there is no history of mankind, there is only an indefinite number of histories
of all kinds of aspects of human life. and one of these is the history of political
power. this is elevated into the history of the world."
sir karl popper

"one would expect people to remember the past and to imagine the future.
but in fact … they imagine… [history] in terms of their own experience, and
when trying to gauge the future they cite supposed analogies from the past:
till, by a double process of repetition, they imagine the past and remember
the future."
sir lewis namier

"i mean, don't forget the earth's about five
million years old, at least. who can afford
to live in the past."
harold pinter

who?!

The young man was sitting by the bed nearest the door. I saw him as I entered the ward, but he did not see me. He was reading a book, with eyes blinded to the life about him.

I noticed, then, the pile of novels by his side: Tolstoy and Balzac, in translation; Dickens and George Eliot. Not for him, in his illness, the literature that is known as 'escapist', offering a temporary eradication of the painful here-and-now. Pip and Dorothea, Anna and Vautrin, would make uneasy company, even in health.

'Who is he?' I asked the friend I had come to visit.

He said he would tell me later, when we took a walk.

What my friend told me, in the corridor, was that the skinny young man in the next bed had only days to live. He was suffering from a rare kind of wasting disease, and the doctors were as perplexed as they were helpless to save him. He knew his fate. On one of the few occasions he had spoken – between books – he had answered a question my friend couldn't voice. 'I don't want any visitors. **There's no point. I told them all not to come.'**

(Going home from the hospital that evening, I recalled, with distaste, how I had once believed I would die young. I had had Keats in mind, and Mozart and Schubert, as well as those awesomely gifted musicians who perished, one after another, in the 1950s – Dinu Lipatti, Kathleen Ferrier, Guido Cantelli, Ginette Neveu. 'He was cut off in his brilliant prime,' I had my obituarist write, 'but his **legendary Hamlet and Richard II will long outlive him.'**

I remembered, too, thanks to the youth with the books, the icy fear of not-being I had experienced on learning, in my late thirties, that the lump by my jaw was a tumour. With panic came a feeling of displacement, as if I had been removed from the ordinary world with its small but sustainable concerns. Nowhere loomed.

And now here I was on a crowded Underground train, ten years on, marvelling at the young man's need for the complexities of great fiction at such a time, and hoping that he would reach the end of the pile at least, before his anticipated darkness claimed him.)

My friend was released from hospital the following day, so I saw no more of the curious reader, urgently turning the pages of *Lost Illusions*. There was no point, he said, in relatives and friends visiting him – and I cannot presume to imagine what he meant. Yet I wondered then, and I wonder still, why he didn't consider that last, urgent need of his short life to be pointless, too. He might have stared at the wall; he might have chatted, as the other patients chatted, of commonplace things. He chose to read instead – furiously, hastily – and to live, for a short while, among the undying. That, he might have explained to me, had I been crass enough to ask, is the whole point, precisely.

Paul Bailey

'Great!' \
first.' The\
the truth\
denying

But she\
around \
hilarious\
a great\
banned

I unders\
the mod\
times, s\

There w\
it was th\
bedside\
comfort,\
obvious

Ruth and\
that we\
at Christ\
pregnan\
some in\
solution.

Someho\
to make

Even Ru\
a heavy\
yourself

First, it\
had Stag\
system\
the char\
always\
the canc

Needles\
I though\
the requ\
everywh

To me,\
bitterly b\
much, t

If Ruth\
process\
to her, i\
trial – all\
delicate\
of her a

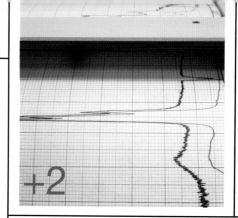

'Great!' wrote Ruth in her column of 3 August, 'I'm going to die, but I'm going to go bonkers first.' There was a bravado about Ruth's black humour: it was a way not so much of facing the truth, but of trying to face it down; a means of both acknowledging the inevitable and denying it, in a shriek of raucous laughter.

But she did it for us, too: if there was one thing she couldn't stand, it was people hanging around with long faces, not knowing what to say. Before she became really ill, Ruth was hilariously impatient with people she felt were inadequate in dealing with her cancer. Always a great compiler of lists, she started and discarded several notes of those who were to be banned from her funeral on the grounds of failing the C-test.

I understood her exasperation, but I knew from experience it wasn't always easy to judge the mood. Sometimes Ruth would be furious with people for ignoring the subject; at other times, she'd declare herself sick of talking about it.

There was no right way for any of us. If I learned one thing over the weeks that followed, it was that the illusions one holds about a peaceful, dignified death and the family's perfect bedside farewell will almost certainly be tugged away. If one is left with any shreds of comfort, then they must be unlooked-for blessings. Dying is nasty, ugly and painful; it's so obvious, isn't it?

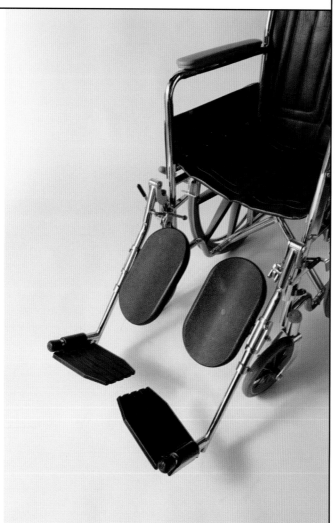

Ruth and I were always optimistic people. Perhaps we believed a little too much in our luck, that we somehow deserved a providentially good life. After the misery of facing childlessness, at Christmas 1994 we were dealt the most fantastic backslap of fortune when Ruth became pregnant with twins on the first attempt at IVF. This was perfect: since conception was, for some inexplicable reason, difficult for us, then having two children at once was the ideal solution.

Somehow I felt it was almost expected of us, in having twins, to do something a bit special, to make a statement.

Even Ruth having cancer didn't cure us of our optimism. Every bit of bad news came like a heavyweight's punch that would throw you on the canvas; but you would always pick yourself up before the count. Like suckers, perhaps, but what else can you do?

First, it was secondary cancer, then Stage III. A few weeks later, it was confirmed that she had Stage IV: the cancer had made that vital, fatal leap from her left breast and its lymphatic system into another tissue type, the bone of her sternum. She already suspected it, from the characteristic pain of bone cancer that had begun. This set a pattern in which she always knew the bad news before the hospital tests confirmed it; her body told her – about the cancer in her lungs, her liver, and finally her brain.

Needless to say, Ruth had done nothing to invite this. She was always a fit, active person. I thought of her romantically as my Amazon; she was once, she was fond of boasting (with the requisite irony), junior high-jump champion of South Glamorgan, and she used to cycle everywhere, even into her sixth month of pregnancy.

To me, trying to put myself in her position as a cancer patient, I knew I would have felt so bitterly betrayed by my own body – my friend-turned-assassin. But she never admitted as much, to me at least. She just spent more on clothes and face creams.

If Ruth did fall out of love with her body, then perhaps it had been so imperceptible a process, predating her cancer, that she did not fully recognise it. Pregnancy was laborious to her, in every sense; childbirth, ultimately by Caesarean, a trauma; and breastfeeding a trial – all those physical metamorphoses and hormonal mutations threw into turbulence the delicate dialectic between body-as-fact and body-as-image that exists for virtually all women of her age.

- Her will and her capacity to lose her post-partum tummy unsurprisingly flagged; it became another object of dismay which she turned into the subject of hilarity. To some, it must have seemed that she simply lacked inhibitions, but she chose to put them aside. One of the goading little ironies when she became ill with the brain tumours in August was that she did become, in the technical parlance of pyschiatry, 'disinhibited'. Her sense of what was socially appropriate behaviour lapsed.

- The curious thing was that being careless about whether she'd put on knickers under her nightshirt when she sat up to talk to a doctor, or being rude to the oncology professor, was both Ruth and not-Ruth. And there she was again, making lists – so Ruth. Except now, her lists were the desperate attempt of her drowning mind to order its thoughts and maintain some purchase on reality.

- Ruth usually looked after the children on Fridays. She worked the rest of the week, but taking a long weekend was the honourable compromise she'd worked out between career and motherhood. She hadn't been sleeping well for several weeks, but then, I'd thought recklessly, who does – either with small children or the anxiety of having terminal cancer, let alone both?

- I didn't know it, but she had been struggling to write her *Observer* column that week; the rough draft, unfinished, was, as it turned out, her last. Writing was so swift and sure and natural to her, that it must have been part of the cause of her anxiety that suddenly she couldn't stitch it together.

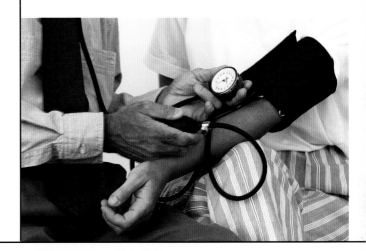

4

I left for work that Friday with no more sense of foreboding than the usual dull, grey, back-of-the-mind awareness of our predicament. Her mother called me that afternoon to tell me that Ruth had checked herself into Guy's Hospital, where she had received all her treatment, because she was in terror of her rising panic. She'd even spoke of her fear of losing control and jumping out of the window. By the time I got there, the doctors had posted a registered mental nurse outside her door.

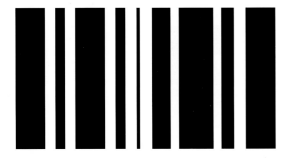

+5 *That evening Ruth was prescribed Valium to help her sleep. My first thought, evidently the psychiatrist's too, was that sleep deprivation and anxiety about terminal cancer had precipitated a sort of nervous breakdown. And yet, that just didn't seem Ruth. As the weekend wore on, her nights were better, but the woman we knew was replaced by this dull, flat, compliant person I didn't recognise at all.*

+6

I became haunted by Ruth's blank expression and uncomprehending, frightened eyes: they reminded me of nothing so much as footage of a cow in the final stages of BSE, lurching and stumbling, knowing nothing but incomprehension and fear. If that seems a terrible way to speak, even figuratively, of one's wife, think how it felt to witness.

She was going bonkers after all, and it wasn't to be the lurid paranoia of schizophrenia or the affective excess of mania; it was the blunted, stupid morbidity of the lobotomised. For that was what the brain tumour was doing, stealthily performing its own crude version of a frontal lobotomy.

+7

It took the doctors several days to reach a collective agreement about Ruth's condition and its best treatment. A week after her admission to Guy's, she had the first of two doses of cobalt radiation to the front portion of her brain. How effective this might prove, no one could tell us. Radiotherapy does not always work, and in any case, only a palliative course was prescribed. And all the time Ruth's liver function was steadily deteriorating.

In the meantime, Ruth had been put on a low dose of an anti-psychotic drug to damp down the agitated behaviour she'd begun to display. For most of the week, she had decided that either I or her sisters were 'in charge'. So that she would always know at least this, and the day and date, she wrote it down on her hand.

+8

In reality, though, she was still in charge: by Thursday she had decided that she was coming home, and – though we were waiting anxiously for the say-so of the psychiatrist – Ruth reached such a pitch of desperation that she marched out of the hospital, and insisted on walking the mile or so from Guy's to our house. We held hands and Ruth smiled all the way home, triumphant and happy as she could be. A nurse followed at a discreet fifteen paces behind, in case Ruth bolted. We must have made an odd little parade, and a pathetic one, but like many terrible things it has its humorous aspect with hindsight.

Home worked its soothing balm on Ruth's mind for only a few hours. It soon became obvious that her dissociated thoughts and her agitation were not an unwanted side-effect of hospitalisation. With the children in danger of seeing their mother distressed by her own inability to make sense, it was obvious we needed another solution. We were advised about Trinity Hospice in Clapham and it was there that I took Ruth that Friday morning.

+9

The next couple of days saw Ruth pull back from dementia. She became calm and gentle; but this spaced-out, tranquillised Ruth, emptied her of her fierce will, was no more her than the raving one had been. For a week now, we had been coming to terms with the possibility that the person we loved might be gone for good, her brain irreparably damaged by the intruding mass of rogue cells. In the peaceful surroundings of the hospice's beautiful garden, I choked back my tears: I'd learned that they only confused and upset her as she tried to empathise without being able to understand the reason for my breaking heart.

+10

After a few days more, she gradually found some of that will again, some of her essential self – enough at least to insist on reducing her drug intake and coming back home. And so, for a couple of weeks, we bounced backwards and forwards from home to hospice – under the endlessly kind, compassionate guidance of the doctors and nurses there. It was still a stressful and often miserable phase: she often treated her mother, her sister and I – her primary guardians and carers – more with impatience and irritation than anything else. The survivors have their guilt, the dying a justifiable anger. Since I now found myself making decisions for her, with only her grudging consent, I was often her 'gaoler'. I wrote a series of long, self-pitying e-mails to a faraway friend. She had the courage to tell me what I already knew: that I had probably had as much love now from Ruth as I was going to have.

+11

Hard as this was to accept then, I can find some pattern, some rationality, in it now. The dying person has to break her bonds with the world, to separate herself. I was seeing this happening slowly in front of my eyes with the children. Day by day, as Ruth weakened physically under the load of her liver tumour, she could do less and less for the twins: no more bending to pick them up, no more rising at night to settle them, no more being the climbing frame and punch bag. Gradually, they too became accustomed to Mummy being sick.

On the night before the night she died, she struggled up the stairs in my parents' house, resting every other step, to help me put the children to bed. We were visiting there as a consolation for the fact that we'd finally cancelled a weekend in Ireland which Ruth had planned for months as another carrot of survival. (I hadn't confronted her with my misgivings about the Irish expedition: to cross her about anything felt like pulling the last cigarette from the condemned man's lips.)

+12

I lifted Joe to be cradled on her lap, and moved away to an adjacent bed to give Lola her milk. With the lights down, our bedtime ritual would always include singing the children nursery rhymes and lullabies. Ruth would usually lead and berate me at some point for my bum notes or tuneless dirging. Now I led, and she palely followed.

After a few minutes, Joe simply got up off Ruth's lap, came over and lay down on the bed by me and Lola. The sight of Ruth's poor, hunched silhouette, half-lit by a shaft of light from the door, still faintly finishing the lines of our song, was the saddest thing I ever hope to see. I knew then that, like Eurydice, she was lost to the underworld, and that the true meaning of dying is its absolute loneliness.

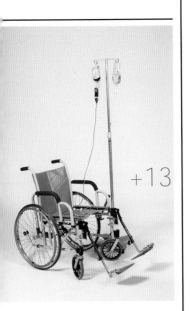

+13

As the children started their night's sleep, I looked for signs in Ruth of the bitter sorrow I felt. I found none; I think she had already made her peace with all that.

JOHN BAYLEY

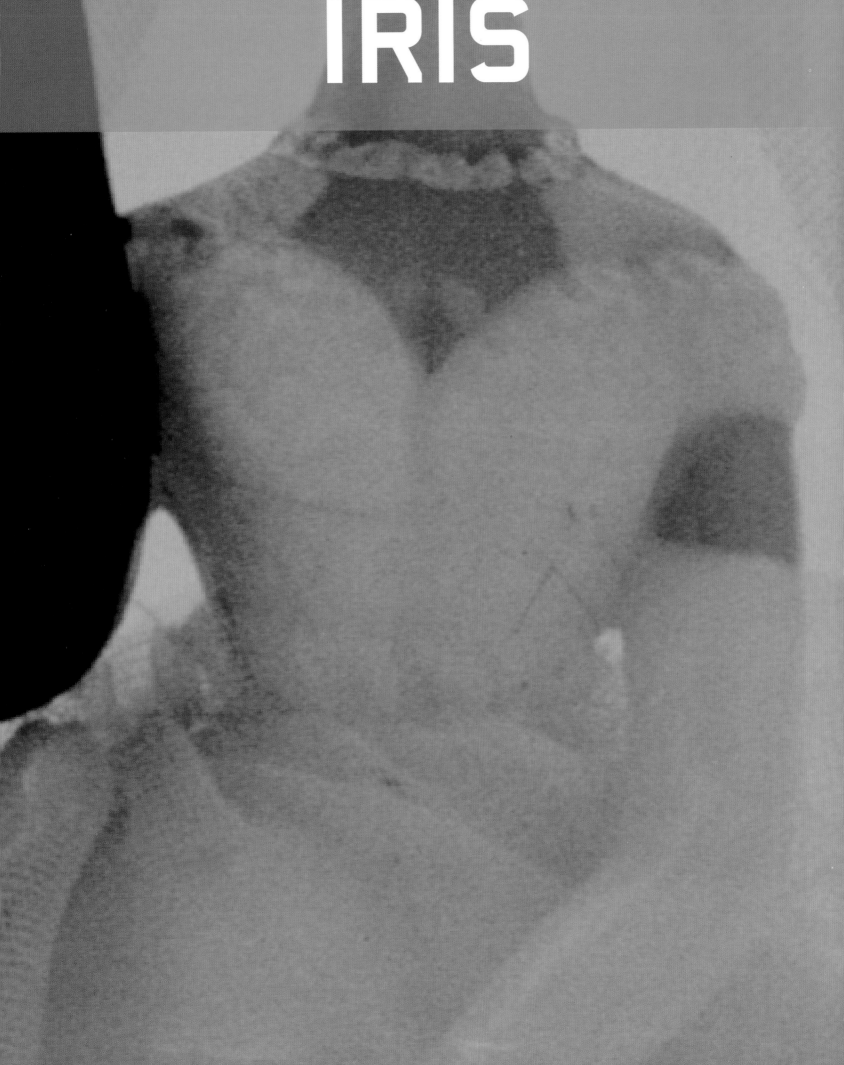

I THINK THIS ATTEMPT AT
TO IS ALSO A REMINDER OF
ALTHOUGH REMINDER IS HA
ALZHEIMER PATIENT IS NOT
ANY DEFINABLE WAY OF WHA
WERE OTHERWISE THE PROCE
IT BECOMES IN THE END, W
ALONG DIFFERENT LINES, I
SUFFERERS DO REMAIN CO
PARADOXICAL AS THIS SEEMS
THAT YOU CANNOT SPEAK
MUST BE INTOLERABLE, AN
WHOM SUCH A TORMENT IS
IRIS TALKS TO ME THE RES
AND TO ME SURPRISINGLY F
LISTEN TO WHAT IS BEING
A MATRIMONIAL WAY, AS THE
THUS OF RECOGNITION.

READING AND BEING READ

F THE LOSS OF IDENTITY;
RDLY THE WORD, FOR AN
T USUALLY CONSCIOUS IN
AT HAS HAPPENED. IF IT
ESS, HOWEVER IRREVERSIBLE
OULD HAVE DEVELOPED
N A DIFFERENT FORM. SOME
NSCIOUS OF THEIR STATE,
S. THE TORMENT OF KNOWING
OR THINK WHAT YOU WANT
ID I HAVE MET PATIENTS IN
CLEARLY VISIBLE. BUT WHEN
ULT SEEMS NORMAL TO HER
LUENT, PROVIDED I DO NOT
SAID BUT APPREHEND IT IN
VOICE OF FAMILIARITY, AND

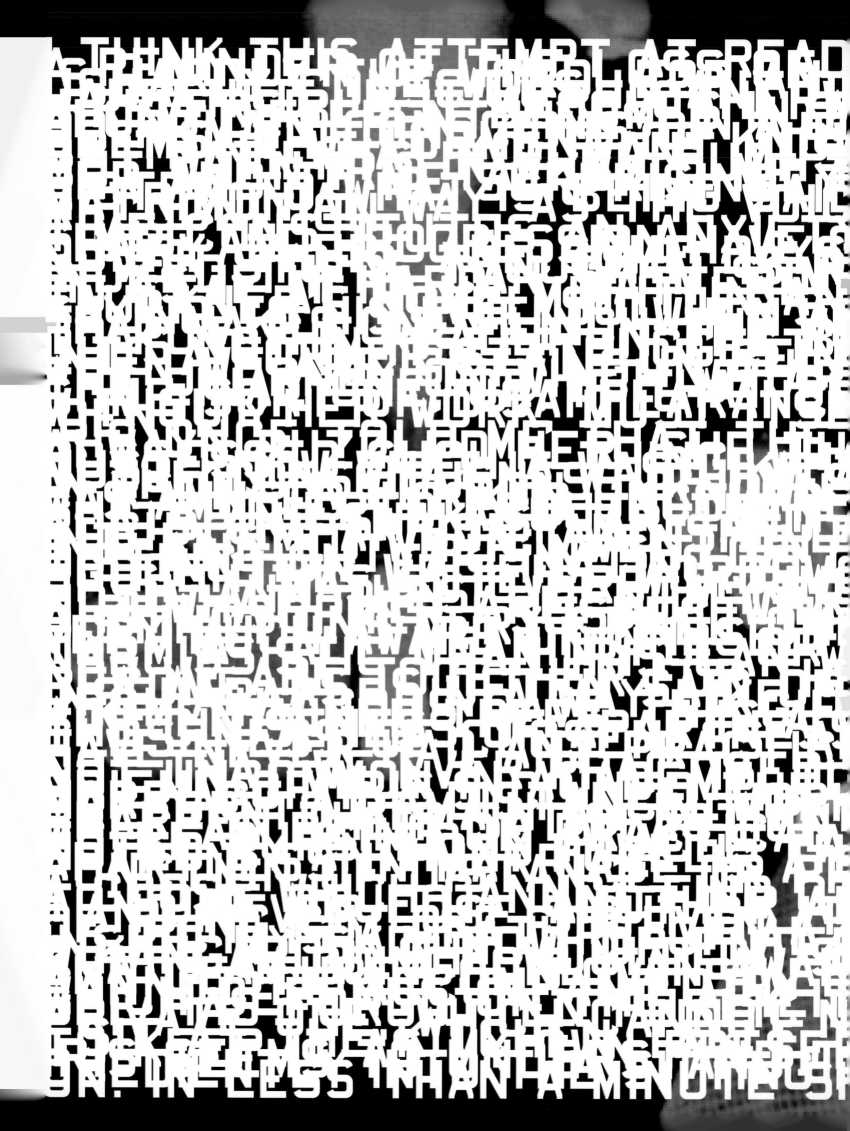

TIME CONSTITUTES AN ANXIETY BECAUSE ITS CONVENTIONAL SHAPE AND PROGRESSION HAVE GONE, LEAVING ONLY A PERPETUAL QUERY. THERE ARE SOME DAYS WHEN 'WHEN ARE WE LEAVING?' NEVER STOPS, THOUGH IT IS REPEATED WITHOUT AGITATION. INDEED THERE CAN SEEM SOMETHING QUITE PEACEFUL ABOUT IT, AS IF IT HARDLY MATTERED WHEN WE WENT, OR WHERE, AND TO STAY AT HOME MIGHT IN ANY CASE BE PREFERABLE. IN FAULKNER'S NOVEL SOLDIER'S PAY THE BLINDED AIRMAN KEEPS SAYING TO HIS FRIEND, 'WHEN ARE THEY GOING TO LET ME OUT?' THAT MAKES ONE FLINCH: THE WRITER HAS CONTRIVED UNERRINGLY TO PUT THE READER IN THE BLIND MAN'S PLACE. IRIS'S QUERY DOES NOT IN ITSELF SUGGEST DESIRE FOR CHANGE OR RELEASE INTO A FORMER STATE OF BEING; NOR DOES SHE WANT TO KNOW WHEN WE ARE GETTING IN THE CAR AND GOING OUT TO LUNCH. THE JOURNEY ON WHICH WE ARE LEAVING MAY FOR HER MEAN THE FINAL ONE; OR, IF THAT SOUNDS TOO PORTENTOUS, SIMPLY SOME SORT OF DISAPPEARANCE FROM THE DAILY LIFE WHICH, WITHOUT HER WORK, MUST ITSELF HAVE LOST ALL SENSE AND IDENTITY.

IRIS ONCE TOLD ME THAT THE QUESTION OF IDENTITY HAD ALWAYS PUZZLED HER. SHE THOUGHT SHE HERSELF HARDLY POSSESSED SUCH A THING, WHATEVER IT WAS. I SAID THAT SHE MUST KNOW WHAT IT WAS LIKE TO BE ONESELF, EVEN TO REVEL IN THE CONSCIOUSNESS OF ONESELF, AS A SECRET AND SEPARATE PERSON – A PERSON UNKNOWN TO ANY OTHER. SHE SMILED, WAS AMUSED, LOOKED UNCOMPREHENDING. IT WAS NOT SOMETHING SHE BOTHERED ABOUT. 'THEN YOU LIVE IN YOUR WORK? LIKE KEATS AND SHAKESPEARE AND ALL THAT?' SHE DISCLAIMED ANY SUCH COMPARISON; AND SHE DID NOT SEEM PARTICULARLY INTERESTED WHEN I WENT ON TO SPEAK (I WAS AFTER ALL IN THE ENG. LIT. BUSINESS) OF THE WELL-KNOWN ROMANTIC DISTINCTION, FASCINATING TO COLERIDGE, BETWEEN THE GREAT EGOCENTRIC WRITERS, WORDSWORTH AND MILTON, WHOSE SENSE OF SELF WAS SO OVERPOWERING THAT IT INCLUDED EVERYTHING ELSE, AND THESE IDENTITY-FREE SPIRITS FOR WHOM BEING IS NOT WHAT THEY ARE, BUT WHAT THEY LIVE IN AND REVEAL. AS A PHILOSOPHER I SUSPECT THAT SHE FOUND ALL SUCH DISTINCTIONS VERY CRUDE ONES. PERHAPS ONE HAS TO BE VERY MUCH AWARE OF ONESELF AS A PERSON IN ORDER TO FIND THEM AT ALL MEANINGFUL OR INTERESTING. NOBODY LESS NARCISSISTIC THAN IRIS CAN WELL BE IMAGINED.

NOW WE ARE TOGETHER FOR THE FIRST TIME. WE HAVE ACTUALLY BECOME, AS IS OFTEN SAID OF A HAPPY MARRIED COUPLE, INSEPARABLE, IN A WAY LIKE OVID'S BAUCIS AND PHILEMON, TO WHOM THE GODS GAVE THE GIFT OF GROWING OLD TOGETHER LIKE ENTWINED TREES. IT IS A WAY OF LIFE THAT IS UNFAMILIAR. THE CLOSENESS OF APARTNESS HAS NECESSARILY BECOME THE CLOSENESS OF CLOSENESS. AND WE KNOW NOTHING OF IT; WE HAVE NEVER HAD ANY PRACTICE.

NOT THAT WE EVER PRACTISED THE OPPOSITE: THE WAY OF LIFE, NOT UNCOMMON IN ACADEME, TO DEFINE WHICH A PHILOSOPHICAL FRIEND OF IRIS'S COINED THE WORD TELEGAMY. TELEGAMY, MARRIAGE AT A DISTANCE, WORKS WELL FOR SOME PEOPLE, WHO PREFER TO REMAIN AN INDEPENDENT PART OF AN ITEM. IT MAY SHARPEN THEIR SATISFACTION IN TIME SPENT TOGETHER, AS WELL AS BEING OF PRACTICAL CONVENIENCE IF CAREERS ARE TO BE PURSUED IN PLACES FAR APART. BUT IT IS NOT, AS NOTED BY ANTHONY POWELL, THE SAME THING AS BEING MARRIED. APARTNESS IN MARRIAGE IS A STATE OF LOVE; AND NOT A FUNCTION OF DISTANCE, OR PREFERENCE, OR PRACTICALITY.

A GOOSE WHICH CANNOT FIND OTHER GEESE WILL ATTACH ITSELF TO SOME OBJECT – ANOTHER ANIMAL, EVEN A STONE OR A POST – AND NEVER LOSE SIGHT OF IT. THIS TERROR OF BEING ALONE, OF BEING CUT OFF FOR EVEN A FEW SECONDS FROM THE FAMILIAR OBJECT, IS A FEATURE OF ALZHEIMER'S. IF IRIS COULD CLIMB INSIDE MY SKIN NOW, OR ENTER ME AS IF I HAD A POUCH LIKE A KANGAROO, SHE WOULD DO SO. SHE HAS NO AWARENESS OF WHAT I AM DOING, ONLY AN AWARENESS OF WHAT I AM. THE WORDS AND GESTURES OF LOVE STILL COME NATURALLY, BUT THEY CANNOT BE ACCOMPANIED BY THAT WORDLESS COMMUNICATION WHICH DEPENDS ON THE ABILITY TO USE WORDS. IN ANY CASE SHE HAS FORGOTTEN PUBLIC LANGUAGE, ALTHOUGH NOT OUR PRIVATE ONE, WHICH CANNOT NOW GET US FAR.

I SIT AT THE KITCHEN TABLE, AND MAKE DESPERATE EFFORTS TO KEEP IT AS MY OWN PRESERVE, AS IT HAS ALWAYS BEEN. IRIS SEEMS TO UNDERSTAND THIS, AND WHEN PROMPTED GOES OBEDIENTLY INTO THE SITTING-ROOM WHERE THE TV IS SWITCHED ON. IN LESS THAN A MINUTE SHE IS BACK AGAIN.

Have you any notion how many books are written about women in the course of one year? Have you any notion how many are written by men? Are you aware that you are, perhaps, the most discussed animal in the universe? Here had I come with a notebook and a pencil proposing to spend a morning reading, supposing that at the end of the morning I should have transferred the truth to my notebook. But I should need to be a herd of elephants, I thought, and a wilderness of spiders, desperately referring to the animals that are reputed longest lived and must multitudinously eyed, to cope with all this. I should need claws of steel and beak of brass even to penetrate the husk. How shall I ever find the grains of truth embedded in all this mass of paper? I asked myself, and in despair began running my eye up and down the long list of titles. Even the names of the books gave me food for thought. Sex and its nature might well attract doctors and biologists; but what was surprising and difficult of explanation was the fact that sex – woman, that is to say – also attracts

Virginia Woolf

A Room of One's Own

agreeable essayists, light-fingered novelists, young men who have taken the MA degree; men who have taken no degree; men who have no apparent qualification save that they are not women. Some of these books were, on the face of it, frivolous and facetious; but many, on the other hand, were serious and prophetic, moral and hortatory. Merely to read the titles suggested innumerable schoolmasters, innumerable clergymen mounting their platforms and pulpits and holding forth with a loquacity which far exceeded the hour usually allotted to such discourse on this one subject. It was a most strange phenomenon; and apparently – here I consulted the letter M one confined to the male sex. Women do not write books about men – a fact that I could not help welcoming with relief, for if I had first to read all that men have written about women, then all that women have written about men, the aloe that flowers once in a hundred years would flower twice before I could set pen to paper. So, making a perfectly arbitrary choice of a dozen volumes or so, I sent my slips of paper to lie in the wire tray, and waited in my stall, among the other seekers for the essential oil of truth.

What could be the reason, then, of this curious disparity, I wondered, drawing cart-wheels on the slips of paper provided by the British taxpayer for other purposes. Why are women, judging from this catalogue, so much more interesting to men than men are to women? A very curious fact it seemed, and my mind wandered to picture the lives of men who spend their time in writing books about women; whether they were old or young,

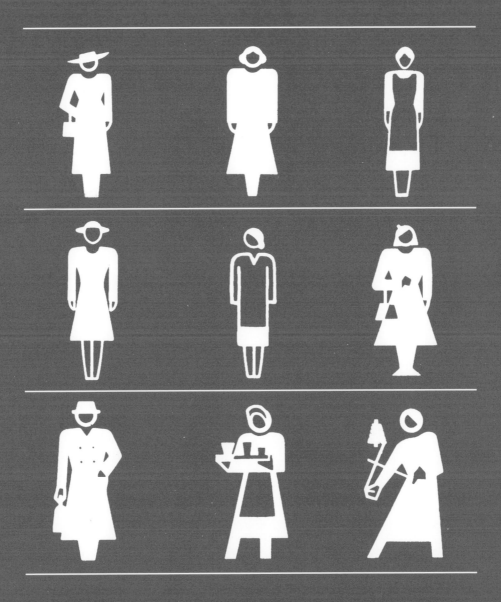

PICTOGRAPH CORPORATION SYMBOLS

married or unmarried, red-nosed or hump-backed – anyhow, it was flattering, vaguely, to feel onself the object of such attention, provided that it was not entirely bestowed by the crippled and infirm – so I pondered until all such frivolous thoughts were ended by an avalanche of books sliding down on to the desk in front of me. Now the trouble began. The student who has been trained in research at Oxbridge has no doubt some method of shepherding his question past all distractions till it runs into its answer as a sheep runs into its pen. The student by my side, for instance, who was copying assiduously from a scientific manual, was, I felt sure, extracting pure nuggets of the essential ore every ten minutes or so. His little grunts of satisfaction indicated so much. But if, unfortunately, one has had no training in a university, the question far from being shepherded to its pen flies like a frightened flock hither and thither, helter-skelter, pursued by a whole pack of hounds. Professors, schoolmasters, sociologists, clergymen, novelists, essayists, journalists, men who had no qualification save that they were not women, chased my simple and single question – Why are women poor? – until it became fifty questions; until the fifty questions leapt frantically into mid-stream and were carried away. Every page in my notebook was scribbled over with the notes. To show the state of mind I was in, I will read you a few of them, explaining that the page was headed quite simply, women and poverty, in block letters; but what followed was something

like this; ——————————

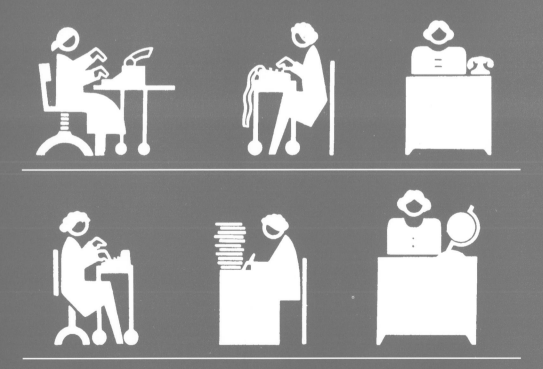

Condition in Middle Ages of,

Habits in the Fiji Islands of,

Worshipped as goddesses by,

Weaker in moral sense than,

Idealism of,

Greater conscientiousness of,

South Sea Islanders, age of puberty among,

Attractiveness of,

Offered as sacrifice to,

Smaller size of brain of,

Profounder sub-consciousness of,

Less hair on the body of,

Mental, moral and physical inferiority of,

Love of children of,

Greater length of life of,

Weaker muscles of,

Strength of affections of,

Vanity of,

Higher education of,

Shakespeare's opinion of,

Lord Birkenhead's opinion of,

Dean Inge's opinion of,

La Bruyère's opinion of,

Dr Johnson's opinion off,

Mr Oscar Browning's opinion of ...

Here I drew breath and added, indeed, in the margin, Why does Samuel Butler say, 'Wise men never say what they think of women?' Wise men never say anything else apparently. But, I continued, leaning back in my chair and looking at the vast dome in which I was a single but by now somewhat harassed thought, what is so unfortunate is that wise men never think the same thing about women.

fig. 1 yap dog

fiasco

steve
aylett

When mobster Harry Fiasco looked in the mirror he didn't see the tentacled mass of soupy horror the rest of us see in ours. He considered his appearance the highlight about which the rest of the world should arrange its colour scheme. His hair was his religion and compared to its over-arching control he found the city of Beerlight chaotic and wanting. But he stepped out to exemplify rather than indict. He was a simple man.

One day he saw a shrunk old woman with a little skittering dog, about to step into a blurring streetful of cars.

He snatched the dog from the path of a speeding cab. 'Slowly does it now, yapdog,' he said, and took ahold of the gran's arm. 'Road's pretty busy here, ma'am.'

Miss Kiddie Kaufman was known to be a little reactionary. On this occasion, she reacted by screaming for the cops and Harry ran as fast as his arms and legs could take him. When the gran's description resulted in a photofit of an Armani mannequin the cops hauled Harry in for a line-up.

Chief Henry Blince, whose belly was one of the few objects visible from space, fired up a Hindenburg and laid out the shocking facts in a yelling cell. It seemed the old lady thought she'd detected a hidden message in Harry's remark - when phonetically reversed, 'Slowly does it now, yapdog. Road's pretty busy here, ma'am' became the more threatening 'Ma'am, he is a biter so you gotta pay one thousand dollars.'

Blince gave a deep chuckle, looking down his cigar at the suspect. 'This here's a Stari Trg con, boy. Gratuitous. Scam like that'd make more money than war, eh? Or some other monkey-puzzle o' motives. You're wet behind the eyes, Fiasco. Shoulda stuck with something simple - Found Money or Shortchange.'

Though Harry shot Blince an eye, his cuff rail blunted the impact, what with the kneeling and all. 'I don't know rightly what you mean, Mr Blince.'

'Sure yuh don't, Harry - you're a little mob boy gone walkabout. Your steamers say so - Stigmata Hardball and a Daewoo 51, weren't it? Korean semi in an ankle pull - perfect for sayin' hello to a spaniel. You're a sick one alright. Don't a hairstyle like that hurt?'

'No pain no gain.'

'Like I said, sick. Enjoy the parade.'

In the observation room a half hour later, Blince and Miss Kiddie Kaufman looked through a double-paned window as six men filed into the duck room and faced forward, slouched and shuffling, backs against the height-marked wall.

All six wore similar garb. Fiasco was the third.

6' 0"

5' 6"

'Can't beat a screen test in the crime studio. Nobody that side o' the glass can see us, granny. Pick a number and don't expect any cooperation from these bastards.'

Kaufman peered, making faces like bubbling gruel.

'Take your time, Miss Kaufman, your grave's waited this long.'

'He was stood next to me - can they turn side-on?'

'Turn to your left, boys,' ordered Blince over the speaker, and they grudgingly did so, every limb heavy as a sap.

'He scared me when he asked for the cash. Could you make 'em shout?'

'Demand a grand, boys,' rumbled Blince down the speaker.

The boys took turns at asking for the cash, with varying degrees of disinterest.

'Guess he must be an original thinker pullin' a smart ploy like that.'

Blince bent to the mike.'State an original idea, boys.'

Suspect number one, chewing gum, drawled 'A flyin' saucer's concave, not convex.'

Rolling his eyes, number two shuffled and then stated flatly 'Water flows down the plughole counterclockwise in the southern hemisphere. If clocks had been invented in Australia, would this observation have resulted in clockhands rotating the other way today.'

Harry Fiasco gave a hefty sigh, and piped up. 'Er under our lives our death continues like the blank tape under a recording.' He looked up at the striplights, embarrassed.

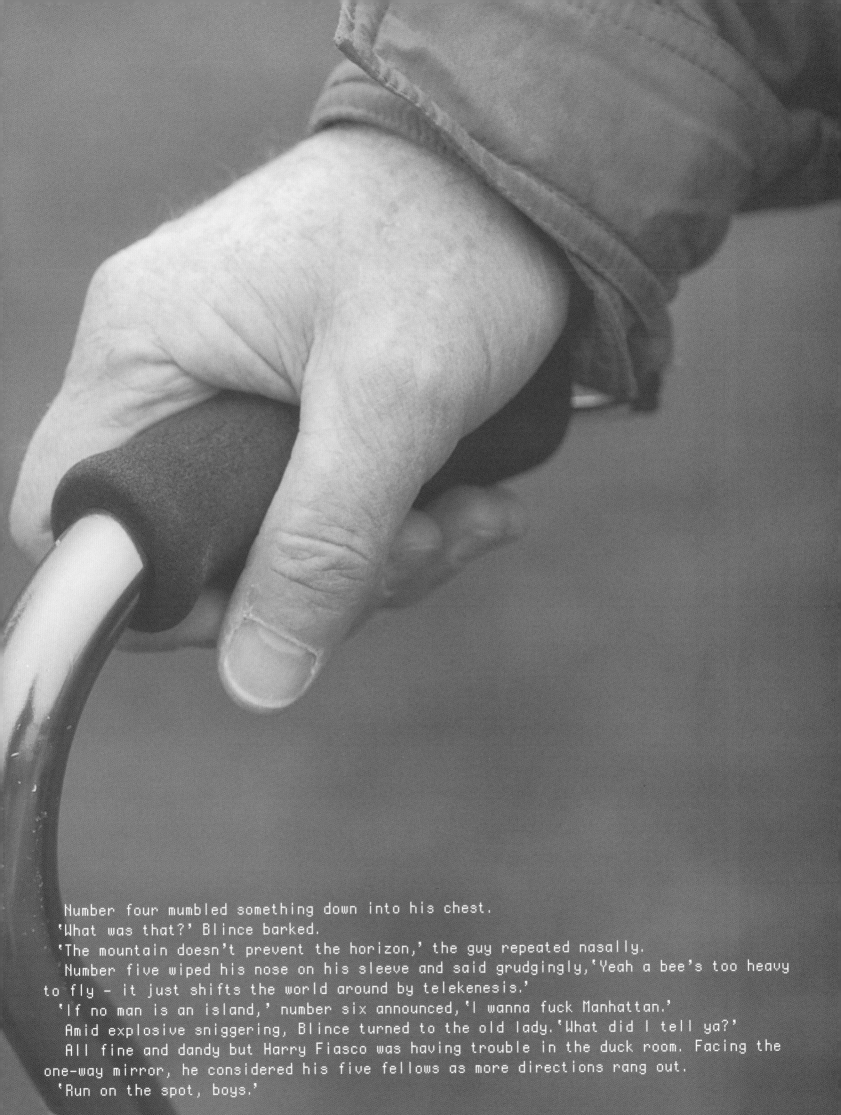

    Number four mumbled something down into his chest.
   'What was that?' Blince barked.
   'The mountain doesn't prevent the horizon,' the guy repeated nasally.
    Number five wiped his nose on his sleeve and said grudgingly,'Yeah a bee's too heavy
to fly — it just shifts the world around by telekenesis.'
   'If no man is an island,' number six announced,'I wanna fuck Manhattan.'
    Amid explosive sniggering, Blince turned to the old lady.'What did I tell ya?'
    All fine and dandy but Harry Fiasco was having trouble in the duck room. Facing the
one-way mirror, he considered his five fellows as more directions rang out.
   'Run on the spot, boys.'

The point of an ID parade was that everyone in the line-up should be dressed alike so the witness was picking out the person instead of the clobber. But the threads on these guys were of such poor quality there was no contest. The colours were duplicated at the crudest level. The fit was farcical. One guy seemed to be wearing a lobster bib. As Harry ran on the spot, he also shook his head grimly. They weren't giving him any credit.

'Sweep your arm from your face like an elephant's trunk.'

They were meant to avoid wildly different body types too, but these guys barely conformed to the same basic anatomy. Flying saucer boy was a case in point. Drenched in Mace, his face was a riot of clashing species. He'd clearly shaved his favourite chin but left the other two to seed. From the centre of his stretch-satin forehead bloomed a zit like a thistle. His clothing was a T-shirt parody of Harry's own.

The face of the guy to Harry's immediate right appeared to be transparent. His head was a mass of veins and puce tissue from which the eyes peered as though from a punishment tarring. His personality was an unsuccessful pizza experiment of diced starfruit and scorched interface leads, his pants bubbling with nutty slack. But he seemed quite happy.

'Act like you're bailin' large bundles o' hay into a barn.'

Number four was a gubbing marine tart who would have felt fully at home if the chamber were flooded and the glass fogged with algae upon which he could feed with slow, pullulating gob movements. An enhanced nose area was specially flared for suction attachment to manhole covers, clanging removal of the latter and subsequent drooping exhaustion in the knowledge of a difficult job well done. They thought he resembled these freaks?

'You're conductin' an orchestra, boys, but suddenly there's a fire in the theatre and you have to direct people to the exits. Go.'

The more he considered it, the more insulting and unacceptable the situation seemed. Quivering and fiddling its limbs like a violinist, number five was an oversized worker ant capable of hauling twice its weight in cars and drifting huge distances in a light breeze. It looked like a living tollbooth, barbed with flaring airvalves and topped with a face like a split cinder-block. Puffs of hot ash blew from its wooden ears. Its eyes slammed open, leaking alcohol. What were the odds?

'You're eight years old. You're openin' a present on Christmas mornin'. You're excited. You tear off the bow, the wrapping, the last layers, revealin' a box that's all the colours o' the rainbow. You shake it – is it the skateboard you wanted? When you open the box, a jack-on-a-spring leaps out at you, givin' you a scare. You cry with fright and disappointment. Your mom and dad don't understand why you're upset. They try to console you but already you're plottin' your revenge. Work with it, boys.'

The evolutionary equivalent of a strangled cry, number six was a huge sentient intestine stood upright in a localised cloud of swamp gas. Stolen eyebrows were taped to a frown of pulsing gut. It was a breathing wedge of smoked salmon.

Sweating like a bastard, Harry gasped in demented outrage. He broke ranks, yelling incoherently about

lard, gills, tusks.

He hammered on the opaque window. 'I'm not like these people!' he spluttered, and sank sobbing to his knees. 'I don't belong here!'

In the observation room, Blince and Kiddie Kaufman watched Harry slide out of sight, leaving a track of hair gel down the glass. 'That's the guy, right?' Blince rumbled.

'Nah,' croaked the old lady, disgusted. 'The guy I met was real cool.'

THE STEREOTYPE IS THE ETERNAL FEMININE. SHE IS THE SEXUAL OBJECT SOUGHT BY ALL MEN, AND BY ALL WOMEN.

SHE is of neither sex, for she has herself no sex at all. Her value is solely attested by the demand she excites in others. All she must contribute is her existence. She need achieve nothing, for she is the reward of achievement. She need never give positive evidence of her moral character because virtue is assumed from her loveliness, and her passivity. If any man who has no right to her be found with her she will not be punished, for she is morally neuter. The matter is solely

one of male rivalry. Innocently she may drive men to madness and war. The more trouble she can cause, the more her stocks go up, for possession of her means more the more demand she excites. Nobody wants a girl whose beauty is imperceptible to all but him; and so men welcome the stereotype because it directs their taste into the most commonly recognised areas of value, although they may protest because

SOME ASPECTS OF IT DO NOT TALLY WITH THEIR FETISHES.

154

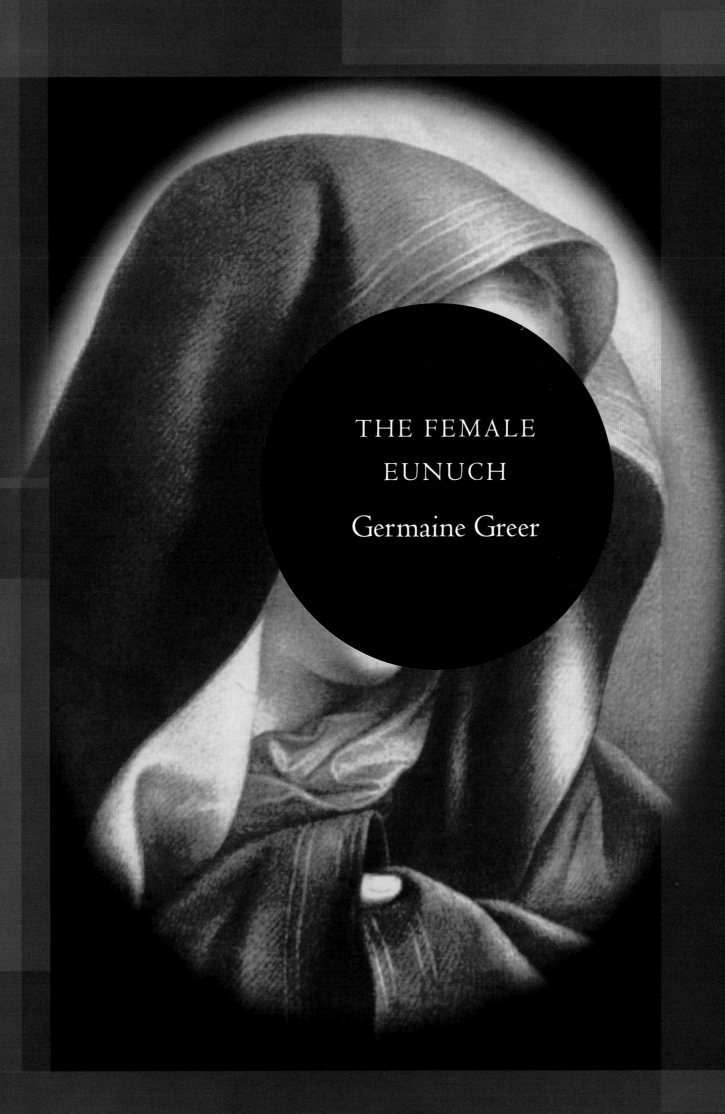

THE FEMALE
EUNUCH

Germaine Greer

"if we assume that the last breath of, say, julius caesar has by now become thoroughly
scattered through the atmosphere, then the chances are that each of us inhales one
molecule of it with every breath we take."
james jeans

"that men do not learn very much from the lessons of history is the most important
of all the lessons that history has to teach."
aldous huxley

"who controls the past controls the future: who controls the present
controls the past."
george orwell

home:

The Lion and the Unicorn
George Orwell

When you come back to England from any foreign country, you have immediately the sensation of breathing a different air. Even in the first few minutes dozen of small things conspire to give you this feeling. The beer is bitterer, the coins are heavier, the grass is greener, the advertisements are more blatant. The crowds in the big towns with their mild knobby faces, their bad teeth and gentle manners, are different from a European crowd. Then the vastness of England swallows you up, and you lose for a while your feeling that the whole nation has a single identifiable character.

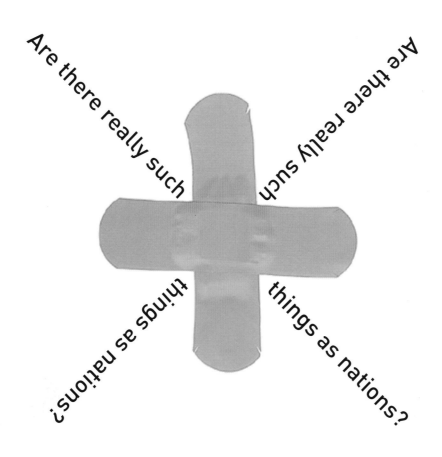

Are there really such things as nations? Are there really such things as nations?

Are we not forty-six million individuals, all different? And the diversity of it, the chaos! The clatter of clogs in the Lancashire mill towns, the to-and-fro of the lorries on the Great North Road, the queues outside the Labour Exchanges, the rattle of pin-tables in the Soho pubs, the old maids biking to Holy Communion through the mists of autumn morning - all these are not only fragments, but **characteristic** fragments, of the English scene. How can one make a pattern out of this muddle?

I left the Río Negro and went on south to Port Madryn. § A hundred and fifty-three Welsh colonists landed here off the brig Mimosa in 1865. They were poor people in search of a New Wales, refugees from cramped coal-mining valleys, from a failed independence movement, and from Parliament's ban on Welsh in schools. Their leaders had combed the earth for a stretch of open country uncontaminated by Englishmen. They chose Patagonia for its absolute remoteness and foul climate; they did not want to get rich.

Bruce Chatwin

La Patagonia Galesa

GADEWAIS Y RIO NEGRO A THROI TUA'R DE I GYFEIRIAD PORTH MADRYN.

YN 1865, HWYLIODD CANT A PHUM DEG TRI O GYMRY YMA AR Y *MIMOSA*. POBL DLAWD OEDDYNT AR DRYWYDD Y WALIA NEWYDD, YN FFOI O GYFYNGDERAU'R CYMOEDD GLO, O FETHIANT EU HYMGYRCH AM ANNIBYNIAETH, AC O WAHARDDIAD Y SENEDD AR GYMRAEG MEWN YSGOLION. ROEDD EU HARWEINWYR WEDI CHWILIO PEDWAR BAN Y BYD AM DDARN O DIR AGORED NAD OEDD WEDI'I LYGRU GAN SAESON. DEWISWYD PATAGONIA AM EI LLEOLIAD CWBL ANGHYSBELL A'I THYWYDD GARW; NID OEDD EU BRYD AR GYFOETH.

Partí de Río Negro y me fui al sur, a Puerto Madryn. § Ciento cincuenta y tres colonos galeses desembarcaron aquí del bergantín Mimosa en 1865. Era gente pobre que buscaba una Nueva Gales, refugiados provenientes de atestados valles donde se explotaban minas de carbón, de un movimiento por la independencia que había fracasado, y de la prohibición del idioma galés en las escuelas, impuesta por el Parlamento. Sus líderes habían buscado en todo el mundo una extensión de terreno abierto no contaminado por ingleses. Eligieron la Patagonia por lo apartado del lugar y por

la inclemencia de su clima. No deseaban enriquecerse.

Cawsant dir ar lannau'r Afon Chubut gan Lywodraeth yr Ariannin. O Borth Madryn, roedd taith o ddeugain milltir ar draws diffeithwch garw. A phan ddaethant o'r diwedd i olwg y dyffryn, rhodd Duw, meddent hwy, ac nid y Llywodraeth, oedd y tir o'u blaen. § Roedd Porth Madryn yn dref o adeiladau concrid di-raen, byngalos tun, warysau tun a gardd wedi'i sathru gan y gwynt. Roedd yno fynwent o goed cypres du a cherrig beddau o farmor du sgleiniog. Roedd y Calle Saint-Exupéry yn dwyn i gof bod y storm yn *Vol de Nuit* yn rhywle yn y parthau hyn. § Cerddais ar hyd glan y môr gan edrych draw at y llinell wastad o glogwyni oedd yn ymestyn o gylch y bae. Roedd lliw'r clogwyni yn oleuach llwyd na llwyd y môr a'r awyr. Roedd y traeth yn llwyd ac yn frith o bengwiniaid marw. Tua hanner ffordd ar draws safai cofgolofn concrid er cof am y Cymry. Edrychai fel mynedfa i gell danddaearol. Yn ei hochrau gosodwyd cerfwedd efydd a gynrychiolai Anwaredd a Gwareiddiad. Roedd Anwaredd yn dangos criw o Indiaid o lwyth y Tehuelche - oll yn noethlymun, gyda slabiau o gyhyrau yn eu cefnau yn yr arddull Sofietaidd. Roedd y Cymry ar ochr Gwareiddiad - henwyr penfrith, llanciau gyda phladurau a merched bronnog yn nyrsio'u hepil. § Amser swper gwisgai'r gweinydd fenig gwynion a'i arlwy oedd twmpyn o oen wedi llosgi a drybowndiai ar y plât. Ar draws wal y bwyty roedd cynfas anferth yn dangos *gauchos* yn gyrru gwarttheg i ryw fachlud oren. Rhoddodd rhyw flonden henffasiwn y gorau i'r oen a dechreuodd beintio'i hewinedd. Daeth Indiad meddw i mewn ac yfodd dri llond jwg o win. Pefriai ei lygaid main ym mwgwd coch a gwydn ei wyneb. Plastig gwyrdd ar siâp pengwiniaid oedd y jwgiau. § Cafwyd dechrau gwael i'r Nadolig pan aeth Mr. Caradog Williams, yr orsaf-feistr ers ugain mlynedd, i'r Hen Fethel i ymofyn y bwyler i ferwi dŵr ar gyfer te parti'r plant. Digwyddodd edrych yn yr afon a gwelodd gorff noethlymun, wedi chwyddo'n dew, ac yn gaeth yn erbyn boncyff coeden helyg oedd wedi cwympo. Nid Cymro ydoedd. § "Twrist fwy na thebyg" meddai'r heddwas. § Aeth Anselmo a minnau i dreulio'r diwrnod gyda'r teulu Davies ar fferm Ty-Isaf, un o'r lleiniau can erw gwreiddiol. Roedd y teulu Davies yn gefndryd i'r Powelliaid, ond yn fwy cefnog. Roedd y fferm yn cynnal chwe pherson, heb gynnwys y peon o Chile: Mrs Davies yr hynaf, ei mab Ivor, ei wraig yntau a'u dau fab, ac Euan, brawd di-briod Ivor. § Roedd Mrs Davies yr hynaf yn byw yn y tŷ mawr pum ystafell. Hen wraig fach grebachlyd oedd hi gyda'r wen gynhesaf a welodd neb erioed a'i gwallt yn bleth dorchog ar ei phen.

Gwyddech ei bod hi'n wraig gadarn iawn yn y bôn. Yn y prynhawn byddai'n eistedd ar y portsh dwyreiniol, allan o ddannedd y gwynt, yn gwylio'r hocys a'r peianau yn newid o ddydd i ddydd. Nid oedd yr ystafell fyw wedi newid nemor ddim ers pan ddaeth yma'n wraig ifanc yn 1913. Yr un oedd y waliau pinc. Ar y pentan yn ymyl y ddau smwtgi pridd roedd rhai o'i hanrhegion priodas – dau hambwrdd o blât Sheffield. O boptu'r seld roedd lluniau melynwyn o rieni ei gŵr, a ddaeth draw o Ffestiniog. Yno y buont, ac yno y byddent ar ôl ei dyddiau hi.

The Argentine Government gave them land along the Chubut River. From Madryn it was a march of forty miles over the thorn desert. And when they did reach the valley, they had the impression that God, and not the Government, had given them the land.

Port Madryn was a town of shabby concrete buildings, tin bungalows, tin warehouses and a wind-flattened garden. There was a cemetery of black cypresses and shiny black marble tombstones. The Calle Saint-Exupéry was a reminder that the storm in Vol de Nuit was somewhere in these parts.

I walked along the esplanade and looked out at the even line of cliffs spreading round the bay. The cliffs were a lighter grey than the greys of the sea and sky. The beach was grey and littered with dead penguins. Half-way along was a concrete monument in memory of the Welsh. It looked like the entrance to a bunker. Let into its sides were bronze reliefs representing Barbarism and Civilisation. Barbarism showed a group of Tehuelche Indians, naked, with slabby back muscles in the Soviet style. The Welsh were on the side of Civilization – greybeards, young men with scythes, and big-breasted girls with babies.

El Gobierno argentino les dio tierras junto al Río Chubut. Desde Madryn era una marcha de cuarenta millas por el desierto lleno de espinos. Y, cuando finalmente llegaron al valle, tuvieron la impresión de que Dios, y no el Gobierno, les había dado las tierras.

Puerto Madryn era un pueblo de edificios de hormigón venidos a menos, casas de zinc de un solo piso, depósitos de zinc y un jardín aplastado por el viento. Había un cementerio de cipreses negros y lápidas brillosas de mármol negro. La Calle Saint-Exupéry hacía recordar que la tormenta de Vol de Nuit había ocurrido en algún sitio de estos lugares.

Caminé por la costanera y observé la línea pareja de acantilados diseminados alrededor de la bahía. Los acantilados eran de un gris más claro que los grises del mar y del cielo. La playa era gris y estaba llena de pingüinos muertos. A mitad de camino había un monumento de hormigón a la memoria de los galeses. Parecía la entrada a un búnker. En los costados tenía relieves de bronce que representaban a la Civilización y a la Barbarie. La Barbarie mostraba a un grupo de indios tehuelches, desnudos de espaldas fláccidas, al estilo soviético. Los galeses estaban del lado de la Civilización: barbas grises hombres jóvenes con guadañas y muchachas de senos grandes con bebés. A la hora de la cena el mozo, que tenía puestos guantes blancos, sirvió un pedazo de cordero quemado que rebotaba en el plato. Por toda la pared del restaurant había un lienzo inmenso de gauchos que arriaban ganado rumbo a un atardecer naranja. Una rubia de estilo anticuado renunció al cordero y se quedó sentada pintándose las uñas. Entró un indio que se tomó tres jarras de vino. Sus ojos eran rendijas brillantes en el escudo de cuero rojo que era su rostro. Las jarras eran de plástico verde y tenían forma de pingüino.

EL DIA DE NAVIDAD empezó mal cuando el Sr. Caradog Williams, jefe de estación desde hacia veinte años, fue al Old Bethel y sacó el caldero para hervir agua para el té de los niños. Se le ocurrió mirar al río y vio el cadáver de un hombre desnudo, todo hinchado y atrapado contra el tronco de un sauce caído. No era un galés.

"Probablemente un turista", dijo el policía.

Anselmo y yo fuimos a pasar el día con la familia Davies en su quinta, Ty-Ysaf, uno de los terrenos originales de cien acres. Los Davies eran primos de los Powell pero más ricos. La quinta daba de comer a seis personas, sin contar al peón chileno. La Sra. de Davies Madre, su hijo Ivor, la esposa de éste y sus dos hijos, y Euan, el hermano soltero de Ivor.

La anciana Sra. de Davies vivía en la casa grande de cinco habitaciones. Era una anciana encogida, de sonrisa magnífica y con el cabello recogido en trenzas. Se adivinaba que era muy fuerte en el fondo. Por las tardes solía sentarse en el porche que daba al este, al abrigo del viento, y miraba las malvas locas y las peonias. La sala no había cambiado desde su llegada, de recién casada joven, en 1913. Las paredes rosadas eran las mismas. Las dos bandejas Sheffield enchapadas - regalos de casamiento - estaban en la repisa de la chimenea, con los dos doguillos de loza. A cada lado del aparador había fotografías coloreadas de sus suegros, que eran de Ffestiniog. Siempre habían estado colgadas allí, y seguirían colgadas allí después de que ella desapareciera.

El anciano Sr. Davies murió el año pasado. Tenía ochenta y tres años. Pero ella siempre había tenido a Euan de compañía. Era un hombre musculoso de ojos color avellana y cabello pelirrojo oscuro, de rostro alegre y pecoso.

"No", dijo la Sra. de Davies. "Euan no se ha casado todavía, pero en cambio canta. Tiene una voz maravillosa de tenor. Los hizo llorar a todos en el Eisteddfod cuando ganó el premio. Anselmo lo acompañaba, y los dos se lucieron. Ay, cómo toca el piano ese chico. Me alegro mucho de que Euan le haya dado ese lindo plato para Navidad. El pobre parece tan perdido y solo, y no es nada divertido vivir en Chubut si la familia no lo ayuda".

"Sí. Euan tiene que casarse algún día, pero ¿con quién? Hay escasez de señoritas y tiene que ser la apropiada. ¿Qué pasaría si se peleara con los demás? ¿Qué pasaría si la quinta no diera para mantener a dos familias? Habría que dividir, y eso sería terrible. Un grupo tendría que irse y empezar en otro lugar".

La Sra. de Davies esperaba que no ocurriera mientras ella estuviera con vida.

Ivor Davies vivía con su familia en la casa más chica de ladrillos de barro y tres habitaciones. Era un hombre alto y erguido, que se estaba quedando calvo y tenía ojos muy hundidos. Era religioso y sobre su aparador había folletos de la Sociedad Bíblica Galesa. Ivor Davies no podía creer que el mundo fuera tan malo como todos decían.

Ivor y Euan hacían todo el trabajo de la quinta. Lo más duro era excavar las zanjas de riego. El peón casi no hacía nada. Vivía en el galpón de las herramientas desde hacía cinco años. Plantaba su propias chauchas y hacía trabajitos suficientes como para poder comprar mate y azúcar. Nunca había vuelto a Chile y la gente se preguntaba si habría matado a algún hombre.

Ymadawodd Mr Davies yr hynaf â'r fuchedd hon y llynedd, yn dair a phedwar ugain. Ond roedd Euan yn gwmni iddi o hyd. Dyn cyhyrog oedd ef gyda llygaid gwinau, gwallt browngoch a wyneb llawen, brycheulyd.

"Na", meddai Mrs Davies. "Dydi Euan ddim wedi priodi eto, ond mae'n canu yn lle hynny. Mae o'n denor gwych. Daeth dagrau i lygaid pawb yn yr Eisteddfod pan gafodd y wobr gyntaf. Anselmo oedd y cyfeilydd, a dyna i chi bâr! Ew, does debyg i'r bachgen yna am ganu'r piano. Rwy'n falch iawn bod Euan wedi rhoi'r plât neis yna iddo'r Nadolig. Mae'r truan bach yn edrych mor amddifad a digalon a dydi byw yn Chubut yn fawr o hwyl os nad yw eich teulu yn helpu.

"Oes, mae'n rhaid i Euan briodi rhyw ddydd, ond pwy? Mae merched ifanc yn brin iawn, ac ar ben hynny wnaiff rhywun-rhywun mo'r tro. Beth petai hi'n cweryla gyda'r lleill? Beth petai'r fferm yn methu cynnal dau deulu? Byddai'n rhaid iddyn nhw wahanu a byddai hynny'n drychineb. Byddai'n rhaid i un teulu symud i ffwrdd a dechrau o'r newydd yn rhywle arall."

Roedd Mrs Davies yn gobeithio na fyddai hynny'n digwydd tra byddai hi fyw.

Roedd Ivor Davies yn byw gyda'i deulu yn y tŷ priddfaen tair ystafell. Roedd yn ddyn tal, unionsyth, a'i ben yn moeli uwchben y llygaid dyfnion. Dyn crefyddol ydoedd yntau, ac ar ei seld roedd pamffledi Cymdeithas y Beibl. Allai Ivor Davies ddim credu bod y byd cynddrwg ag yr honnai pawb.

Ivor ac Euan oedd yn gwneud holl waith y fferm. Y gwaith caletaf oedd cloddio'r ffosydd dyfrhau. O'r braidd na chodai'r peon flaen ei fys bach i helpu. Bu'n byw yn y gweithdy ers pum mlynedd. Plannai ei glwt ei hun o ffa a gwnâi ddigon o fân waith yma ac acw i'w gadw mewn mate a siwgr. Nid aeth fyth yn ôl i Chile ac roeddynt yn dyfalu tybed a oedd wedi lladd rhywun.

𝔄t dinner the waiter wore white gloves and served a lump of burnt lamb that bounced on the plate. 𝔖pread over the restaurant wall was an immense canvas of gauchos herding cattle into an orange sunset. 𝔄n old-fashioned blonde gave up on the lamb and sat painting her nails. 𝔄n 𝔍ndian came in drunk and drank through three jugs of wine. 𝔥is eyes were glittering slits in the red leather shield of his face. 𝔗he jugs were of green plastic in the shape of penguins. § 𝔠hristmas 𝔇ay began badly when 𝔐r 𝔠aradog 𝔚illiams, the station master for twenty years, went to the 𝔒ld 𝔅ethel and got out the cauldron to boil water for the children's tea-party. 𝔥e happened to look in the river and saw the corpse of a naked man, all bloated up and caught against the trunk of a fallen willow. 𝔍t was not a 𝔚elshman.

'Probably a tourist,' the policeman said. § Anselmo and I went to spend the day with the Davies family on their farm, Ty-Ysaf, one of the original hundred-acre lots. The Davieses were cousins of the Powells but better off. The farm supported six people, not counting the Chilean peon: Mrs Davies Senior, her son Ivor, his wife and their two boys, and Ivor's bachelor brother Euan. § Old Mrs Davies lived in the big house of five rooms. She was a shrunken old lady with the nicest smile and her hair worn up in braids. You could tell she was very tough underneath. In the afternoons she sat on the east porch, out of the wind, and watched the hollyhocks and peonies changing day by day. The living-room hadn't changed since she came here as a young bride in 1913. The pink walls were the same. The two Sheffield-plate trays – they were wedding presents – were on the mantelpiece, and the two pottery pug-dogs. On either side of the dresser were tinted photographs of her husband's parents, who came out from Ffestiniog. They had always hung there and they'd hang there when she'd gone. § Old Mr Davies passed on last year. He was eighty-three. But she always had Euan for company. He was a brawny man with hazel eyes and dark red hair and a cheerful, freckled face. § 'No,' Mrs Davies said. 'Euan hasn't married yet, but he sings instead. He's a wonderful tenor. He made them all cry at the Eisteddfod when he carried off the prize. Anselmo was the accompanist and they made a fine pair. Oh, how that boy plays the piano. I'm so pleased Euan gave him the nice plate for Christmas. The poor thing looks so lost and lonely and it's no fun living in Chubut if your family doesn't help. § 'Yes. Euan must get married one day, but who to? There's a shortage of young ladies and she has to be the right one. Suppose she quarrelled with the others? Suppose the farm couldn't support two families? They'd have to split and that would be terrible. One lot would have to go away and start somewhere else.' § Mrs Davies hoped that would not happen as long as she were alive. § Ivor Davies lived with his family in the smaller mudbrick house of three rooms. He was a tall upright man, balding, with eyes set well back into the skull. He was a religious man himself, and on his dresser were pamphlets from the Welsh Bible Society. Ivor Davies could not believe the world was as bad as everyone said. § Ivor and Euan did all the work on the farm. The hardest work was digging out the irrigation ditches. The peon hardly did a thing. He had lived in the tool shed for five years. He planted his own patch of beans and did enough odd jobs to keep him in maté and sugar. He never went back to Chile and they wondered if he'd killed a man.

La Sra. de Ivor Davies era una italiana alegre. Sus padres eran genoveses. Tenía cabello negro y ojos azules y una tez rosa que uno no asociaba con el clima. Repetía constantemente qué lindo era todo: "¡Qué linda familia"! [Nota de la traductora: en castellano en el original], aunque los niños fueran feos. "¡Qué lindo día"! [Nota de la traductora: en castellano en el original] aunque lloviera a cántaros. Si algo no era lindo, ella hacía que lo pareciera. La comunidad galesa le parecía especialmente linda. Hablaba galés y cantaba en galés. Pero, en tanto italiana, no podía hacer que los niños fueran galeses. Estaban aburridos de la comunidad y querían irse a Norteamérica.

"Ese es el problema", dijo Gwynneth Morgan, fina mujer celta de cabello dorado recogido en un rodete. "Cuando los galeses se casan con extranjeras, pierden la tradición". Gwynneth Morgan era soltera. Quería que el valle se mantuviera galés, tal cual era. "Pero se está viniendo todo abajo", dijo.

Porque la Sra. de Ivor Davies soñaba con Italia, y con Venecia en particular. Una vez había visto Venecia y el Puente de los Suspiros. Y cuando dijo la palabra sospiri, lo dijo tan fuerte y con tanta insistencia que uno se daba cuenta de que anhelaba ir a Italia. Chubut estaba tan lejos de Venecia, y Venecia era mucho más lindo que cualquier otro lugar que ella conociera.

Después del té, fuimos todos a cantar himnos en la Capilla Bryn-Crwn. Ivor llevó a su mujer y a su madre en la pickup, y los demás fuimos en el Dodge. El padre de Ivor había comprado el Dodge en la década del 20 y no se había descompuesto todavía, pero la maquinaria era mejor en esa época que ahora.

La Capilla Bryn-Crwn había sido construida en 1896 y estaba en medio de un campo. Seis galeses de traje oscuro y gorra estaban alineados contra la pared de ladrillo rojo. Dentro del anexo, las mujeres ponían la mesa para el té.

Eidales hynaws iawn ei natur oedd Mrs Ivor Davies. Brodoriaid o Genoa oedd ei rhieni. Roedd ganddi wallt du a llygaid glas a chroen rhosbinc nad oedd rhywsut yn cyd-fynd â'r tywydd. Dywedai drosodd a thro mor brydferth yr oedd popeth - "Qué linda familia!" hyd yn oed os oedd y plant yn rhai digon plaen. "Qué lindo dia!" meddai os oedd hi'n diwel y glaw. Waeth beth a welai, roedd yn brydferth yn ei golwg hi. Roedd hi'n meddwl bod y gymuned Gymraeg yn arbennig o brydferth. Roedd hi'n siarad Cymraeg ac yn canu caneuon Cymraeg. Ond, a hithau'n Eidales, allai hi ddim gwneud y bechgyn yn Gymry. Roeddynt wedi hen ddiflasu â'r gymuned ac eisiau mynd i'r Unol Daleithiau.

Mrs Ivor Davies was an Italian woman of the happiest disposition. Both her parents were Genoese. She had black hair and blue eyes and a rose-pink complexion you somehow didn't associate with the climate. She kept saying how beautiful everything was – 'Qué linda familia!' even if the children were ugly. 'Qué lindo dia!' if it poured with rain. Whatever was not beautiful she made it seem so. She thought the Welsh community especially beautiful. She spoke Welsh and sang in Welsh. But, as an Italian, she couldn't make the boys Welsh. They were bored with the community and wanted to go to the States.

'That's the trouble,' said Gwynneth Morgan, who was a fine Celtic woman with golden hair tied in a bun. 'When Welshmen marry foreigners, they lose the tradition.' Gwynneth Morgan was unmarried. She wanted to keep the valley Welsh, the way it was. 'But it's all going to pieces,' she said.

For Mrs Ivor Davies was dreaming of Italy, and of Venice in particular. She had once seen Venice and the Bridge of Sighs. And when she said the word sospiri, she said it so loudly and insistently that you knew she was pining for Italy. Chubut was so very far from Venice and Venice was far more beautiful than anything else she knew.

"Dyna'r trwbwl," meddai Gwynneth Morgan, dynes Geltaidd landeg a thorch o wallt eurfelyn ar ei phen. "Pan fydd y Cymry yn priodi tramorwyr, maent yn colli'r traddodiad." Hen ferch oedd Gwynneth Morgan. Roedd hi eisiau cadw'r dyffryn yn gwbl Gymreig, fel yr arferai fod. "Ond mae popeth yn mynd rhwng y cŵn a'r brain," meddai. § Roedd Mrs Ivor Davies yn breuddwydio am Yr Eidal, ac am Fenis yn fwyaf arbennig. Roedd hi wedi gweld Fenis a Phont yr Ochneidiau unwaith, a phan oedd hi'n ynganu'r gair *sospiri*, gwnâi hynny mor uchel ac mor bendant fel y gwyddech bod ei hiraeth am Yr Eidal yn fawr. Roedd Chubut mor bell o Fenis ac roedd Fenis yn brydferthach o lawer nag unrhyw beth arall a wyddai. § Ar ôl te aeth pob un ohonom i'r gymanfa yng Nghapel Bryn-Crwn. Teithiodd Ivor a'i wraig a'i fam yn y tryc ac aeth y gweddill ohonom yn y Dodge. Roedd tad Ivor wedi prynu'r Dodge yn y 1920'au ac nid oedd wedi methu unwaith, ond roedd gwell graen ar bethau y dyddiau hynny. § Adeiladwyd Capel Bryn-Crwn yn 1896, a safai ynghanol cae. Yn un llinell yn erbyn y wal frics goch, safai chwe Chymro mewn siwtiau tywyll a chapiau brethyn. Yn y festri roedd y merched wrthi'n hwylio'r bwrdd erbyn te.

After tea we all went to the hymn-singing at Bryn-Crwn Chapel. Ivor took his wife and mother in the pick-up, and the rest of us went in the Dodge. Ivor's father bought the Dodge in the 1920s and it hadn't broken down yet, but machinery was better then than now. § Bryn-Crwn Chapel was built in 1896 and sat in the middle of a field. Six Welshmen in dark suits and flat caps stood in line against the red brick wall. Inside the annexe the women were laying the table for tea.

Anselmo played the harmonium and the wind howled and the rain beat on the windows and the teros screamed. The Welsh sang John Wesley's hymns and the sad songs of God's promise to Cymry, the high-pitched trebles and sopranos, and the old men growling at the back. There was old Mr Hubert Lloyd-Jones, who could hardly walk; and Mrs Lloyd-Jones in a straw-flowered hat; and Mrs Cledwyn Hughes, the one they call Fattie; and Nan Hammond and Dai Morgan. All the Davies and Powell families were present, even Oscar Powell 'the wild boy', who wore a T-shirt with: Llanfairpwllgwyngyllgogerychwyrndrobwllllantysiliogogogoch in red letters around a Welsh dragon.

Canodd Anselmo yr harmoniwm dros gwynfan y gwynt a phitran-patran y glaw ar y ffenestri a sgrechiadau'r *teros*. Canodd y Cymry emynau John Wesley a chaneuon hiraethus am addewid Duw i'r Cymry, gyda lleisiau treiddgar y bechgyn a'r sopranos yn gymysg â lleisiau dyfnion y dynion penfrith yn y cefn. Yno, roedd yr hen Mr Hubert Lloyd-Jones, a oedd yn prin gerdded; a Mrs Lloyd-Jones mewn het wellt flodeuog; a Mrs Cledwyn Hughes, yr un a alwent Fattie; a Nan Hammond a Dai Morgan. Roedd holl deulu'r Davies a'r Powelliaid yn bresennol, hyd yn oed Oscar Powell, "y bachgen gwyllt" a wisgai grys-T ag arno'r enw Llanfairpwllgwyngyllgogerychwyrndrobwllllantysiliogogogoch mewn llythrennau coch o gylch draig y Cymry.

The service ended. The old people chatted and the children played hide-and-seek among the pews. Then we all trooped in to tea. It was the second tea of the day, but Christmas was a day of teas. The women poured tea from black pottery teapots. Mrs Davies had brought a pizza and the Welsh tried a little of that. Anselmo was talking and laughing with Euan. They were close friends. He was full of vitality, but it was a borrowed vitality, for the Welshmen cheered up all who saw their bright and weatherbeaten faces.

Daeth y gwasanaeth i ben. Sgwrsiai'r hen bobl gyda'i gilydd tra'r oedd y plant yn chwarae cuddio ymhlith y corau. Yna aeth pawb yn un trŵp i gael te. Hwn oedd ail de'r dydd, ond y Nadolig oedd hi wedi'r cyfan. Arllwysodd y merched de o debotiau pridd du. Roedd Mrs Davies wedi dod â *pizza* a rhoddodd y Cymry gynnig ar hwnnw. Roedd Anselmo yn siarad ac yn chwerthin gydag Euan. Roeddynt yn ffrindiau da. Roedd yn llawn bywyd, ond bywiogrwydd ail-law ydoedd serch hynny, gan fod y Cymry yn llonni pob un a welai eu hwynebau rhuddgoch, geirwon.

Anselmo tocaba el armonio y el viento aullaba y la lluvia golpeaba contra las ventanas y los teros gritaban. Los galeses cantaban los himnos de John Wesley y las canciones tristes de la promesa de Dios a Cymry, los tonos agudos de tenor y soprano, y los viejos gruñendo atrás. Allí estaba el viejo Sr. Hubert Lloyd-Jones, que apenas podía caminar; y la Sra. de Lloyd-Jones con un sombrero de flores de paja, y la Sra. de Gledwyn Hughes, a la que le dicen Fattie; y Nan Hammond y Dai Morgan. Todos los de las familias Davies y Powell estaban presentes, hasta Oscar Powell, "el alocado", que tenía puesta una remera que decía Llanfairpwllgwyngyllgogerychwyrndrobwllllantysiliogogogoch en letras rojas alrededor de un dragón galés.

El servicio terminó. Los viejos charlaban y los niños jugaban a la escondida entre los bancos. Después fuimos todos a tomar el té. Era el segundo té del día, pero Navidad era un día de tés. Las mujeres servían el té con teteras de cerámica negra. La Sra. de Davies había traído una pizza y los galeses probaron un poquito. Anselmo hablaba y se reía con Euan. Eran amigos cercanos. Tenía mucha vitalidad, pero era una vitalidad prestada porque los galeses daban ánimos a todos los que veían sus rostros llenos de vida y curtidos.

FILLING	Bagel	Baguette
BUTTER	£ 0.30	£ 0.48
CHEDDAR CHEESE	£ 0.80	£ 1.45
CREAM CHEESE	£ 0.85	£ 1.55
CREAM C. & SALMON	£ 1.50	£ 2.25
HOT CHILLI TUNA	£ 1.25	£ 1.95
TUNA MAYONNAISE	£ 1.05	£ 1.95
SMOKED SALMON	£ 1.25	£ 1.85
EGG MAYONNAISE	£ 0.75	£ 1.25
OMELETTE	£ 0.95	£ 1.50
CHICKEN MAYONNAISE	£ 1.40	£ 2.25
CHICKEN SUPREME	£ 1.85	£ 2.85
ROAST TURKEY	£ 1.95	£ 2.65
ACKEE & SALTFISH	£ 1.60	£ 2.25
SALT BEEF	£ 1.95	£ 2.65
JERK CHICKEN	£ 1.55	£ 2.25

It is surprising to most newcomers to find that in Jamaica there is hardly a more popular dish among the natives, and often among the upper classes, than the despised salt fish, eaten at home not from choice but as a sort of penitential dish. Here it is the almost daily, and certainly the favourite, food of the people generally, and cooked as they cook it cannot fail to please the most fastidious.

Salt Fish and Ackees
One pound of salt fish
The fruit of twelve ackee pods
Lard
Butter
Black pepper

Soak the salt fish overnight. Put it on to boil in cold water, otherwise it hardens; throw off the first water and put it on again to boil. Carefully pick the ackees free from all red inside, which is dangerous, and boil them for about twenty minutes; add them to the salt fish which is then cut in small pieces; add some lard, butter and pepper. Some prefer the salt fish and ackees mashed together and the melted lard and butter poured over the top.

Salt Fish and Rice
This is a favourite native dish. The salt fish and rice, about half a pound of salt fish to a pint of rice, are boiled together with the usual bit of salt pork and a little butter.

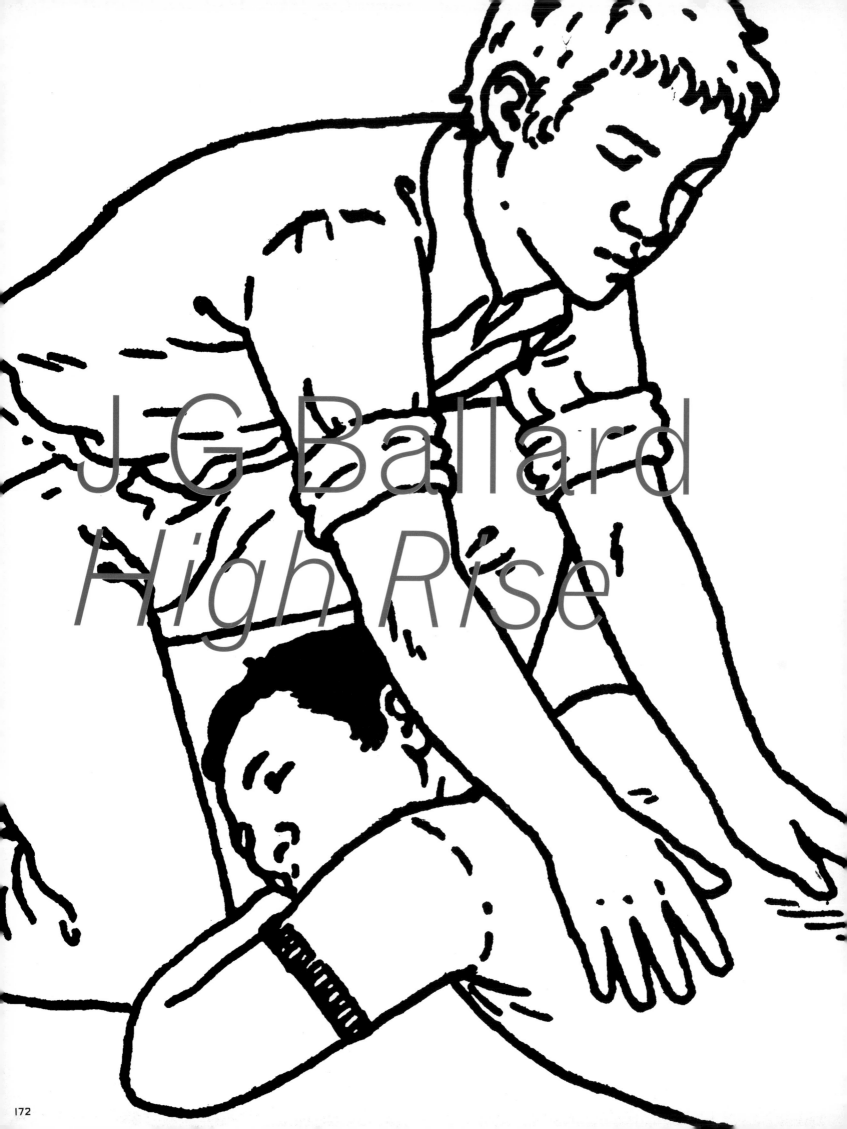

as he sat on his

balcony eating

the dog,

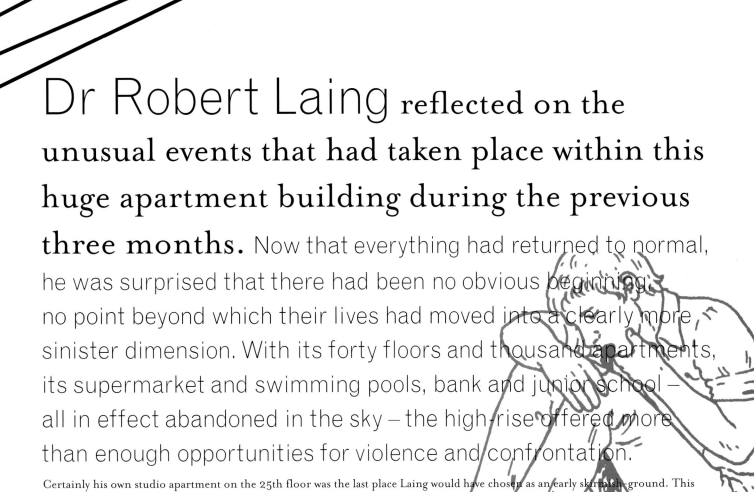

Dr Robert Laing reflected on the unusual events that had taken place within this huge apartment building during the previous three months.

Now that everything had returned to normal, he was surprised that there had been no obvious beginning, no point beyond which their lives had moved into a clearly more sinister dimension. With its forty floors and thousand apartments, its supermarket and swimming pools, bank and junior school – all in effect abandoned in the sky – the high-rise offered more than enough opportunities for violence and confrontation.

Certainly his own studio apartment on the 25th floor was the last place Laing would have chosen as an early skirmish-ground. This over-priced cell, slotted almost at random into the cliff face of the apartment building, he had bought after his divorce specifically for its peace, quiet and anonymity. Curiously enough, despite all Laing's efforts to detach himself from his two thousand neighbours and the régime of trivial disputes and irritations that provided their only corporate life, it was here if anywhere that the first significant event had taken place – on this balcony where he now squatted beside a fire of telephone directories, eating the roast hindquarter of the Alsatian before setting off to his lecture at the medical school.

While preparing breakfast soon after eleven o'clock one Saturday morning three months earlier, Dr Laing was startled by an explosion on the balcony outside his living-room. A bottle of sparkling wine had fallen from a floor fifty feet above, ricocheted off an awning as it hurtled downwards, and burst across the tiled balcony floor.

The living-room carpet was speckled with foam and broken glass. Laing stood in his bare feet among the sharp fragments, watching the agitated wine seethe across the cracked tiles. High above him, on the 31st floor, a party was in progress. He could hear the sounds of deliberately over-animated chatter, the aggressive blare of a record-player. Presumably the bottle had been knocked over the rail by a boisterous guest. Needless to say, no one at the party was in the least concerned about the ultimate destination of this missile — but as Laing had already discovered, people in high-rises tended not to care about tenants more than two floors below them.

Trying to identify the apartment, Laing stepped across the spreading pool of cold froth. Sitting there, he might easily have found himself with the longest hangover in the world.

He leaned out over the rail and peered up at the face of the building, carefully counting the balconies. As usual, though, the dimensions of the forty-storey block made his head reel. Lowering his eyes to the tiled floor, he steadied himself against the door pillar. The immense volume of open space that separated the building from the neighbouring high-rise a quarter of a mile away unsettled his sense of balance. At times he felt that he was living in the gondola of a ferris wheel permanently suspended three hundred feet above the ground.

None the less, Laing was still exhilarated by the high-rise, one of five identical units in the development project and the first to be completed and occupied. Together they were set in a mile-square area of abandoned dockland and warehousing along the north bank of the river. The five high-rises stood on the eastern perimeter of the project, looking out across an ornamental lake — at present an empty concrete basin surrounded by parking-lots and construction equipment. On the opposite shore stood the recently completed concert-hall, with Laing's medical school and the new television studios on either side. The massive scale of the glass and concrete architecture, and its striking situation on a bend of the river, sharply separated the development project from the run-down areas around it, decaying nineteenth-century terraced houses and empty factories already zoned for reclamation.

For all the proximity of the City two miles away to the west along the river, the office buildings of central London belonged to a different world, in time as well as space. Their glass curtain-walling and telecommunication aerials were obscured by the traffic smog, blurring Laing's memories of the past. Six months earlier, when he had sold the lease of his Chelsea house and moved to the security of the high-rise, he had travelled forward fifty years in time, away from crowded streets, traffic hold-ups, rush-hour journeys on the Underground to student supervisions in a shared office in the old teaching hospital.

Here, on the other hand, the dimensions of his life were space, light and the pleasures of a subtle kind of anonymity. The drive to the physiology department of the medical school took him five minutes, and apart from this single excursion Laing's life in the high-rise was as self-contained as the building itself. In effect, the apartment block was a small vertical city, its two thousand inhabitants boxed up into the sky. The tenants corporately owned the building, which they administered themselves through a resident manager and his staff.

For all its size, the high-rise contained an impressive range of services. The entire 10th floor was given over to a wide concourse as large as an aircraft carrier's flight-deck, which contained a supermarket, bank and hairdressing salon, a swimming-pool and gymnasium, a well-stocked liquor store and a junior school for the few young children in the block. High above Laing, on the 35th floor, was a second, smaller swimming-pool, a sauna and a restaurant.

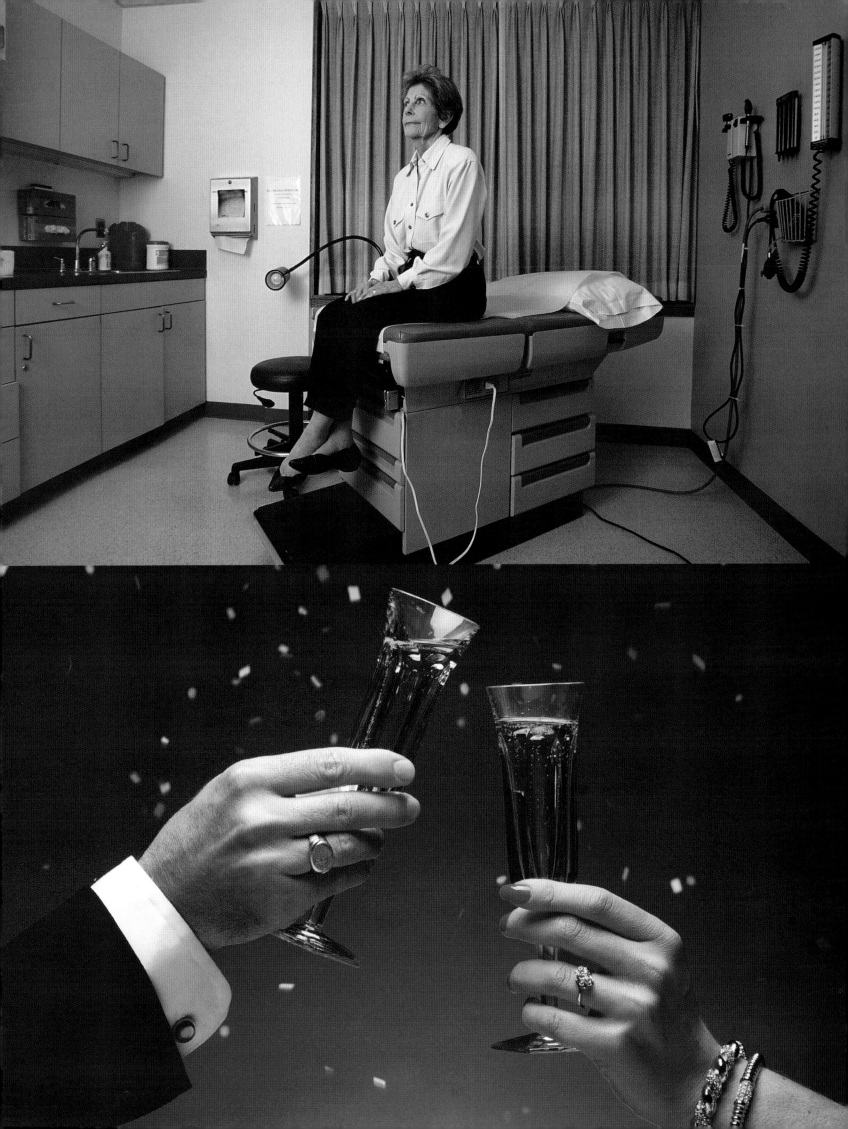

Delighted by this glut of conveniences, Laing made less and less effort to leave the building.

He unpacked his record collection and played himself into his new life, sitting on his balcony and gazing across the parking-lots and concrete plazas below him. Although the apartment was no higher than the 25th floor, he felt for the first time that he was looking down at the sky, rather than up at it.

Each day the towers of central London seemed slightly more distant, the landscape of an abandoned planet receding slowly from his mind. By contrast with the calm and unencumbered geometry of the concert-hall and television studios below him, the ragged skyline of the city resembled the disturbed encephalograph of an unresolved mental crisis.

The apartment had been expensive, its studio living-room and single bedroom, kitchen and bathroom dovetailed into each other to minimise space and eliminate internal corridors. To his sister Alice Frobisher, who lived with her publisher husband in a larger apartment three floors below, Laing had remarked, 'The architect must have spent his formative years in a space capsule – I'm surprised the walls don't curve ...'

At first Laing found something alienating about the concrete landscape of the project – an architecture designed for war, on the unconscious level if no other. After all the tensions of his divorce, the last thing he wanted to look out on each morning was a row of concrete bunkers.

However, Alice soon convinced him of the intangible appeal of life in a luxury high-rise. Seven years older than Laing, she made a shrewd assessment of her brother's needs in the months after his divorce. She stressed the efficiency of the building's services, the total privacy. 'You could be alone here, in an empty building – think of that, Robert.' She added, illogically, 'Besides, it's full of the kind of people you ought to meet.'

Here she was making a point that had not escaped Laing during his inspection visits. The two thousand tenants formed a virtually homogeneous collection of well-do-do professional people – lawyers, doctors, tax consultants, senior academics and advertising executives, along with a smaller group of airline pilots, film-industry technicians and trios of air-hostesses sharing apartments. By the usual financial and educational yardsticks they were probably closer to each other than the members of any conceivable social mix, with the same tastes and attitudes, fads and styles – clearly reflected in the choice of automobiles in the parking-lots that surrounded the high-rise, in the elegant but somehow standardised way in which they furnished their apartments, in the selection of sophisticated foods in the supermarket delicatessen, in the tones of their self-confident voices. In short, they constituted the perfect background into which Laing could merge invisibly. His sister's excited vision of Laing along in an empty building was closer to the truth than she realised. The high-rise was a huge machine designed to serve, not the collective body of tenants, but the individual resident in isolation. Its staff of air-conditioning conduits, elevators, garbage-disposal chutes and electrical switching systems provided a never-failing supply of care and attention that a century earlier would have needed an army of tireless servants.

Besides all this, once Laing had been appointed senior lecturer in physiology at the new medical school, the purchase of an apartment nearby made sense. It helped him as well to postpone once again any decision to give up teaching and take up general practice. But as he told himself, he was still waiting for his real patients to appear – perhaps he would find them here in the high-rise? Rationalising his doubts over the cost of the apartment, Laing signed a ninety-nine-year lease and moved into his one-thousandth share of the cliff face.

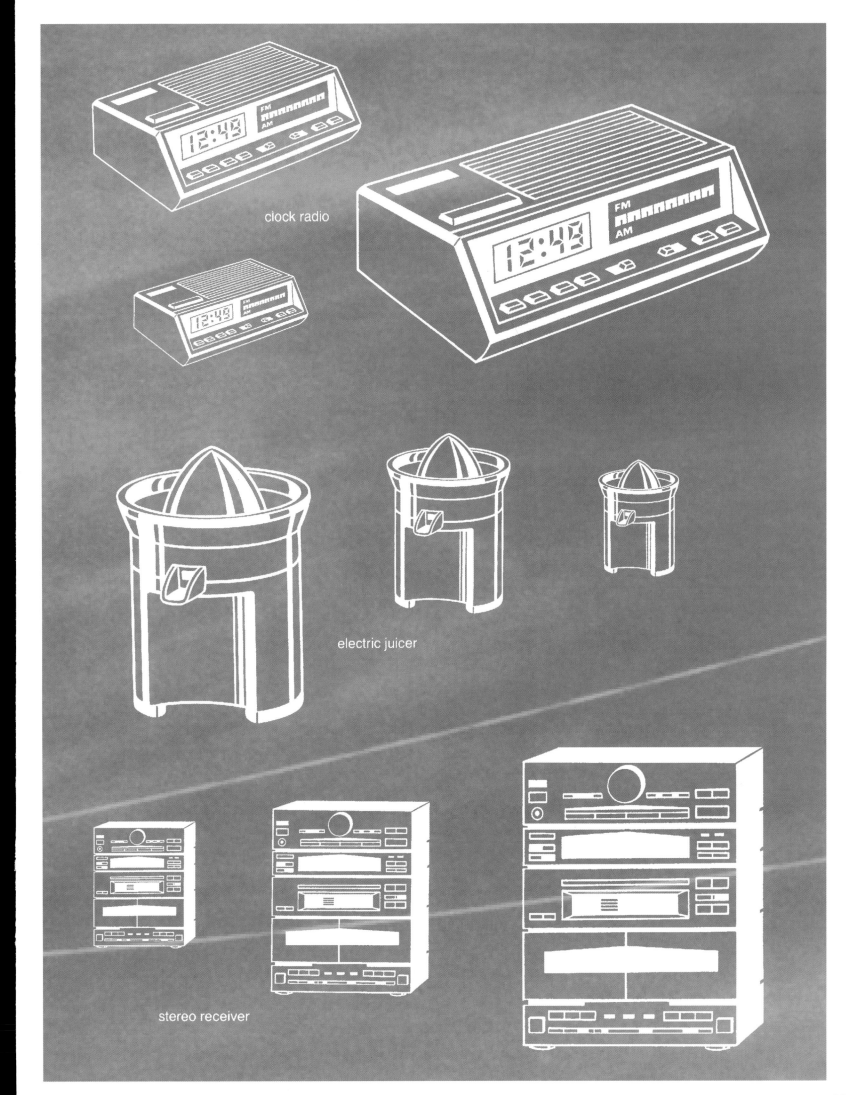

clock radio

electric juicer

stereo receiver

The sounds of the party continued high over his head, magnified by the currents of air that surged erratically around the building. The last of the wine rilled along the balcony gutter, sparkling its way into the already immaculate drains. Laing placed his bare foot on the cold tiles and with his toes detached the label from its glass fragment. He recognised the wine immediately, a brand of expensive imitation champagne that was sold pre-chilled in the 10th floor liquor store and was its most popular line.

They had been drinking the same wine at Alice's party the previous evening, in its way as confused an affair as the one taking place that moment over his head. Only too keen to relax after demonstrating all afternoon in the physiology laboratories and with an eye on an attractive fellow guest, Laing had inexplicably found himself in a minor confrontation with his immediate neighbours on the 25th floor, an ambitious young orthodontic surgeon named Steele and his pushy fashion-consultant wife. Half-way through a drunken conversation Laing had suddenly realised that he had managed to offend them deeply over their shared garbage-disposal chute. The two had cornered Laing behind his sister's bar, where Steele fired a series of pointed questions at him, as though seriously disturbed by a patient's irresponsible attitude towards his own mouth. His slim face topped by a centre parting —always an indication to Laing of some odd character strain — pressed even closer, and he half-expected Steele to ram a metal clamp or retractor between his teeth. His intense, glamorous wife followed up the attack, in some way challenged by Laing's offhand manner, his detachment from the serious business of living in the high-rise. Laing's fondness for pre-lunch cocktails, his nude sunbathing on the balcony and his generally raffish air obviously unnerved her. She clearly felt that at the age of thirty Laing should have been working twelve hours a day in a fashionable consultancy, and be in every way as respectably self-aggrandising as her husband. No doubt she regarded Laing as some kind of internal escapee from the medical profession, with a secret tunnel into a less responsible world.

This low-level bickering surprised Laing, but after his arrival at the apartment building he soon recognised the extra-ordinary number of thinly veiled antagonisms around him. The high-rise had a second life of its own. The talk at Alice's party moved on two levels — never far below the froth of professional gossip was a hard mantle of personal rivalry. At times he felt that they were all waiting for someone to make a serious mistake.

After breakfast, Laing cleared the glass from the balcony. Two of the decorative tiles had been cracked. Mildly irritated, Laing picked up the bottle neck, still with its wired cork and foil in place, and tossed it over the balcony rail. A few seconds later he heard it shatter among the cars parked below.

Pulling himself together, Laing peered cautiously over the ledge — he might easily have knocked in someone's windscreen. Laughing aloud at this aberrant gesture, he looked up at the 31st floor. What were they celebrating at eleven-thirty in the morning? Laing listened to the noise mount as more guests arrived. Was this a party that had accidentally started too early, or one that had been going on all night and was now getting its second wind? The internal time of the high-rise, like an artificial psychological climate, operated to its own rhythms, generated by a combination of alcohol and insomnia.

On the balcony diagonally above him one of Laing's neighbours, Charlotte Melville, was setting out a tray of drinks on a table. Queasily aware of his strained liver, Laing remembered that at Alice's party the previous evening he had accepted an invitation to cocktails. Thankfully, Charlotte had rescued him from the orthodontic surgeon with the disposal-chute obsessions. Laing had been too drunk to get anywhere with this good-looking widow of thirty-five apart from learning that she was a copywriter with a small but lively advertising agency. The proximity of her apartment, like her easy style, appealed to Laing, exciting in him a confusing blend of lechery and romantic possibility — as he grew older, he found himself becoming more romantic and more callous at the same time.

Sex was one thing, Laing kept on reminding himself, that the high-rise potentially provided in abundance. Bored wives, dressed up as if for a lavish midnight gala on the observation roof, hung around the swimming pools and restaurant in the slack hours of the early afternoon, or strolled arm-in-arm along the 10th floor concourse. Laing watched them saunter past him with a fascinated but cautious eye. For all his feigned cynicism, he knew that he was in a vulnerable zone in this period soon after his divorce — one happy affair, with Charlotte Melville or anyone else, and he would slip straight away into another marriage. He had come to the high-rise to get away from all relationships. Even his sister's presence, and the reminders of their high-strung mother, a doctor's widow slowly sliding into alcoholism, at one time seemed too close for comfort.

However, Charlotte had briskly put all these fears to rest. She was still preoccupied by her husband's death from leukaemia, her six-year-old son's welfare and, she admitted to Laing, her insomnia – a common complaint in the high-rise, almost an epidemic. **All the residents he had met, on hearing that Laing was a physician, at some point brought up their difficulties in sleeping.** At parties people discussed their insomnia in the same way that they referred to the other built-in design flaws of the apartment block. In the early hours of the morning the two thousand tenants subsided below a silent tide of *seconal*.

POM

Laing had first met Charlotte in the 35th

floor swimming-pool where he usually

swam, partly to be on his own, and partly

to avoid the children who used the 10th

floor pool.

When he invited her to a meal in the restaurant she promptly accepted, but as they sat down at the table she said pointedly, "Look, I only want to talk about myself."

Laing had liked that.

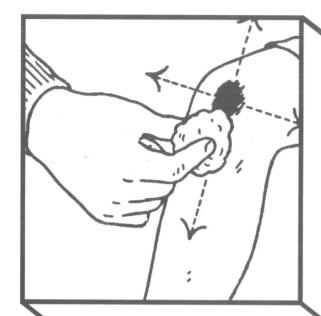

At noon, when he arrived at Charlotte's apartment, a second guest was already present,

a television producer named Richard Wilder. A thick-set, pugnacious man who had once been a professional rugby-league player, Wilder lived with his wife and two sons on the 2nd floor of the building.

The noisy parties he held with his friends on the lower levels – airline pilots and hostesses sharing apartments – had already put him at the centre of various disputes. To some extent the irregular hours of the tenants on the lower levels had cut them off from their neighbours above. In an unguarded moment Laing's sister had whispered to him that there was a brothel operating somewhere in the high-rise. The mysterious movements of the air-hostesses as they pursued their busy social lives, particularly on the floors above her own, clearly unsettled Alice, as if they in some way interfered with the natural social order of the building, its system of precedences entirely based on floor-height. Laing had noticed that he and his fellow tenants were far more tolerant of any noise or nuisance from the floors above than they were from those below them. However, he liked Wilder, with his loud voice and rugby-scrum manners. He let a needed dimension of the unfamiliar into the apartment block. His relationship with Charlotte Melville was hard to gauge – his powerful sexual aggression was overlaid by a tremendous restlessness. No wonder his wife, a pale young woman with a postgraduate degree who reviewed children's books for the literary weeklies, seemed permanently exhausted.

As Laing stood on the balcony, accepting a drink from Charlotte, the noise of the party came down from the bright air, as if the sky itself had been wired for sound. Charlotte pointed to a fragment of glass on Laing's balcony that had escaped his brush.

'Are you under attack? I heard something fall.' She called to Wilder, who was lounging back in the centre of her sofa, examining his heavy legs. 'It's those people on the 31st floor.'

'Which people?' Laing asked. He assumed that she was referring to a specific group, a clique of over-aggressive film actors or tax consultants, or perhaps a freak aggregation of dipsomaniacs. But Charlotte shrugged vaguely, as if it was unnecessary to be more specific. Clearly some kind of demarcation had taken place in her mind, like his own facile identification of people by the floors on which they lived.

'By the way, what are we all celebrating?' he asked as they returned to the living-room.

'Don't you know?' Wilder gestured at the walls and ceiling. 'Full house. We've achieved critical mass.'

'Richard means that the last apartment has been occupied,' Charlotte explained. 'Incidentally, the contractors promised us a free party when the thousandth apartment was sold.'

I'll be interested to see if they hold it,' Wilder remarked. Clearly he enjoyed running down the high-rise. 'The elusive Anthony Royal was supposed to provide the booze. You've met him, I think,' he said to Laing. 'The architect who designed our hanging paradise.'

'We play squash together,' Laing rejoined. Aware of the hint of challenge in Wilder's voice, he added, 'Once a week – I hardly know the man, but I like him.'

Wilder sat forward, cradling his heavy head in his fists. Laing noticed that he was continually touching himself, for ever inspecting the hair on his massive calves, smelling the backs of his scarred hands, as if he had just discovered his own body. 'You're favoured to have met him,' Wilder said. 'I'd like to know why. An isolated character – I ought to resent him, but somehow I feel sorry for the man, hovering over us like some kind of fallen angel.'

'He has a penthouse apartment,' Laing commented. He had no wish to become involved in any tug of war over his brief friendship with Royal. He had met this well-to-do architect, a former member of the consortium which had designed the development project, during the final stages of Royal's recovery from a minor car accident. Laing had helped him to set up the complex callisthenics machine in the penthouse where Royal spent his time, the focus of a great deal of curiosity and attention. As everyone continually repeated, Royal lived 'on top' of the building, as if in some kind of glamorous shack.

'Royal was the first person to move in here,' Wilder informed him. 'There's something about him I haven't put my finger on. Perhaps even a sense of guilt – he hangs around up there as if he's waiting to be found out. I expected him to leave months ago. He has a rich young wife, so why stay on in this glorified tenement?' Before Laing could protest, Wilder pressed on. 'I know Charlotte has reservations about life here – the trouble with these places is that they're not designed for children. The only open space turns out to be someone else's car-park. By the way, doctor, I'm planning to do a television documentary about high-rises, a really hard look at the physical and psychological pressures of living in a huge condominium such as this one.'

'You'll have a lot of material.'

'Too much, as always. I wonder if Royal would take part – you might ask him, doctor. As one of the architects of the block and its first tenant, his views would be interesting. Your own, too …'

As Wilder talked away rapidly, his words over-running the cigarette smoke coming from his mouth. Laing turned his attention to Charlotte. She was watching Wilder intently, nodding at each of his points. Laing liked her determination to stick up for herself and her small son, her evident sanity and good sense. His own marriage, to a fellow physician and specialist in tropical medicine, had been a brief but total disaster, a reflection of heaven-only-knew what needs. With unerring judgement Laing had involved himself with this highly strung and ambitious young doctor, for whom Laing's refusal to give up teaching – in itself suspicious – and involve herself directly in the political aspects of preventive medicine had provided a limitless opportunity for bickering and confrontation. After only six months together she had suddenly joined an international famine-relief organisation and left on a three-year tour. But Laing had made no attempt to follow her. For reasons he could not yet explain, he had been reluctant to give up teaching, and the admittedly doubtful security of being with students who were still almost his own age.

Charlotte, he guessed, would understand this. In his mind Laing projected the possible course of an affair with her. The proximity and distance which the high-rise provided at the same time, that neutral emotional background against which the most intriguing relationships might develop, had begun to interest him for its own sake. For some reason he found himself drawing back even within this still imaginary encounter, sensing that they were all far more involved with each other than they realised. An almost tangible network of rivalries and intrigues bound them together.

As he guessed, even this apparently casual meeting in Charlotte's apartment had been set up to test his attitude to the upper-level residents who were trying to exclude children from the 35th-floor swimming-pool.

'The terms of our leases guarantee us equal access to all facilities,' Charlotte explained. 'We've decided to set up a parents' action group.'

'Doesn't that leave me out?'

'We need a doctor on the committee. The paediatric argument would come much more forcefully from you, Robert.'

'Well, perhaps …' Laing hesitated to commit himself. Before he knew it, he would be a character in a highly charged television documentary, or taking part in a sit-in outside the office of the building manager. Reluctant at this stage to be snared into an inter-floor wrangle, Laing stood up and excused himself. As he left, Charlotte had equipped herself with a checklist of grievances. Sitting beside Wilder she began to tick off the complaints to be placed before the building manager, like a conscientious teacher preparing the syllabus for the next term.

When Laing returned to his apartment, the party on the 31st floor had ended. He stood on his balcony in the silence, enjoying the magnificent play of light across the neighbouring block four hundred yards away. The building had just been completed, and by coincidence the first tenants were arriving on the very morning that the last had moved into his own block. A furniture pantechnicon was backing into the entrance to the freight elevator, and the carpets and stereo-speakers, dressing-tables and bedside lamps would soon be carried up the elevator shaft to form the elements of a private world.

Thinking of the rush of pleasure and excitement which the new tenants would feel as they gazed out for the first time from their aerial ledge on the cliff face, Laing contrasted it with the conversation he had just heard between Wilder and Charlotte Melville. However reluctantly, he now had to accept something he had been trying to repress – that the previous six months had been a period of continuous bickering among his neighbours, of trivial disputes over the faulty elevators and air-conditioning, inexplicable electrical failures, noise, competition for parking space and, in short, that host of minor defects which the architects were supposed specifically to have designed out of these over-priced apartments. The underlying tensions among the residents were remarkably strong, damped down partly by the civilized tone of the building, and partly by the obvious need to make this huge apartment block a success.

Laing remembered a minor but unpleasant incident that had taken place the previous afternoon on the 10th floor shopping concourse. As he waited to cash a cheque at the bank an altercation was going on outside the doors of the swimming-pool. A group of children, still wet from the water, were backing away from the imposing figure of a cost-accountant from the 17th floor. Facing him in this unequal contest was Helen Wilder. Her husband's pugnacity had long since drained any self-confidence from her. Nervously trying to control the children, she listened stoically to the accountant's reprimand, now and then making some weak retort.

Leaving the bank counter, Laing walked towards them, past the crowded check-out points of the supermarket and the lines of women under the driers in the hair-dressing salon. As he stood beside Mrs Wilder, waiting until she recognised him, he gathered that the accountant was complaining that her children, not for the first time, had been urinating in the pool.

Laing briefly interceded, but the accountant slammed away through the swing doors, confident that he had sufficiently intimidated Mrs Wilder to drive her brood of children away for ever.

'Thanks for taking my side – Richard was supposed to be here.' She picked a damp thread of hair out of her eyes. 'It's becoming impossible – we arrange set hours for the children but the adults come anyway.' She took Laing's arm and squinted nervously across the crowded concourse. 'Do you mind walking me back to the elevator? It must sound rather paranoid, but I'm becoming obsessed with the idea that one day we'll be physically attacked ...' She shuddered under her damp towel as she propelled the children forward. 'It's almost as if these aren't the people who really live here.'

During the afternoon Laing found himself thinking of this last remark of Helen Wilder's. Absurd though it sounded, the statement had a certain truth. Now and then his neighbours, the orthodontic surgeon and his wife, stepped on to their balcony and frowned at Laing, as if disapproving of the relaxed way in which he lay back in his reclining chair. Laing tried to visualise their life together, their hobbies, conversation, sexual acts. It was difficult to imagine any kind of domestic reality, as if the Steeles were a pair of secret agents unconvincingly trying to establish a marital role. By contrast, Wilder was real enough, but hardly belonged to the high-rise.

Laing lay back on his balcony, watching the dusk fall across the façades of the adjacent blocks. Their size appeared to vary according to the play of light over their surfaces. Sometimes, when he returned home in the evening from the medical school, he was convinced that the high-rise had managed to extend itself during the day. Lifted on its concrete legs, the forty-storey block appeared to be even higher, as if a group of off-duty construction workers from the television studios had casually added another floor. The five apartment buildings on the eastern perimeter of the mile-square project together formed a massive palisade that by dusk had already plunged the suburban streets behind them into darkness.

The high-rises seemed almost to challenge the sun itself – Anthony Royal and the architects who had designed the complex could not have foreseen the drama of confrontation each morning between these concrete slabs and the rising sun. It was only fitting that the sun first appeared between the legs of the apartment blocks, raising itself over the horizon as if nervous of waking this line of giants. During the morning, from his office on the top floor of the medical school, Laing would watch their shadows swing across the parking-lots and empty plazas of the project, sluice-gates opening to admit the day. For all his reservations, Laing was the first to concede that these huge buildings had won their attempt to colonize the sky.

Soon after nine o'clock that evening, an electrical failure temporarily blacked out the 9th, 10th and 11th floors. Looking back on this episode, Laing was surprised by the degree of confusion during the fifteen minutes of the blackout. Some two hundred people were present on the 10th floor concourse, and many were injured in the stampede for the elevators and staircases.

A number of absurd but unpleasant altercations broke out in the darkness between those who wanted to descend to their apartments on the lower levels and the residents from the upper floors who insisted on escaping upwards into the cooler heights of the building. During the blackout two of the twenty elevators were put out of action. The air-conditioning had been switched off, and a woman passenger trapped in an elevator between the 10th and 11th floors became hysterical, possibly the victim of a minor sexual assault — the restoration of light in due course revealed its crop of illicit liaisons flourishing in the benevolent conditions of total darkness like a voracious plant species.

Laing was on his way to the gymnasium when the power failed. Uneager to join the mêlée on the concourse, he waited in a deserted classroom of the junior school. Sitting alone at one of the children's miniature desks, surrounded by the dim outlines of their good-humoured drawings pinned to the walls, he listened to their parents scuffling and shouting in the elevator lobby. When the lights returned he walked out among the startled residents, and did his best to calm everyone down. He supervised the transfer of the hysterical woman from the elevator to a lobby sofa. The heavy-boned wife of a jeweller on the 40th floor, she clung powerfully to Laing's arm, only releasing him when her husband appeared. As the crowd of residents dispersed, their fingers punching the elevator destination buttons, Laing noticed that two children had sheltered during the blackout in another of the classrooms. They were standing now in the entrance to the swimming-pool, backing away defensively from the tall figure of the 17th floor cost-accountant. This self-appointed guardian of the water held a long-handled pool skimmer like a bizarre weapon.

Angrily, Laing ran forward. But the children were not being driven from the pool. They stepped aside when Laing approached. The accountant stood by the water's edge, awkwardly reaching the skimmer across the calm surface. At the deep end three swimmers, who had been treading water during the entire blackout, were clambering over the side. One of them, he noticed without thinking, was Richard Wilder. Laing took the handle of the skimmer. As the children watched, he helped the accountant extend it across the water.

Floating in the centre of the pool was the drowned body of an Afghan hound.

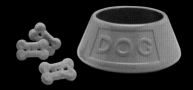

The famous fish fried in batter, which the Jews eat cold, and which has become the English national dish (the chef Alexis Soyer and other nineteenth-century writers described it as a Jewish way of cooking fish), is a Portuguese import.

Best Wishes
Claudia Roden. XXX

Greetings From 'Working Class Britain' ™

Kazuo Ishiguro | Butlers | It is sometimes said that butlers only truly exist in England this is true. Continentals are unable to be butlers because they are as a breed incapable by and large the Celts, as you will no doubt agree) — are as a rule unable

d. Other countries, whatever title is actually used, have only manservants. I tend to believe of the emotional restraint which only the English race is capable of. Continentals — and e to control themselves in moments of strong emotion, and are thus unable to

stephen gill, the flying turban, indian cuisine. 1999

maintain a professional demeanour other than in the least challenging of situations. If I are like a man who will, at the slightest provocation, tear off his suit and his shirt and important advantage over foreigners in this respect and it is for this reason that when

stephen gill, casablanca, lebanese cuisine. 1999

may return to my earlier metaphor — you will excuse my putting it so coarsely — they run about screaming. In a word, 'dignity' is beyond such persons. We English have an you think of a great butler, he is bound, almost by definition, to be an Englishman.

imagine picture of **sandy loaning** here

I would begin with the Greek word, **omphalos**, meaning the navel, and hence the stone that marked the centre of the world, and repeat it, **omphalos, omphalos, omphalos**, until its blunt and falling music becomes the music of somebody pumping water at the pump outside our back door. It is Co. Derry in the early 1940s. The American bombers groan towards the aerodrome at Toomebridge, the American troops manoeuvre in the fields along the road, but all of that great historical action does not disturb the rhythms of the yard. There the pump stands, a slender, iron idol, snouted, helmeted, dressed down with a sweeping handle, painted a dark green and set on a concrete plinth, marking the centre of another world. Five households drew water from it. Women came and went, came rattling between empty enamel buckets, went evenly away, weighed down by silent water. The horses came home to it in those first length-ening evenings of spring, and in a single draught emptied one bucket and then another as the man pumped and pumped, the plunger slugging up and down,

omphalos, omphalos, omphalos.

I do not know what age I was when I got lost in the pea-drills in a field behind the house, but it is a half-dream to me, and I've heard about it so often that I may even be imagining it. Yet, by now, I have imagined it so long and so often that I know what it was like: a green web, a caul of veined light, a tangle of rods and pods, stalks and tendrils, full of assuaging earth and leaf smell, a sunlit lair. I'm sitting as if just wakened from a winter sleep and gradually become aware of voices, coming closer, calling my name, and for no reason at all I have begun to weep.

All children want to crouch in their secret nests. I loved the fork of a beech tree at the head of our lane, the close thicket of a boxwood hedge in the front of the house, the soft, collapsing pile of hay in a back corner of the byre; but especially I spent time in the throat of an old willow tree at the end of the farmyard. It was a hollow tree, with gnarled, spreading roots, a soft, perishing bark and a pithy inside. Its mouth was like the fat and solid opening in a horse's collar, and, once you

squeezed in through it, you were at the heart of a different life, looking out on the familiar yard as if it were suddenly behind a pane of strangeness. Above your head, the living tree flourished and breathed, you shouldered the slightly vibrant bole, and if you put your forehead to the rough pith you felt the whole lithe and whispering crown of willow moving in the sky above you. In that tight cleft, you sensed the embrace of light and branches, you were a little Atlas shouldering it all, a little Cerunnos pivoting a world of antlers.

The world grew. Mossbawn, the first place, widened. There was what we called the Sandy Loaning, a sanded pathway between old hedges leading in off the road, first among fields and then through a small bog, to a remote farmhouse. It was a silky, fragrant world there, and for the first few hundred yards you were safe enough. The sides of the lane were banks of earth topped with broom and ferns, quilted with moss and primroses. Behind the broom, in the rich grass, cattle munched reassuringly. Rabbits occasionally broke cover and ran ahead of

seamus heaney
omphalos

you in a flurry of dry sand. There were wrens and goldfinches. But, gradually, those lush and definite fields gave way to scraggy marshland. Birch trees stood up to their pale shins in swamps. The ferns thickened above you. Scuffles in old leaves made you nervous and you dared yourself always to pass the badger's set, a wound of fresh mould in an overgrown ditch where the old brock had gone to earth. Around that badger's hole, there hung a field of dangerous force. This was the realm of bogeys. We'd heard about a mystery man who haunted the fringes of the bog here, we talked about mankeepers and mosscheepers, creatures un-catalogued by any naturalist, but none the less real for that. What was a mosscheeper, anyway, if not the soft, malicious sound the word itself made, a siren of collapsing sibilants coaxing you out towards bog pools lidded with innocent grass, quicksands and quagmires? They were all there and spreading out over a low, birch-screened apron of land towards the shores of Lough Beg.

That was the moss, forbidden ground. Two families lived at the heart of it, and a recluse, called Tom Tipping, whom we never saw, but in the morning on the road to school we watched his smoke rising from a clump of trees, and spoke his name between us until it was synonymous with mystery man, with unexpected scuttlings in the hedge, with footsteps slushing through long grass.

To this day, green, wet corners, flooded wastes, soft rushy bottoms, any place with the invitation of watery ground and tundra vegetation, even glimpsed from a car or a train, possess an immediate and deeply peaceful attraction. It is as if I am betrothed to them, and I believe my betrothal happened one summer evening, thirty years ago, when another boy and myself stripped to the white country skin and bathed in a moss-hole, treading the liver-thick mud, unsettling a smoky muck off the bottom and coming out smeared and weedy and darkened. We dressed again and went home in our wet clothes, smelling of the ground and the standing pool, somehow initiated.

Beyond the moss spread the narrow reaches of Lough Beg, and in the centre of Lough Beg lay Church Island, a spire rising out of its yew trees, a local mecca. St. Patrick, they said, had fasted and prayed there fifteen hundred years before. The old graveyard was shoulder-high with meadow-sweet and cow parsley, overhung with thick, unmolested yew trees and, somehow, those yews fetched me away to Agincourt and Crécy, where the English archers' bows, I knew, were made of yew also. All I could ever manage for my bows were tapering shoots of ash or willow from a hedge along the stackyard, but even so, to have cut a bough from that silent compound on Church Island would have been a violation too treacherous to contemplate.

If Lough Beg marked one limit of the imagination's nesting ground, Slieve Gallon marked another. Slieve Gallon is a small mountain that lies in the opposite direction, taking the eye out over grazing and ploughed ground and the distant woods of Moyola Park, out over Grove Hill and Back Park and Castledawson. This side of the country was the peopled, communal side, the land of

imagine picture of the **shores of lough beg** here

imagine picture of **grove hill** here

haycock and corn-stook, of fence and gate, milk-cans at the end of lanes and auction notices on gate pillars. Dogs barked from farm to farm. Sheds gaped at the roadside, bulging with fodder. Behind and across it went the railway, and the noise that hangs over it constantly is the heavy shunting of an engine at Castledawson station.

I have a sense of air, of lift and light, when this comes back to me. Light dancing off the shallows of the Moyola River, shifting in eddies on the glaucous whirlpool. Light changing on the mountain itself, that stood like a barometer of moods, now blue and hazy, now green and close up. Light above the spire, away at Magherafelt. Light frothing among the bluebells on Grove Hill. And the lift of the air is resonant, too, with vigorous musics. A summer evening carries the fervent and melancholy strain of hymn-singing from a gospel hall among the fields, and the hawthorn blooms and the soft, white patens of the elderflower hang dolorous in the hedges. Or the rattle of Orange drums from Aughrim Hill sets the heart alert and watchful as a hare.

For if this was the country of community, it was also the realm of division. Like the rabbit pads that loop across grazing, and tunnel the soft growths under ripening corn, the lines of sectarian antagonism and affiliation followed the boundaries of the land. In the names of its fields and townlands, in their mixture of Scots and Irish and English etymologies, this side of the country was redolent of the histories of its owners. Broagh, The Long Rigs, Bell's Hill; Brian's Field, the Round Meadow, the Demesne; each name was a kind of love made to each acre. And saying the names like this distances the places, turns them into what Wordsworth once called a prospect of the mind. They lie deep, like some script indelibly written into the nervous system.

I always remember the pleasure I had in digging the black earth in our garden and finding, a foot below the surface, a pale seam of sand. I remember, too, men coming to sink the shaft of the pump and digging through that seam of sand down into the bronze riches of the gravel, that soon began to puddle with the spring water. That pump marked an original descent into earth, sand, gravel, water. It centred and staked the imagination, made its foundation the foundation of the **omphalos** itself. So I find it altogether appropriate that an old superstition ratifies this hankering for the underground side of things. It is a superstition associated with the Heaney name. In Gaelic times, the family were involved with ecclesiastical affairs in the diocese of Derry, and had some kind of rights to the stewardship of a monastic site at Banagher in the north of the county. There is a St. Muredach O'Heney associated with the old church at Banagher; and there is also a belief that sand lifted from the ground at Banagher has beneficent, even magical, properties, if it is lifted from the site by one of the Heaney family name. Throw sand that a Heaney has lifted after a man going into court, and he will win his case. Throw it after your team as they go out on to the pitch, and they will win the game.

Vindaloo
FAT LES

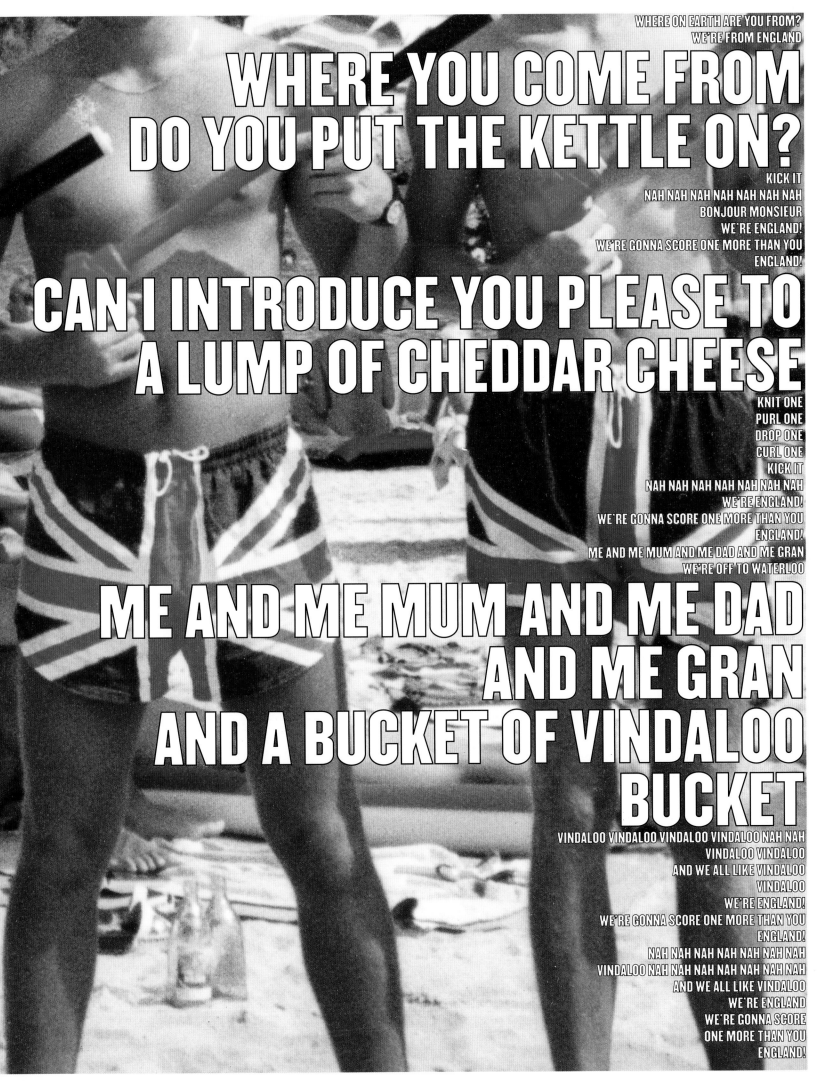

WHERE ON EARTH ARE YOU FROM?
WE'RE FROM ENGLAND

WHERE YOU COME FROM DO YOU PUT THE KETTLE ON?

KICK IT
NAH NAH NAH NAH NAH NAH NAH
BONJOUR MONSIEUR
WE'RE ENGLAND!
WE'RE GONNA SCORE ONE MORE THAN YOU
ENGLAND!

CAN I INTRODUCE YOU PLEASE TO A LUMP OF CHEDDAR CHEESE

KNIT ONE
PURL ONE
DROP ONE
CURL ONE
KICK IT
NAH NAH NAH NAH NAH NAH NAH
WE'RE ENGLAND!
WE'RE GONNA SCORE ONE MORE THAN YOU
ENGLAND!
ME AND ME MUM AND ME DAD AND ME GRAN
WE'RE OFF TO WATERLOO

ME AND ME MUM AND ME DAD AND ME GRAN AND A BUCKET OF VINDALOO BUCKET

VINDALOO VINDALOO VINDALOO VINDALOO NAH NAH
VINDALOO VINDALOO
AND WE ALL LIKE VINDALOO
VINDALOO
WE'RE ENGLAND!
WE'RE GONNA SCORE ONE MORE THAN YOU
ENGLAND!
NAH NAH NAH NAH NAH NAH NAH
VINDALOO NAH NAH NAH NAH NAH NAH NAH
AND WE ALL LIKE VINDALOO
WE'RE ENGLAND
WE'RE GONNA SCORE
ONE MORE THAN YOU
ENGLAND!

"what we know of the past is mostly not worth knowing. what is worth knowing is mostly uncertain. events in the past may roughly be divided into those which probably never happened and those which do not matter."

w.r. inge (dean of st. paul's 1911-1934)

"why kill time when you can kill yourself."

tony hancock

in & out of love:

THE QUAIL

BY

SARAH

LEFANU

The Quail: Coturnix Coturnix Coturnix: In general appearance much like a very small, delicately built Partridge, which it also resembles in flight if flushed, but presence is more often detected by characteristic note of male (see 'Voice') than by bird being seen.

Last year it was ducks. This year it is quails. And because I feel anxious about the changes I am about to inflict on my children and grasp at any semblance of continuity, even quailine continuity, I say, yes: don't send them all back to the city farm once they're hatched. I'll have one, with pleasure. My daughter's teacher is delighted.

Nicholas moved out of our house, although not out of my life, a year ago. I forced him to. It was either that, or murder him; and while the flesh was willing and my hand itched to pour weedkiller into his tomato soup on the few occasions when he was home in the evenings in time to eat with me, the spirit baulked. I dreamt about killing him, often, and each time struggled towards consciousness burdened with an immense weight of guilt. Poisoning is, apparently, a peculiarly female mode of murder. It inspires horror in the hearts of judges: they see it as coldly premeditated, not realising that with the alternative, lashing out in rage, women are more likely to get themselves killed than to kill. Or maybe that's our justification, and the truth is women are drawn atavistically to poisoning by their witchy past. But think of the poor children: a dead father and a murderess (infinitely more sinister than murderer) for a mother.

My daughter is delighted. She is almost as pleased at the prospect of having one of these speckled little brown birds for her very own as she is excited at the prospect of moving house and school. My children seem to love change. The other day I heard them chanting in a kind of nasal sing-song the names of their father's girl-friends of the last year: Mi-chelle, A-nnabel, A-dele, then they creased up and fell about on the floor shrieking. None of my friends have names like that: we're all simple Jo or Viv or Kate. Nicholas prefers the Annabels of this world. Sexy, young, childless.

Nicholas would have liked me to have other lovers. Correction: he would have liked me to have lovers. That side of marriage, as I remember my mother quaintly calling it in reference to my raffish father, hadn't existed for us since the birth of our daughter six years ago. And that was a fluke, if not semi-miraculous. Nicholas thought that my taking a lover (to take a lover: like an examination) would even things up - this was after the discovery that brought it out in the open - but why should I act to satisfy his balance sheet? Nicholas is an accountant.

And as he gets older, his women get younger.

The family Phasianidae comprises about 170 species of quails, partridges, pheasants, peafowl and jungle fowl. The group is a very mixed one, showing marked variation in size and plumage; e.g. the splendour of the peacock and the dull, drab coloration of the partridge, and it is difficult to find a common denominator. One such attempt at classification has been to divide the birds into polygamous and monogamous, the brightly coloured species belonging to the first group, the duller, drab ones to the second.

Moving day draws near. The teacher is distraught. One of the baby quails (eight of them hatched out, only one casualty, they heard its beak tap-tapping inside the shell, growing fainter and fainter until it stopped) has had an accident. The roof of the cage slipped out of her hands as she replaced it after feeding them, its leg was trapped and now is dangling in a sickeningly broken fashion. It will wither away, she says: a one-legged quail won't survive unless it has a special home. Could we possibly? She tails off, her eyes are still wet, her vocation is to care for small creatures (my daughter adores her) and look what's happened.

Of course, I say. I mean who can refuse a home to a one-legged quail? She goes on: But you must have your own one too. They all look the same to me (apart from the one with the dangling leg), but I say: Fine. My daughter is further delighted. Two quails are even better than one. I hope there will be no more injuries.

The one I found him with in our bed was in her early twenties. I felt as if I'd been punched in the stomach. I couldn't breathe, it was like falling off a horse, being winded, desperately trying to draw in breath and thinking you'll die of suffocation. Then I was sick, copiously, in the bathroom where I'd locked myself in, and he was knocking on the door and calling my name in his special concerned voice. He must have hustled Rosie, I think her name was, or perhaps Rosalie, out of the house pretty smartly. You think vomiting in the lav is a bit of an overreaction, do you? I mean what's the big fuss? There're probably statistics like with the birth and death rate: one adulterous fornication is committed every two seconds. Or every one second.

It wasn't so much the shock of finding him there doing it in our bed. It was the instant realisation that he'd been doing just this for years, if not in this bed, then in beds all over the place; and with that realisation the simultaneous admission, and this is what seemed to hit me in the stomach, that I had known it all along. When I opened the bedroom door there was a moment of utter clarity; it was as if I was seeing him for the first time and my vision wasn't fogged by desire, or fear, or habit, and then I was doubled over, wheezing and retching.

I wonder: are all men like Nicholas, but less obvious about it? Did my father have mistresses? Did my mother know? Did she feel powerless, out of control, like Nicholas makes me feel?

Nicholas now wants to buy a house, and although he is, in my view, grossly overpaid, he says he can't afford a new mortgage on top of what he pays for this house. So the children and I are going somewhere smaller, and I'll manage most of the new mortgage although local arts administration is not exactly lucrative. Particularly part-time and so no chance of promotion. Equal opportunities, what a joke.

Bernard, who has been in the office only eighteen months, is about to get some flashy regional job. He's a nice enough bloke, but hardly out to set the world on fire. I suspect his baldness has something to do with it; it seems to give men an air of authority. It's not quite the same if you're a woman, is it? Even grey puts you at a disadvantage, let alone no hair. Nicholas lovingly tends his thick dark curls. How did I ever fall for a man so vain? Maybe his vanity spoke to mine; my narcissism mirrored in his gaze.

As always, however, there are exceptions to the rule: some quails, even though their plumage is dull, leave the hen immediately after copulation.

Nicholas has said he'll help me move, but something comes up. Or someone.

It doesn't matter, as my old schoolfriend Kate is coming the day before and will spend the night and help with the final packing-up.

A skip full of rubbish is parked outside the front door; the baby clothes have all gone to the CancerCare shop; summer clothes have been washed and put away, they won't be needed for another year (perhaps I should have got rid of more of them, well, it's too late now). Most of the big pieces of furniture have already gone, and I thought I'd be left with just beds and kitchen equipment to deal with. But instead I am afloat in a sea of rubbish. It's as if I've sieved the contents of the house over and over, catching smaller and smaller items: this to be chucked, that to be packed, this to be discreetly lost when the children are safely out of the way, and what I'm left with is objects old, dusty, worn, but somehow not easily classifiable as rubbish. Such as: that nice old faded Asian pheasant serving dish my mother gave me which I broke two years ago and could easily be mended but hasn't been. A dusty heap of Lego pieces revealed when the large pieces of furniture went this morning. Six and a half pairs of shoes, that might or might not fit someone, from the cupboard under the stairs. I feel incapable of any further decisions.

Covey or pack of partridges; brood, eye (obs), nye or bouquet (when a number cross the guns at once) of pheasants; bevy of quails.

The scaffolding at the back of the house should have come down two months ago, when Viv and the girls finished mending the roof, but the scaffolder to whom they had subcontracted, a harmless-looking fellow, I thought, when he put it up, has since been arrested and charged with threatening behaviour. With a shotgun. He's now out on bail, but can't or won't remove the scaffolding. It must go by tomorrow, completion day. I'm not happy being left in possession of something that belongs to a man rampaging with a shotgun (sawn-off, of course, aren't they all?), but Viv says not to worry, it was a family affair. Oh well, that's OK, then, isn't it?

Kate thinks that I am cynical about men. She tells me that it is hopelessly old-fashioned of me to see men as the enemy, that that went out with the ark and I am stuck in a time-warp. Men, too, can be loving and faithful. The trouble is that while I can believe that Kate's Peter, for example, is loving, faithful, clean and has all sorts of other sterling qualities, he's always struck me as a dull dog and I could never imagine what clever, pretty Kate saw in him. I do not say this.

I ask Kate to put everything into boxes as best she can. Meanwhile I start to empty the filing cabinet, then remember that the removals men said not to bother. I unlock the door of the back room to check on the quails, collected earlier from school and looking rather cramped in their temporary home, a disused gerbil cage. The crippled quail has made a remarkable recovery. In fact I can't tell the two apart. So much for withering away. They've knocked their water bowl over again. Oh well, I expect they'll survive the night without water. I hope. I lock the door behind me, then suddenly think: where's the cat? Have I locked it in with them? I open the door again, and peer under the table. Yes. I drag it out.

Kate is carefully wrapping each piece of the broken serving dish in a separate piece of newspaper. I stifle my irritation. Kate has a close and loving relationship with her mother. They swap recipes.

The doorbell rings. It's the man next door. He's an ex-Hell's Angel, but mellowed since he had a heart attack two years ago. He offers to ring up some of his mates and ask them to come and take down the scaffolding. In a couple of hours' time, he says: when it's dark. No questions asked. I decline the offer politely, but I can see he's annoyed. I explain that it isn't mine to get rid of, that it was hired by Viv the builder, and I don't want to get her into trouble. This doesn't seem to cut much ice with him, but I manage to get him out of the door, while I grovellingly express thanks for his kind offer.

I am now full of fear that he'll do it anyway, that he'll send his mates over the garden wall at midnight. If that's the case, I'll just have to let it go: his mates have not suffered heart attacks as far as I know and are far from mellowed.

Half an hour later Viv arrives. She's spent the whole evening ringing round scaffolding firms to find someone to take it down. None of them will touch it. They've all heard he's on an

attempted murder charge. What a network these scaffolders must have, says Kate, like the early days of the women's movement. But on the eighth call Viv found somebody who would take it down, first thing tomorrow morning, but they won't store it. They said it was probably stolen, and they don't want any trouble. Who does?

I hope that this move will get me out of trouble. Nicholas trouble and money trouble all at once. I want quiet. I want to be untouched.

I make us each a bowl of spaghetti, which we eat with some pesto I find lurking in the fridge. I open a bottle of red wine and pour out a glass for Kate and myself. Viv doesn't drink. She only smokes dope.

I look around the kitchen. On the draining board stand a cluster of old plastic cups, stained and dusty, a jam jar of paintbrushes and three children's paintboxes, none of which has a lid. A pile of paperbacks leans against the fridge, thrillers mostly. Where on earth did they come from? I thought I'd packed all the books last week. There is still an awful lot of crockery on the shelves. The lampshade over the table is thick with dust. Mustn't forget to take that: it's the most expensive lampshade Nicholas and I ever bought - Italian, wide-brimmed, made of thick, heavy, clear glass with a black border.

Could you hoover the lampshades, Kate, and then pack them? I ask.

Hoover them? says Kate. She gives me an odd look.

I can't bear the thought of taking all this dust and dirt with me. I feel like a huge bear just coming out of hibernation, a six-year-long hibernation; I want to shake off the leaves and cobwebs, the mould of old attachments, that cling to my fur, I want to delouse myself and go out clean.

By midnight Kate has hoovered and packed all the lampshades. I notice she is looking a little pale. I check on the quails one last time. They are huddled in a corner of the cage, one on top of the other. Keeping themselves warm, I think. I put the cat out, am struck with fear that it might be so upset by the emptying of the house that it will run away, open the door for it to come in again and then decide against it. I don't want to be clearing up cat crap tomorrow morning. I check on the children: fast asleep. Then I go to bed. There are no curtains, and I lie there watching the dance of clouds, glowing an eerie orange, behind the solid black criss-cross of the scaffolding poles.

But-for-but, Cheshire; corncrake, Sussex; deadchick, Shetland Isles; landrail, Sussex; quailzie, Scotland; quick-me-Dick, Oxon; rine, Cornwall; sofliar, Wales; throsher; wandering quail; wet-my-feet, Ireland, Scotland; wet-my-lips, Norfolk, Sussex; wet weather, Sussex.

The scaffolders arrive at eight-thirty the next morning. When the removals men arrive, fifteen minutes later, there is nowhere for them to park their van, which is as tall, or so it seems, as the scaffolders' lorry is long. This makes the removals men rather surly. They attempt to remove the covered trailer belonging to the man next door, which has been parked outside ever since Nicholas and I moved in; and has been moved only once, when some lads dragged it to a nearby hill in the middle of the night and let it career to the bottom. The man next door throws up a window on the first floor, leans out and lets rip a string of abuse at the removals men, me and a couple of passers-by. I ask Kate if she will take the children to school for their last morning. They are reluctant to go, and stand by the gate goggle-eyed. The man next door is leaning further out of his window, and obviously has no clothes on.

He shuts the window with a crash. The removals men shrug their shoulders, and manage to back their van into the space now cleared. They are not yet cheerful, and cast dark looks at the scaffolders, who are being noisy and insouciant.

I lurk unhappily in the kitchen, feeling that I have set in motion a series of events that I no longer control. Couldn't I have managed to stay on here somehow? I remember all the articles I've read recently about the dire necessity of providing stability for your children, some of them hinting at the consequences of failure: criminal tendencies, inability to form lasting relationships, even (God spare us) a marked swing towards fundamentalist religious beliefs. Well, at least I don't parade a series of lovers in front of them like their father does. No, I don't do that.

A bejeaned pair of legs swings down outside the window, followed by an unpromising buttock cleavage, then a face peers in and shouts at me through the glass: Put the kettle on, love, would you? I give him the V-sign as his legs disappear upwards, but only as a matter of form - after all, he is removing the scaffolding,

and for that I am grateful. I ask the removals men if they too would like tea but, frostily polite, they say they're not yet ready for it.

Viv arrives. She has found somewhere for the scaffolding to be stored, and within half an hour all the poles are down and the men are gone. There are not many boxes left to go, most of the rooms are bare though thick with dust and fluff. I feel as if I've been cleaning for weeks already. I never realised we lived in such a sea of dirt, it must act as excellent insulation. The sloppy housewife as saver of energy, friend of the earth. Viv returns with an industrial hoover and starts at the top of the house, joint hanging from the corner of her mouth. I think I could fall in love with Viv.

The removals men are all smiles now. One of them tells me, primly, that the scaffolders were unsavoury characters. He should have met the original one.

Voice: Call of male a liquid 'quic, quic-ic' usually repeated several times and very faintly suggested by the popular 'wet-mi-lips'. Ordinary note of female a soft 'peu, peu'. When flushed birds call 'crwee-crwee' or a more croaking 'crucc-crucc'. Naumann describes the alarm-note when flushed as 'trul-reck-reck-reck', which might represent a combination of these notes. He also describes 'callnotes', 'bubibi' and 'brubrub', a soft 'trulilil, trulil' and a faint 'gurr-gurr'gurr' not unlike purring of cat.

I'll miss the bathroom in this house. It's on the first floor, and as the house is in a terrace that snakes around the edge of a steep hill, when you lie in the bath you see just sky, the clouds chasing across it, and on summer evenings hot air balloons in bright primary colours, in red and blue and yellow stripes, waft past, giving a sudden roar as the balloonists open up the fire. In the new house the bath is tucked into a corner of the room and you can't see out of the window unless you lie with your head at the tap end - not conducive to watery daydreaming. In the early days Nicholas and I used to bath together, uncomfortably but excitingly, skin slipping and sliding over skin. That was before the babies were born. He has other skin to slip and slide over now, and probably did even then. Later, he was never home in the evenings - work, he used to say - and came home smelling of

sweat and sex. I ignored it: I couldn't admit the idea of sharing his body, his lips, the soft down on his belly, his tongue, his cock, with other women. Are men naturally polygamous? Do women only want babies? I used not to have these heretical thoughts. Kate would be horrified.

Cheeper: young bird.

Viv is still hoovering as Kate and I start to pack the car. Three sleeping bags, one ragged sheep that used to bleat when turned upside-down but now only rattles (son's), one raccoon Fluppet (daughter's: she likes to stroke its fat tail against her cheek), one box of food for tonight with a few knives, forks and plates, the pile of books that once again missed being packed, one suitcase containing a change of clothes for all of us, assorted coats (it is an unseasonably hot autumn day), a basket full of dirty clothes, my bulging handbag, cat scratching in cat basket and miaowing in plaintive and pitiful fashion, and the quails. The straw in the cage looks damp and filthy, oh Christ I hope they survive the journey.

It's only half an hour's drive, Kate points out reassuringly. I'm feeling tight and tense, I hear my teeth grinding together.

Mustn't forget the children, says Kate. The children, oh Christ again, I had forgotten them. All their accoutrements, but no actual children. We're going to collect them from school and go straight on.

The removals men have gone, Viv has finished hoovering, the house is clean, empty, there is nothing of me in it any longer. I rush into each room one last time. Do I want to cry? No, there isn't time. If I start crying now I might never stop. I find the old wooden stepladder leaning in a lonely pose against the kitchen wall. Curses. What on earth am I going to do with it? Viv says she'll take it to her house and bring it round to me in a few days' time. Oh wonderful Viv.

I lock the door for the last time. Good riddance, Nicholas, I hiss as I climb into the car.

About time too, says Kate, sitting beside me with the cat basket on her lap. Kate thinks I should have left him years ago. Well, she's probably right. But I don't feel joyously free. I feel sick. Keys to the estate agent, then to school to pick up the children. They are full of the anticipated pleasure of sleeping bags tonight.

The Common or Migratory Quail: Northern populations migrate to Africa and southern Asia, many of them perishing on the way either in the sea or at the hands of sportsmen in some countries where they are netted and shot in vast numbers.

One of the quails has died. I looked in on them earlier and saw them snuggled up in a corner, one on top of the other, and thought they were asleep. Then wandering round the garden just before I went to bed, I went into the shed again and one of them was still in the corner, looking sort of flattish, and the other one was hopping about the cage. I opened the cage and the flattish one didn't move. I picked it up. It seemed to have shrunk.

Deadchick.

For a moment I think this is a bad omen, a death on our first night in the new house. Then I tell myself not to be so silly. Animals die and that's all there is to it. Maybe it was the crippled one, maybe it had suffered some other injury in the accident and its days were numbered anyway. Maybe it wasn't my fault. What shall I do with it? I'd better not get rid of it tonight, maybe the children will want to see it. I must let them express their grief. What about the other one? I hope it won't pine for its companion. Maybe it was trying to resuscitate it when I saw them earlier, keeping its cold body warm.

The next morning I tell the children. Both become tearful.

Would you like to see it? I ask gently.

Yuk. No way, they chorus.

I'm not going in that shed till you've got rid of it, says my son.

Yuk, says my daughter again.

Later I dig a deep hole and bury the quail. I don't want the cat digging it up and bringing it into the house.

At work I mention to Bernard my worries that my children are not normal. They show no affect, I say. Complete inability to grieve over parents' separation, death of beloved pet, etc. I keep on looking out for signs of disturbed behaviour, I complain, but there's not a trace.

Bernard laughs. Hard-hearted like you, he says.

Hard-hearted? Me?

What do you mean? I say, annoyed.

You keep yourself apart, he says. We've worked together for eighteen months and you still treat me like a stranger, with

polite tolerance.

I don't like this one bit, and I grab a floating piece of paper from my desk and fall to a concentrated study of it. It's something about a new community theatre.

I don't think it's because you dislike me, he goes on.

He's right. I don't. But I'll start disliking him soon if there's any more of this uncalled for personal comment.

I reach for the telephone.

We avoid each other for the rest of the day. Then, just as I'm about to go home, he says, You do know about quails, don't you?

Know about them?

Bernard smiles. He has a crooked smile that makes him look rather schoolboyish despite his lack of hair.

You have to be careful to provide the male with at least five or six females, he says. Or else ...

Or else?

Well, the female dies.

Good God, I cry. Of exhaustion, you mean? How awful. To think I kept that poor female shut up in a tiny cage with a voracious male and no means of escape. And to think that I thought that he was keeping her warm.

I look at Bernard and I start to laugh.

When I get home I go and cast my beady eye on the beady eye of the remaining quail. I decide it has a rough and vicious look to it. What's more, it has waxed fat and is now strutting round its cage in what can only be described as a self-important fashion. None the less, I throw it some corn. I can hardly let it starve to death. Although being eaten is what it deserves.

Quails from the Sea: And there went forth a wind from the Lord, and brought quails from the sea, and let them fall by the camp, as it were a day's journey on this side, and as it were a day's journey on the other side, round about the camp, and as it were two cubits high upon the face of the earth. And the people stood up all that day, and all that night, and all the next day, and they gathered the quails: he that gathered least gathered ten homers; and they spread them all abroad for themselves round about the camp. And whilst the flesh was yet between their teeth, ere it was chewed, the wrath

of the Lord was kindled against the people, and the Lord smote the people with a very great plague.

Were they not meant to eat them? Are quails unclean, as fowls that creep, going upon all four, that shall be an abomination? Why then pile them as it were two cubits high?

My daughter worries that the quail is lonely and pesters me to get another one. I repress my shudders and put her off by saying we can't get another one until we make a bigger hutch: they need room to flap around in and they'd like to have some branches to fly up to and perch on, I tell her. That means putting it off for a long time, perhaps until this one dies of old age, I secretly hope. What is a quail's lifespan, assuming it is not drowned, netted, shot or eaten?

It is now illegal to kill wild quail. Japanese quail are bred for the table: they can be browned in butter and braised with a little stock, port wine and orange peel.

The following weekend Bernard comes round and builds a new quail house. Quite how this has come about I'm not too sure. The children watch delightedly as he saws, planes, hammers, fixes. They are both so busy helping Bernard they barely squabble all day. Hmph, I think. The murderous quail is put into its new house. Yet another example of vice rewarded, I say to Bernard, as I present him with a bottle of wine as thanks. Still, my daughter is very fond of it.

The school holidays come and go, and then Kate comes to stay. It's cold outside, one of those early spring cold spells that seem worse than winter because you've begun to expect, foolishly, a bit of warmth. I give the children an early supper, and once they're in bed Kate and I eat in front of the fire in the sitting-room. Kate asked me about Nicholas.

Worse than ever, I say: he's become a weekend raver, driving around the countryside half the night looking for parties. He doesn't turn up to collect the children when he says he will.

Bit old for that kind of thing, isn't he? says Kate.

You'd think so, I say morosely. And he hasn't paid any maintenance since Christmas.

I ponder the iniquity of men for a bit.

Oh look, says Kate, I brought this for you. I thought you'd be amused.

She takes out of her bag a dictionary of historical slang. Look up quail, she says. I do, and read out: *A harlot, or a courtesan, ex the bird's supposed amorousness.*

How disgraceful, I say. How typical, blaming women for male depravity. It's like men accusing women of irrationality, when it's men who have invented and sustained all major religions.

I read some of the other entries. Almost every one refers to women's insatiable sexual appetite. Maybe it's only the Qs; but no, it's everything from A to Z.

Even his own name, says Kate.

Partridge: a harlot.

Kind of obsessive, isn't it? says Kate.

A couple of whiskies later, and Kate tells me that she and Peter make love every night, or almost every night. Good God. I can hardly hide my amazement.

It's so long since I've had sex I can't even remember what it's like, I tell her.

She can hardly hide her amazement.

When the children have left home, I say, I shall probably retire to a convent and live the rest of my life serenely among members of my own sex.

Kate looks unconvinced. Would that be rational? she asks.

One Saturday a few weeks later I am in bed with Bernard. It is the middle of the morning. The children are, amazingly and conveniently, with their father. Bernard and I have just made love for the first time, and now he is gently sucking my nipples, first one, then the other. Trulilil, trulil. Gurr, gurr, gurr. I am almost fainting with pleasure. I roll on my side, hook my legs round his back and pull him inside me again.

This is a relationship begun *ab ovo.* I rang him earlier and invited him over for a cup of coffee - I don't think I had anything else in mind - as there was something I wanted to show him. We stood together in the kitchen looking down at the pale yellow egg richly speckled with brown and purple that lies in my hand.

Look what I've just found, I say.

That rather mucks up your theories, he says.

Your theories, I reply.

Suddenly I know what I want to do. I put the egg down gently on the table and move towards him. He smiles his crooked smile and then we are kissing and I run my hand over the back of his balding head, and I think, I like you. I think: I want you. We stop, and we both laugh.

Well? I say.

Yes, he replies.

Sofliar, throsher, wandering quail. I imagine our quailzie, bonneted, in a croft, baking scones for all her little cheepers. She's such a pretty, plump, brown little thing.

Langouste à l'Americaine

The best recipe for this dish is given by Charles Monselet.

Take a superb and lively crayfish, cut it in pieces, and throw it, still breathing, into finest oil in a saucepan on a very hot fire, add salt, pepper, a little chopped garlic, some good white wine, good sauce of fresh tomatoes, plenty of spices. Cook for about half an hour; put in at the last minute a little demi-glacé stock, and dust lightly with Cayenne pepper. Monselet declares that if the chaste Joseph had been given this dish by Potiphar's wife, she would not have been snubbed on that memorable occasion.

Norman Douglas

212

Purée of Game

Put on the fire in an earthenware pot a partridge, a hare, and a neck of veal in an excellent beef stock; skim it and then add carrots, onions and celery. When the game is cooked take it out of the pot, remove the bones, let it half cool and pound in a mortar. Add some crumbs of bread soaked in the gravy and pound it again; mix everything thoroughly and pass it through a sieve. The purée thus obtained should be thinned with gravy passed through a strainer; then heat it up again without letting it come to the boil. Serve with croûtons.

Americans of a certain age, if they cared more for game than they do, might learn to appreciate the mildly stimulating effects of this purée.

Norman Douglas

hanif kureishi
my son
the fanatic

Surreptitiously, the father began going into his son's bedroom. He would sit there for hours, rousing himself only to seek clues. What bewildered him was that Ali was getting tidier. The room, which was usually a tangle of clothes, books, cricket bats and video games, was becoming neat and ordered; spaces began appearing where before there had been only mess.

Initially, Parvez had been pleased: his son was outgrowing his teenage attitudes. But one day, beside the dustbin, Parvez found a torn shopping bag that contained not only old toys but computer disks, videotapes, new books and fashionable clothes the boy had bought a few months before. Also without explanation, Ali had parted from the English girlfriend who used to come around to the house. His old friends stopped ringing.

For reasons he didn't himself understand, Parvez was unable to bring up the subject of Ali's unusual behaviour. He was aware that he had become slightly afraid of his son, who, between his silences, was developing a sharp tongue. One remark Parvez did make – 'You don't play your guitar anymore' – elicited the mysterious but conclusive reply, 'There are more important things to be done.'

Yet Parvez felt his son's eccentricity as an injustice. He had always been aware of the pitfalls that other men's sons had stumbled into in England. It was for Ali that Parvez worked long hours; he spent a lot of money paying for Ali's education as an accountant. He had bought Ali good suits, all the books he required, and a computer. And now the boy was throwing his possessions out! The TV, video-player and stereo system followed the guitar. Soon the room was practically bare. Even the unhappy walls bore pale marks where Ali's pictures had been removed.

Parvez couldn't sleep; he went more often to the whisky bottle, even when he was at work. He realised it was imperative to discuss the matter with someone sympathetic.

Parvez had been a taxi-driver for twenty years. Half that time he'd worked for the same firm. Like him, most of the other drivers were Punjabis. They preferred to work at night, when the roads were clearer and the money better. They slept during the day, avoiding their wives. They led almost a boy's life together in the cabbies' office, playing cards and setting up practical jokes, exchanging lewd stories, eating takeaways from local balti houses and discussing politics and their own problems.

But Parvez had been unable to discuss the subject of Ali with his friends. He was too ashamed. And he was afraid, too, that they would blame him for the wrong turning his boy had taken, just as he had blamed other fathers whose sons began running around with bad girls, skipping school and joining gangs.

For years, Parvez had boasted to the other men about how Ali excelled in cricket, swimming and football, and what an attentive scholar he was, getting As in most subjects. Was it asking too much for Ali to get a good job, marry the right girl, and start a family? Once this happened, Parvez would be happy. His dreams of doing well in England would have come true. Where had he gone wrong?

One night, sitting in the taxi office on busted chairs with his two closest friends, watching a Sylvester Stallone film, Parvez broke his silence.

'I can't understand it!' he burst out. 'Everything is going from his room. And I can't talk to him any more. We were not father and son – we were brothers! Where has he gone? Why is he torturing me?' And Parvez put his head in his hands.

Even as he poured out his account, the men shook their heads and gave one another knowing glances.

'Tell me what is happening!' he demanded.

The reply was almost triumphant. They had guessed something was going wrong. Now it was clear: Ali was taking drugs and selling his possessions to pay for them. That was why his bedroom was being emptied.

'What must I do, then?'

Parvez's friends instructed him to watch Ali scrupulously and to be severe with him, before the boy went mad, overdosed or murdered someone.

Parvez staggered out into the early-morning air, terrified that they were right. His boy – the drug-addict killer!

To his relief, he found Bettina sitting in his car.

Usually the last customers of the night were local 'brasses', or prostitutes. The taxi-drivers knew them well and often drove them to liaisons. At the end of the girls' night, the men would ferry them home, though sometimes they would join the cabbies for a drinking session in the office. Occasionally, the drivers would go with the girls. 'A ride in exchange for a ride,' it was called.

Bettina had known Parvez for three years. She lived outside the town and, on the long drives home, during which she sat not in the passenger seat but beside him, Parvez had talked to her about his life and hopes, just as she talked about hers. They saw each other most nights.

He could talk to her about things he'd never be able to discuss with his own wife. Bettina, in turn, always reported on her night's activities. He liked to know where she had been and with whom. Once, he had rescued her from a violent client, and since then they had come to care for each other.

Though Bettina had never met Ali, she heard about the boy continually. That night, when Parvez told Bettina that he suspected Ali was on drugs, to Parvez's relief, she judged neither him nor the boy, but said, 'It's all in the eyes.' They might be bloodshot; the pupils might be dilated; Ali might look tired. He could be liable to sweats, or sudden mood changes. 'OK?'

Parvez began his vigil gratefully. Now that he knew what the problem might be, he felt better. And surely, he figured, things couldn't have gone too far?

He watched each mouthful the boy took. He sat beside him at every opportunity and looked into his eyes. When he could, he took the boy's hand, checked his temperature. If the boy wasn't at home, Parvez was active, looking under the carpet, in Ali's drawers, and behind the empty wardrobe – sniffing, inspecting, probing. He knew what to look for: Bettina had drawn pictures of capsules, syringes, pills, powders, rocks.

Every night, she waited to hear news of what he'd witnessed. After a few days of constant observation, Parvez was able to report that although the boy had given up sports, he seemed healthy. His eyes were clear. He didn't – as Parvez expected he might – flinch guiltily from his father's gaze. In fact, the boy seemed more alert and steady than usual: as well as being sullen, he was very watchful. He returned his father's long looks with more than a hint of criticism, of reproach, even – so much so that Parvez began to feel that it was he who was in the wrong, and not the boy.

'And there's nothing else physically different?' Bettina asked.

'No!' Parvez thought for a moment. 'But he is growing a beard.'

One night, after sitting with Bettina in an all-night coffee shop, Parvez came home particularly late. Reluctantly, he and Bettina had abandoned the drug theory, for Parvez had found nothing resembling any drug in Ali's room. Besides, Ali wasn't selling his belongings. He threw them out, gave them away, or donated them to charity shops.

Standing in the hall, Parvez heard the boy's alarm clock go off. Parvez hurried into his bedroom, where his wife, still awake, was sewing in bed. He ordered her to sit down and keep quiet, though she had neither stood up nor said a word. As she watched him curiously, he observed his son through the crack of the door.

The boy went into the bathroom to wash. When he returned to his room, Parvez sprang across the hall and set his ear to Ali's door. A muttering sound came from within. Parvez was puzzled but relieved.

Once this clue had been established, Parvez watched him at other times. The boy was praying. Without fail, when he was at home, he prayed five times a day.

Parvez had grown up in Lahore, where all young boys had been taught the Koran. To stop Parvez from falling asleep while he studied, the maulvi had attached a piece of string to the ceiling and tied it to Parvez's hair, so if his head fell forward, he would instantly jerk awake. After this indignity, Parvez had avoided all religions. Not that the other taxi-drivers had any more respect than he. In fact, they made jokes about the local mullahs walking around with their caps and beards, thinking they could tell people how to live while their eyes roved over the boys and girls in their care.

Parvez described to Bettina what he had discovered. He informed the men in the taxi office. His friends, who had been so inquisitive before, now became oddly silent. They could hardly condemn the boy for his devotions.

Parvez decided to take a night off and go out with the boy. They could talk things over. He wanted to hear how things were going at college; he wanted to tell him stories about their family in Pakistan. More than anything, he yearned to understand how Ali had discovered the 'spiritual dimension', as Bettina called it.

To Parvez's surprise, the boy refused to accompany him. He claimed he had an appointment. Parvez had to insist that no appointment could be more important than that of a son with his father.

The next day, Parvez went immediately to the street corner where Bettina stood in the rain wearing high heels, a short skirt and a long mac, which she would open hopefully at passing cars.

'Get in, get in!' he said.

They drove out across the moors and parked at the spot where, on better days, their view unimpeded for miles except by wild deer and horses, they'd lie back, with their eyes half-closed, saying, 'This is the life.' This time Parvez was trembling. Bettina put her arms around him.

'What's happened?'

'I've just had the worst experience of my life.'

As Bettina rubbed his head Parvez told her that the previous evening, as he and his son had studied the menu, the waiter, whom Parvez knew, brought him his usual whisky-and-water. Parvez was so nervous he had even prepared a question. He was going to ask Ali if he was worried about his imminent exams. But first he loosened his tie, crunched a poppadum, and took a long drink.

Before Parvez could speak, Ali made a face.

'Don't you know it's wrong to drink alcohol?' he had said.

'He spoke to me very harshly,' Parvez said to Bettina. 'I was about to castigate the boy for being insolent, but I managed to control myself.'

Parvez had explained patiently that for years he had worked more than ten hours a day, had few enjoyments or hobbies, and never gone on holiday. Surely it wasn't a crime to have a drink when he wanted one?

'But it is forbidden,' the boy said.

Parvez shrugged. 'I know.'

'And so is gambling, isn't it?'

'Yes. But surely we are only human?'

Each time Parvez took a drink, the boy winced, or made some kind of fastidious face. This made Parvez drink more quickly. The waiter, wanting to please his friend, brought another glass of whisky. Parvez knew he was getting drunk, but he couldn't stop himself. Ali had a horrible look, full of disgust and censure. It was as if he hated his father.

Halfway through the meal, Parvez suddenly lost his temper and threw a plate on the floor. He felt like ripping the cloth from the table, but the waiters and other customers were staring at him. Yet he wouldn't stand for his own son's telling him the difference between right and wrong. He knew he wasn't a bad man. He had a conscience. There were a few things of which he was ashamed, but on the whole he had lived a decent life.

'When have I had time to be wicked?' he asked Ali.

In a low, monotonous voice, the boy explained that Parvez had not, in fact, lived a good life. He had broken countless rules of the Koran.

'For instance?' Parvez demanded.

Ali didn't need to think. As if he had been waiting for this moment, he asked his father if he didn't relish pork pies?

'Well.' Parvez couldn't deny that he loved crispy bacon smothered with mushrooms and mustard and sandwiched between slices of fried bread. In fact, he ate this for breakfast every morning.

Ali then reminded Parvez that he had ordered his wife to cook pork sausages, saying to her, 'You're not in the village now. This is England. We have to fit in.'

Parvez was so annoyed and perplexed by this attack that he called for more drink.

'The problem is this,' the boy said. He leaned across the table. For the first time that night, his eyes were alive. 'You are too implicated in Western civilisation.'

Parvez burped; he thought he was going to choke. 'Implicated!' he said. 'But we live here!'

'The Western materialists hate us,' Ali said. 'Papa, how can you love something which hates you?'

'What is the answer, then,' Parvez said miserably, 'according to you?'

Ali didn't need to think. He addressed his father fluently, as if Parvez were a rowdy crowd which had to be quelled or convinced. The law of Islam would rule the world; the skin of the infidel would burn off again and again; the Jews and Christers would be routed. The West was a sink of hypocrites, adulterers, homosexuals, drug users and prostitutes.

While Ali talked, Parvez looked out the window as if to check that they were still in London.

'My people have taken enough. If the persecution doesn't stop, there will be jihad. I, and millions of others, will gladly give our lives for the cause.'

'But why, why?' Parvez said.

'For us, the reward will be in Paradise.'

'Paradise!'

Finally, as Parvez's eyes filled with tears, the boy urged him to mend his ways.

'But how would that be possible?' Parvez asked.

'Pray,' urged Ali. 'Pray beside me.'

Parvez paid the bill and ushered his boy out of there as soon as he was able. He couldn't take any more.

Ali sounded as if he'd swallowed someone else's voice.

On the way home, the boy sat in the back of the taxi, as if he were a customer. 'What has made you like this?' Parvez asked him, afraid that somehow he was to blame for all this. 'Is there a particular event which has influenced you?'

'Living in this country.'

'But I love England,' Parvez said, watching his boy in the rear view mirror. 'They let you do almost anything here.'

'That is the problem,' Ali replied.

For the first time in years, Parvez couldn't see straight. He knocked the side of the car against a lorry, ripping off the wing mirror. They were lucky not to have been stopped by the police: Parvez would have lost his licence and his job.

Back at the house, as he got out of the car, Parvez stumbled and fell in the road, scraping his hands and ripping his trousers. He managed to haul himself up. The boy didn't even offer him his hand.

Parvez told Bettina he was willing to pray, if that was what the boy wanted - if it would dislodge the pitiless look from his eyes. 'But what I object to,' he said, 'is being told by my own son that I am going to Hell!'

What had finished Parvez off was the boy's saying he was giving up his studies in accounting. When Parvez had asked why, Ali said sarcastically that it was obvious. 'Western education cultivates an anti-religious attitude.'

And in the world of accountants it was usual to meet women, drink alcohol and practise usury.

'But it's well-paid work,' Parvez argued. 'For years you've been preparing!'

Ali said he was going to begin work in prisons, with poor Muslims who were struggling to maintain their purity in the face of corruption. Finally, at the end of the evening, as Ali went up to bed, he had asked his father why he didn't have a beard, or at least a moustache.

'I feel as if I've lost my son,' Parvez told Bettina. 'I can't bear to be looked at as if I'm a criminal, I've decided what to do.'

'What is it?'

'I'm going to tell him to pick up his prayer mat and get out of my house. It will be the hardest thing I've ever done, but tonight I'm going to do it.'

'But you mustn't give up on him,' said Bettina. 'Many young people fall into cults and superstitious groups. It doesn't mean they'll always feel the same way.' She said Parvez had to stick by his boy.

Parvez was persuaded that she was right, even though he didn't feel like giving his son more love when he had hardly been thanked for all he had already given.

For the next two weeks, Parvez tried to endure his son's looks and reproaches. He attempted to make conversation about Ali's beliefs. But if Parvez ventured any criticism, Ali always had a brusque reply. On one occasion, Ali accused Parvez of 'grovelling' to the whites;

in contrast, he explained, he himself was not 'inferior'; there was more to the world than the West, though the West always thought t was best.

'How is it you know that?' Parvez said. 'Seeing as you've never left England?'

Ali replied with a look of contempt.

One night, having ensured there was no alcohol on his breath, Parvez sat down at the kitchen table with Ali. He hoped Ali would compliment him on the beard he was growing, but Ali didn't appear to notice it.

The previous day, Parvez had been telling Bettina that he thought people in the West sometimes felt inwardly empty and that people needed a philosophy to live by.

'Yes,' Bettina had said. 'That's the answer. You must tell him what your philosophy of life is. Then he will understand that there are other beliefs.'

After some fatiguing consideration, Parvez was ready to begin. The boy watched him as if he expected nothing. Haltingly, Parvez said that people had to treat one another with respect, particularly children their parents. This did seem, for a moment, to affect the boy. Heartened, Parvez continued. In his view, this life was all there was, and when you died, you rotted in the earth. 'Grass and flowers will grow out of my grave, but something of me will live on.'

'How then?'

'In other people. For instance, I will continue – in you.'

At this the boy appeared a little distressed.

'And in your grandchildren,' Parvez added for good measure. 'But while I am here on earth I want to make the best of it. And I want you to, as well!'

'What d'you mean by "make the best of it"?' asked the boy.

'Well', said Parvez, 'For a start … you should enjoy yourself. Yes. Enjoy yourself without hurting others.'

Ali said enjoyment was 'a bottomless pit'.

'But I don't mean enjoyment like that,' said Parvez. 'I mean the beauty of living.'

'All over the world our people are oppressed,' was the boy's reply.

'I know,' Parvez answered, not entirely sure who 'our people' were. 'But still – life is for living!'

Ali said, 'Real morality has existed for hundreds of years. Around the world millions and millions of people share my beliefs. Are you saying you are right and they are all wrong?' And Ali looked at his father with such aggressive confidence that Parvez would say no more.

A few evenings later, Bettina was riding in Parvez's car after visiting a client when they passed a boy on the street.

'That's my son,' Parvez said, his face set hard. They were on the other side of town, in a poor district, where there were two mosques.

Bettina turned to see. 'Slow down, then, slow down!'

She said, 'He's good-looking. Reminds me of you. But with a more determined face. Please, can't we stop?'

'What for?'

'I'd like to talk to him.'

Parvez turned the cab round and pulled up beside the boy.

'Coming home?' Parvez asked. 'It's quite a way.'

The boy shrugged and got into the back seat. Bettina sat in the front. Parvez became aware of Bettina's short skirt, her gaudy rings and ice-blue eyeshadow. He became conscious that the smell of her perfume, which he loved, filled the cab. He opened the window.

While Parvez drove as fast as he could, Bettina said gently to Ali, 'Where have you been?'

'The mosque, ' he said.

'And how are you getting on at college? Are you working hard?'

'Who are you to ask me these questions?' Ali said, looking out of the window. Then they hit bad traffic, and the car came to a standstill.

By now, Bettina had inadvertently laid her hand on Parvez's shoulder. She said, 'Your father, who is a good man, is very worried about you. You know he loves you more than his own life.'

'You say he loves me,' the boy said.

'Yes!' said Bettina.

'Then why is he letting a woman like you touch him like that?'

If Bettina looked at the boy in anger, he looked back at her with cold fury.

She said, 'What kind of woman am I that I should deserve to be spoken to like that?'

'You know what kind,' he said. Then he turned to his father. 'Now let me out.'

'Never,' Parvez replied.

'Don't worry, I'm getting out,' Bettina said.

'No, don't!' said Parvez. But even as the car moved forward, she opened the door and threw herself out – she had done this before – and ran away across the road. Parvez stopped and shouted after her several times, but she had gone.

Parvez took Ali back to the house, saying nothing more to him. Ali went straight to his room. Parvez was unable to read the paper, watch television, or even sit down. He kept pouring himself drinks.

At last, he went upstairs and paced up and down outside Ali's room. When, finally, he opened the door, Ali was praying. The boy didn't even glance his way.

Parvez kicked him over. Then he dragged the boy up by the front of his shirt and hit him. The boy fell back. Parvez hit him again. The boy's face was bloody. Parvez was panting; he knew the boy was unreachable, but he struck him none the less. The boy neither covered himself nor retaliated; there was no fear in his eyes. He only said, through his split lip,

'So who's the fanatic now?'

IT WAS A SUNNY SUMMER'S MORNING IN 1980 when for the first time I ascended the spindly staircase, festooned with posters of theatrical triumphs past, that led to Margaret Ramsay Ltd, in Goodwin's Court, off St Martin's Lane, in the centre of the West End of London. I had come to collect a copy of a play in which I had acted a couple of years before, in the theatre, and which I now hoped to persuade the BBC to do on television. Straight ahead of me, at the top of three flights of stairs, was the door with the agency's name on it, under several layers of murky varnish. The last thing I expected or wanted to do was to talk to Peggy Ramsay herself, but when I opened the door, there she unmistakably was, sitting at a desk - or rather *on* one - as she flicked through a script, almost hitting the pages in her impatience to make them turn quicker. Her skirt was drifting up round the middle of her thighs to reveal knee-high stockings. Hearing me enter, she looked up with an expression which seemed to mingle surprise, amusement and challenge, as if she'd been expecting me but had rather doubted I'd have the courage to come. It was a curiously sexy look. ¶ 'Hello,' I said, 'I'm -' ¶ 'I know *exactly* who you are, dear,' she said. 'Tell me,' she continued, as if resuming a conversation rather than beginning one, 'do you think Ayckbourn will *ever* write a *really* GOOD play?' ¶ 'It's an interesting question,' I replied nervously, slightly inhibited by the fact that I was at that moment appearing in a play by the author under discussion, and that he was by far the most successful client of the woman asking the question.

'You'd better come in,' she said, calling over her shoulder for 'tea and *kike*' to one of the young women in the office, as she ushered me into what was evidently her private office. Adjusting and readjusting her skirt - a flowery item, beige, silk and diaphanous - she kicked off her shoes and seated herself at her desk, while I settled down on the sofa. ¶ 'Ah, that sofa ...' she murmured, mysteriously, with many a nod and a smile, as she absent-mindedly combed her fine golden hair. The room had an air of glamorous chaos about it, half work-place, half boudoir. There were shelves and shelves of scripts right up to the ceiling, their authors' names boldly inscribed in red down the spine: in one quick glance I saw Adamov, Bond, Churchill, Hampton, Hare, Rudkin. There were books, in great tottering piles; awards, both framed and in statuette form; posters (all of Orton, Nichols in Flemish, Mortimer on Broadway); plants everywhere, trailing unchecked; discarded knee-high stockings, scarves, hairbrushes, make-up bags, mirrors and hats: huge, wide-brimmed, ribbon-toting hats, four or five of them, draped over the furniture. The air was headily fragrant, confirming the room's overpoweringly feminine aura. ¶ In the midst of it all was Peggy, clearly the source of both the glamour and the chaos. She was now answering the telephone in a startlingly salty manner. 'Well, you'll just have to tell them to fuck off, dear,' she was saying to one caller, 'I shall tell Merrick that we *must* HAVE a million,' to another. 'But your play's *no* GOOD, *dear*,' she cried, to a third, informing me in an entirely audible aside, 'It's Bolt;' I'm telling him his play's no good,' then informing him, 'I've got *Simon Callow* here and I'm telling

LOVE IS WHERE IT FALLS

BY SIMON CALLOW

him your play's *no good*.' Whatever his response was, it made her chuckle richly. 'Well it isn't dear, is it?' There were more calls, all rapidly despatched; to my astonishment, she seemed to think that talking to me and, even more surprising, listening to me, was more important than the day-to-day business of running the most successful play agency in the country, perhaps the world. She dismissed *that* in a phrase. 'The word *agent*,' she said, 'is the most disgusting word in the English language.' ¶ *Names flew about the room, resonant, legendary, as the conversation got under way. She was on, not first but - so much more intimate - last -name terms with them all: Lean, Ionesco, Miller; nor was she confined to the living, or those whom she might have known personally: Proust, Cocteau, Rilke, were all swept up in the torrent of allusion and anecdote. It was immediately evident that she judged her clients, and herself, by direct comparison with the great dead. This gave the conversation uncommon breadth; but it was the least of what made the meeting extraordinary.* ¶ The overwhelming impression was of the airy, fiery presence of the woman herself. She was never still, not for a second, but there was nothing restless about her. She seemed rather to be performing a *moto perpetuo*, choreographed by some innovative genius into the physical representation of a dancing mind. Her long-fingered hands fluttered, her hair flew out of control, her slight frame drew itself up and up as if she were preparing for a high dive, then would suddenly flop down till she was almost horizontal in her chair, arms stretched out, legs shockingly wide apart, nether regions barely concealed by whichever small part of her transparent skirt was theoretically supposed to be covering her. Sometimes, to make a point, she would reach for a book or a script, wrap her fist round the arm of her spectacles, then whisk them off, thrusting her face flush up against the page. When she'd read what it was she was looking for, she'd unceremoniously throw the book or script down and shove her spectacles back onto her face. Even this alarming procedure was somehow gracefully effected. ¶ The incessancy of movement was complemented by a voice as beautiful and expressive as any actress might hope to possess: perfectly modulated, feathery light and caressing, then suddenly rough and emphatic, but never when you expected it. Harsh things were said beautifully, beautiful things harshly; four-letter words were deployed like jewels. 'I always thought,' she said, liltingly, 'how *touching* it was that when Ken and Joe couldn't find anyone else to fuck, they would fuck *each other*.' Her vowels bore the very slightest trace of her native South Africa, which added a touch of the exotic, more a colour than a sound. Conversational life was made even more exciting with the appearance of an occasional hole in the fabric of her talk. A word would suddenly elude her, and she would search furiously for it. The oddity was that while hundreds of unerringly chosen words in several languages, evidence of the widest possible literary culture, would flow past with seamless elegance, there would be a sudden hiatus: 'So I put the book on the - the - what do you call that thing?' 'What thing, Peggy? What sort of thing?' 'You know perfectly well: the *thing* you use when you want to put other *things* on it.' 'Dumb waiter? Sideboard?' 'Ya cha-cha-cha,' she would cry, dismissively. 'Trolley, Peggy?' A look of withering contempt. And then, in desperation, one would say, 'Table?' 'Table. Exactly.' And we were off again. This could apply equally to proper names; again, hardly the ones you'd expect, after disquisitions on Jean-Jacques Bertrand and Montherlant, laced with citations of large slices of Franz Werfel, all perfectly attributed. 'I first met Schneider because he'd done the American première of *Waiting for Godot* and he wanted to meet … he wanted to meet …' (triumphantly) '*whoever it was who wrote it.*' ¶ *She had a characteristic method of phrasing which bore some resemblance to Queen Victoria's epistolary manner. Words were swooped on and singled out for special attention. Her style was essentially musical: a long legato line in the main body of the sentence, and then the crucial words drawn out in a deeper tone, accompanied by noddings of the head and downward floating motions of the hands: 'The important thing in life is to do whatever you want but then … always … to pick up … THE BILL.' The phrase would then hang in the air for silent moments while you both contemplated its majestic truthfulness.* ¶ Life, and its handmaiden, Art, were her topics, even on this first impromptu meeting. She fiercely announced their paradoxical twin demands: on the one hand, discipline, industry and solitude; on the other, a life lived to the hilt, mentally, physically, above all emotionally. Between these two poles, in either art or life, there was, as far as she was concerned, nothing whatever of the slightest value. Marriage, friendship, parties, pastimes: all fruitless and destructive, she insisted. Independence, from people or from things, was the essential: 'Expect nothing, and *everything* becomes a *bonus.*' Whereupon, ever-surprising, she suddenly informed me, having discovered that I had had my start in the theatre in the Box Office, 'Of course, the Box Office is the only truly *romantic* part of the theatre.' And she meant it: she described the excitement of doing a deal, the thrill of watching the money come in; she had, she told me, a kind of Midas touch, and loved playing the Stock Exchange, for which she showed some talent. Clearly though, this was a holiday from the serious business of reminding authors of their sacred obligations, to Art and to Life. ¶

EVERY WORD THAT CAME OUT OF HER MOUTH THAT DAY WAS COMPLETELY UNEXPECTED, AS UNFORESEEN AS OUR MEETING. MY JAW HUNG OPEN MOST OF THE TIME, WHEN, THAT IS, I WASN'T ROARING WITH LAUGHTER, OR SUDDENLY MOVED ALMOST TO TEARS TO FIND SOMEONE WHO SPOKE SO UNASHAMEDLY AND WITH SUCH HARD-EDGED UNSENTIMENTAL ELOQUENCE ABOUT ART, ITS POWER AND ITS DEMANDS. • It was my own view entirely, as was her view of life itself. Agony or ecstasy, I, at the age of 30, thought, and to hell with the bits in between; and so did she at what I later discovered to be 70, though the evidence of my eyes would have rejected that figure, had I been told it, as preposterous. At this first meeting we spurred each other on higher and higher with great thoughts and terrible truths until we finally fell silent, having completely exhausted ourselves. I got up to go and we shook hands, oddly, awkwardly. She sat at her desk, combing her hair and repairing her lipstick as I left the office. Going back through the reception area to pick up the script which I dimly remembered had been the occasion of my being there at all, I caught the eye of the secretaries and blushed. It was as if Peggy and I had been making love.

As I walked away from the office, dazed and exhilarated, back down the perilous staircase, past the announcements of Bond in Oslo and Hare in Bochum, I laughed out loud at the improbability of what had just happened. My eagerness to avoid meeting her when I had first entered the office had been founded on a long-distance brush we'd had some years before, an incident she seemed now, to my great relief, to have totally forgotten. The play I had collected that day was Martin Sherman's *Passing By*, and it was another play by the same author, *Bent*, which had been the cause of the incident. I had been a play-reader for the Royal Court Theatre at the time; Max Stafford-Clark, then running the place, had asked if I had read any new plays I thought worth doing. I recommended *Bent*, which Martin had shown me as soon as he had written it. Max wanted to see a copy; Peggy's office apparently had none. Martin being out of the country at the time, I helpfully taxied at top speed what appeared to be the only copy of the play in London from Shepherd's Bush, where it was, to the theatre in Sloane Square. ¶ The moment this coup of mine was reported to Peggy, she let off a broadside to Martin of such vigour that he and I were both stunned into silence, an extraordinarily fierce display of professional territorialism on the part of the woman who had just told me that *agent* was the most disgusting word in the English language. '*Some actor*,' she wired him, 'is interfering with the agency's work. Stop him immediately, or consider yourself unrepresented.' At Martin's understandably urgent request, I desisted. The play was put on some while later (at the Royal Court Theatre, in fact, as it happens) to enormous acclaim, but the incident had given me a healthy respect for her formidable fire-breathing authority, even at long distance. ¶ *This fierce exchange had not prepared me in the least for my recent encounter at Goodwin's Court.* This was no Wagnerian dragon, far from it. Beauty, fire, passion, sex, brilliance, elegance, charm and a sort of impersonal ego-less force of character, were the qualities that came to mind. Her sheer animation, coupled with the lightest, most graceful of touches, was the single most striking impression, hard to convey except by extravagant simile: a fire-breathing butterfly? A cross between a dolphin and a humming-bird? I felt as if I had met a great figure of the past, a Mme de Sévigné or a Harriet Martineau. Not that there was anything old-fashioned about Peggy, unless you counted her unbreakable conviction that nothing was more important or more powerful than art. In every regard, she seemed years younger than I in her tastes and fascinations. ¶ There was no denying that she was eccentric. Reporting that first encounter, I amused myself, and others, by saying that Peggy had behaved like a madwoman suffering from the delusion that she was the greatest play agent in the world. ¶ What I actually thought was that I'd met someone touched by genius.

I FOUND OUT

EVERYTHING

THAT I COULD ABOUT HER,

WHICH WAS NOT A GREAT DEAL;

MOST OF IT WAS CONTRADICTORY.

THERE WERE STORIES WITHOUT PUNCH-LINES,

VAGUE RUMOURS OF

LIAISONS

WITH IONESCO, WITH ADAMOV, WITH BECKETT;

SOMEONE THOUGHT

SHE'D ONCE BEEN AN ACTRESS,

SOMEONE ELSE THAT SHE'D BEEN A SINGER.

THERE WAS A STORY ABOUT HER

WALKING OUT ON HER HUSBAND

THE MOMENT HE AND SHE

ARRIVED IN LONDON FROM SOUTH AFRICA.

HER AGE WAS SHROUDED IN

MYSTERY;

Christopher Hampton claimed that a secretary who had accidentally found it out when entrusted with her passport had shortly after drowned in mysterious circumstances, taking her secret with her to a watery grave. What was not in doubt was her unique contribution to the British Theatre: she seemed to represent every living playwright of any importance except, I noted with curiosity, those whose names ended in -er: Shaffer, Pinter, Wesker. On examination, in fact, there were plenty of distinguished writers whom she didn't represent (Stoppard, Bennett and Osborne among them); but every agent in London acknowledged her as their doyenne and a model of what an agent might be: putting lead into her writers' pencils and iron into their souls, money in their purses and sometimes roofs over their heads; giving courage to timid producers and advice to certain directors. She had, above all, a positively papal reputation for being *right*. It was very daunting and deeply intriguing. ¶ Shortly after our meeting at Goodwin's Court, I received a letter from her, the first of many in an unbroken flow that only stopped with her death some eleven years later. In this first, almost formal, letter she suggested a play that she thought might interest me, a French piece in which a pig addresses the audience at some length before being taken to the abattoir. It was the first occasion that Peggy attempted to do something for me, also the first of many, many such attempts. I was still playing at the National Theatre in repertory, in *Amadeus*, *As You Like It*, *Galileo* (translated by Peggy's client Howard Brenton) and *Sisterly Feelings* (by Peggy's client Alan Ayckbourn), and I was beginning to do a series of pre-show Platform Performances in which I introduced and performed Shakespeare's Sonnets in a new sequence devised by Dr John Padel, building up to the extraordinary occasion one summer's afternoon when I would perform all 154 in the Olivier Auditorium. I was at the theatre day and night. ¶ One evening quite soon after my first meeting with Peggy I arrived at the theatre to find the stage door staff in a state of some excitement: a crate of vintage wines from Fortnum and Mason had been delivered, simply labelled 'National Theatre Stage Door'. No one knew who it was for or from whom it had come. In the absence of a legitimate claimant, the stage door keepers were already in their mind's eye knocking it back themselves; eventually, to their chagrin, the National's press department placed a piece about the phantom plonk in the Londoner's Diary of the *Evening Standard*. The next day Peggy Ramsay's office called the National with the information that it was she who had sent it, and that the intended recipient was me. I phoned to thank her. She was amazed that neither I nor anyone else had realised that the wine was for me. She had; she said, been walking down Piccadilly, musing on the fact that it was Molière's birthday and that not a single actor in England would know, much less care. Musing on this sad reality, it had suddenly struck her that, yes, there was an actor in England who would know and care: me. And so she had gone into Fortnum's and ordered the wine and had sent it to me, to celebrate, with my actor friends, the great playwright's birthday. I could hardly admit that my ignorance of the anniversary was quite as great as, if not greater than, that of every other actor in England, so instead I spoke passionately about Molière and his work (this at least was not a fraud) and suggested, *en passant*, that she might like to attend a performance of the Shakespeare Sonnets the following week. ¶ The letter she sent me after that performance was quite different from the first one she had written me, quite unlike any letter anyone had ever written me. She had written to Peter Hall, she told me, telling him that I was his rose and that he must look after me. 'In case you don't know the St Exupéry book *Le Petit Prince*,' she wrote, 'the little Prince finds a rose and tends it, and defends it from the wind, and from other dangers, but he complains that it's a strain, and that, after all, *his* rose is only one of many roses. The storyteller then speaks very firmly to the little Prince and says that *because* he has cared for it and protected it, *it is his rose*, and not like any other, and that it is *because* he has taken so much trouble that the rose is so important, and that he is therefore *responsible* for it.' Then she added: 'It's really all about love,' and continued, characteristically, but inaccurately, 'Exupéry was a homosexual, and had, I suppose, these hidden passions for the "forbidden"... he is talking about *responsibility* of loving, even if it is unrequited.' Somewhat unexpectedly she added: 'It is appropriate to the "pure" feeling P Hall has for you and I'm telling him he is *responsible* for you!' She promised to send me a recording Gérard Philippe had made of *Le Petit Prince*, and finally signed off, 'The understanding and passion of your performance was an overwhelming experience. One began by *listening* to the sonnets, and then one *became part of Shakespeare* in the greatest depths. Yours Peggy R'. A day later she wrote to me 'If you've now read the English *Petit Prince* (the tape is being made for you), didn't you love the Fox saying that the PP should warn him when he was coming "so that he could prepare his heart".' Then she added, 'This reminds me of Ionesco, whose wife didn't like him spending much time in my company. After we'd spent an afternoon together and he was preparing to face the dreaded Rosica he turned to me anxiously and said, "Are my eyes too bright?" - "est-ce que mes yeux *brillent* trop?"' ¶

THIS LETTER CAME ACCOMPANIED BY THREE PAGES OF HAND-WRITTEN QUOTATIONS, OF WHICH THE MOST STRIKING WAS A PASSAGE FROM MAUPASSANT: 'WE MUST FEEL, THAT IS EVERYTHING. WE MUST FEEL AS A BRUTE BEAST, FILLED WITH NERVES, FEELS, AND KNOWS THAT IT HAS FELT, AND KNOWS THAT EACH FEELING SHAKES IT LIKE AN EARTHQUAKE. BUT WE MUST NOT SAY THAT WE HAVE BEEN SO SHAKEN. AT THE MOST, WE CAN LET IT BE KNOWN TO A FEW PEOPLE WHO WILL RESPECT THE CONFIDENCE.' Almost equally arresting was another quotation, from Gertrude Stein: 'It is inevitable that when one has great need of something one finds it. What you need you attract like a lover.' Peggy's next letter, a day later, equally full of intense expression, ended 'Yesterday's Shakespeare reading scorched me like a forest fire, and I am finding it hard to recover.' ¶ 'Dear, dear, dear Simon,' her next letter began, 'you have a temperament which vibrates at the fall of a leaf and I seriously question if we should continue to correspond in case we disturb one another. The trouble is that your performance if anything throws out a secret. But what the secret is, one does not know: (This secret whispered to an audience is the mark of the great actor.) I have a kind of ESP and catch reverberations which are not usually heard (like a dog catches notes too high for the human ear). Also my Slav blood compels me to write letters one ought NOT to (like Tatiana in *Onegin*) and I should know better.' Astonished and humbled, I realised that the extraordinary woman I was coming to know had experienced a *coup de foudre*. She had fallen in love with me, completely and instantaneously. Life was imitating art; the Sonnets, after all, are precisely about being taken over by an overpowering love for someone who remains essentially unknown. While I was working on them I had been in the throes of just such an emotion myself, and had been shaken to the core by my work on them. In rehearsal I had sometimes been unable to continue without breaking down. Even in performance, I would sometimes be overwhelmed by waves of feeling which perhaps distorted the meaning of the poems but which, I was convinced, were somehow true to the poet's experience. It was this, I had no doubt, this personal engagement of mine with the experience behind the poems, which had unerringly communicated itself to Peggy. It was because of the relationship that had so devastated me during my work on the Sonnets that I knew with such certainty what had happened. It had happened to me more than once in my life, the love which suddenly arrives, like a god in a chariot, but for once, this time, when I had fallen passionately in love with a young Turkish-Egyptian film-maker, exquisitely graceful and mysteriously elusive, called Aziz Yehia, he had, by what seemed to me the most miraculous good fortune, fallen in love with me, too. ¶ *He was an exquisite individual in many ways, perfect in his manners, acquired in the best Swiss schools and on the international circuit of the dispossessed Turkish and Egyptian haute bourgeoisie, beautiful to behold, bearing more than a passing resemblance to the young Alain Delon, slight, olive-skinned, brown-eyed and long-lashed, seductive in a feminine but not in the least effeminate way.* He was also brilliantly eloquent in the manner of the brightest products of the French educational system: full of paradox, allusion and witty analysis, by turn sententious, semiotic and structuralist, volubly quoting Lacan, Derrida, Lévi-Strauss. In all of these ways, he left me far behind; I thought him a bit of a genius. He was also, as I was just beginning properly to understand, frighteningly aware of a dark emptiness at his centre, a void, a block, a paralysis of the soul, which drove him across ever-wider extremes of emotional experience in search of a sense of personal reality that grew more and more elusive. Highs got higher and lows got lower, until what seemed at first like a perfectly normal oscillation of spirits was unmistakably, even to a layman, and an infatuated one at that, manic depression. Even now, fairly close to the beginning of our time together, there were unexpected losses of centre, as if he had suddenly forfeited all sense of the parameters of his personality. There would be terrible conversational misjudgements, even physical solecisms, a hand too intimately applied, or too roughly. Under the influence of his preferred tipple, the fiercely strong Carlsberg Special Brew lager (he had no taste for wine or spirits), he could become quite vulgar or silly beyond belief, in curious contrast to the charm of his person, the polish of his manners and the sophistication of his wit. I saw but dismissed these occasional and brief aberrations. To know him was to enter what was for me a strange and thrilling new universe, different from anything

I had ever known. It was meat and drink, it was opera and it was a three-volume novel. I could scarcely believe that it was happening to me. ¶ *Our relationship had been going on for three overwhelming months when I met Peggy. I wanted to come clean about it straight away, but first she and I had to meet again, and take stock of our new relationship. Things had been moving forward between us with alarming speed.* We were already becoming prolific correspondents, and now began to have epic telephone conversations, generally during the long hours when I was sitting in my dressing room between my scenes in *Galileo*. I became more and more fascinated by the beauty of her voice, and one day I told her so. The remark stopped her dead. I knew that my simple compliment had pierced her to the core. For the most part, we talked of plays, exhibitions, concerts. She was a great purveyor of high-level literary gossip, much of it concerning the dead. During one of these conversations, I suggested casually that it would be nice to have supper one evening. She offered to cook for me; I accepted, eagerly. ¶ Some time the following week, late on a balmy May night, I went on to her place after my show, and rang the bell of the basement flat in Redcliffe Square with a nervousness which mingled excitement and anxiety. I wanted to know everything I could about this remarkable woman. I had always had a rapport with women of a certain age (my grandmothers had been powerful and formative figures in my childhood), but with Peggy I felt a directness of communication that was different from any relationship in the past, or maybe from any relationship at all. It was almost frighteningly intimate, frighteningly soon. The difference in our circumstances - our ages, our positions in the world - seemed not to matter at all, but I had no model, no framework for what was developing so quickly between us. Evidently there was no question, with this woman, of holding back; it must be all or nothing. There could be no choice but to let it happen: let the dice fall where they may. I rang again; eventually the door opened. ¶

I HOPE PEGGY DIDN'T HEAR MY GASP. SHE HAD TRANSFORMED HERSELF INTO A YOUNG WOMAN, HER HAIR NEWLY COIFFED, HER SILK HOUSECOAT FLUTTERING ABOUT HER. UNDERNEATH WAS VERY LITTLE INDEED, ONLY A SLIP THROUGH WHICH THE OUTLINE OF HER SHAPELY BREASTS WAS PLAINLY VISIBLE. ON IT SHE HAD PINNED AN EXOTIC FLOWER, A GARDENIA OR PERHAPS AN ORCHID.

The smell of the flower enveloped us both as I stooped to peck her cheek. When I did, she started to shake. She tore herself away, talking torrentially, babbling almost, asking questions but not waiting for replies, wafting me down the hall, which like most of the rest of the flat, was plunged in darkness apart from a few strategically-placed candles, one of which she swept up to light the way. She was describing the flat, waving and gesturing with her candle-hand, hot wax flying in all directions. She had no shoes on, nor was she wearing her spectacles, which led to occasional collisions with furniture, but, bobbing and ducking and weaving, she managed to gather up quantities of food - chicken, ham, pâté, cheese, salad, dressing, snatching up bottles of wine as she went - and steered us into the garden. This was a vision in itself. With a hundred candles in small jars placed across the flowerbeds, she had transformed what I took to be a small nondescript space into a shimmering grotto. She produced blankets and we sat down for our midnight picnic. She was an anxious hostess, apologising for the food, the blankets, the garden. I told her that she looked beautiful. So she did, trembling with life and emotion, everything fluttering: hands, gown, heart. My praise again pierced her, seemed almost to hurt her, to give her physical pain. She took breaths in great gusts.

I DON'T KNOW WHAT WE SPOKE ABOUT; NOTHING MUCH, I THINK; THE GREAT CONVERSATIONS CAME LATER. HERE, ON THIS SUMMER NIGHT, I WAS SIMPLY ASTONISHED TO BE SITTING IN THIS CHIMERICAL GROTTO, WITH THIS FRAGILE, EXOTIC CREATURE FUELLED BY A SORT OF HELIUM COMPOUNDED OF EMOTION AND STRONG PHYSICAL NEED.

¶ A black cat suddenly appeared from on high, and sauntered over to partake of a little light collation. Peggy addressed it in cat language: 'Come-eelong, come-eelong, wah wah wah. This is Button,' she told me, 'the little Button. I used to think that Button was a man. But he's not. He's a woman. When I found out that he was a woman, I felt filled with pity for her.' ¶ The evening went on into the small hours. I could see no need for it to end at all, but finally, out of convention, took my leave. When I kissed her good-night, she shook again, and then let out a tremendous sigh. Almost pushing me out of the flat, she shut the door abruptly. I had the impression, as I walked home, that she felt that she had made a fool of herself. She hadn't. She had simply presented herself in the most vulnerable way she possible could have done. Gone was the scourge of lazy writers, gone the searching editor, gone the power-broker, gone the celebrated lover. In their place was a young belle on her first serious assignation, or Tatiana, as she herself had suggested in her letter, receiving Onegin. I only admired her the more for that, loved her for it, in fact. I knew then that I loved her. I did not desire her, as she must have known. I suspect that this al fresco evening had been in some way an unconscious attempt at seduction, regardless of the impossibility of the situation. Though our love grew stronger and stronger, she never ever attempted anything like it again. This evening was, I believe, a farewell to seduction for her, she who must have been the most potent seducer imaginable. ¶ *I had also failed to tell her about Aziz.*

outrageous, fu- ...ite woman, 35, ...h, solvent, prof ...Ring Voicebox

...attractive, sexy, ...brain, for rela- ...xy, English lady ...368 8142

...blonde, sophis- ...n, seeks kind, ...n 40s-50s for ...oilt rotten! Ring

...5in, brown hair, ...communication, ...to one, laughter, ...ybe my soul ma-

...aring, romantic, ...g, dancing, travel ...essional, caring, ...3 1822

...d with children, ...hite male, 28-35, ...ooking for lasting ...asters. Ring Voi-

...ild and pleasant ...eeting new peo- ...a gentleman 50 ...s. Any area. Ring

Women seeking Women

- **Attractive,** bi, black female, 21, size 12, seeks stunning female soul mate, 20-26, for quiet nights in and fun nights out. No male callers please. Watford/Herts area. Ring Voicebox 0906 368 0852
- **Attractive** and feminine, tall, black, gay female, 28, seeks similar, black/mixed race, gay female, 28-40, honest, loyal, for friendship, possibly leading to relationship. No mobiles/time wasters. Vbox 0906 368 8510
- **Bi,** Oriental female, broadminded, sexy, with gsoh, relaxed, vibrant, bubbly character, interesting, attractive, fun, wltm 30-50 year old female, for fun and good times. Ring Voicebox 0906 368 2142
- **Black,** bi female, mid 20s, n/s, occasional drinker, single, no children, likes, RnB, seeks bi or gay female, SE London area, for friendship and romance. Ring Voicebox 0906 368 5130
- **Boisterous** female, 27-32, 5ft 5in to 5ft 6in, slim to medium build, white or black, sought by black single mum, 28, size 12-14, for friendship/longterm relationship, South London area. Ring Voicebox 0906 368 5216
- **Female,** 27, white bi, looking for a sexy, gorgeous, female soulmate for a long term friendship & relationship. You should enjoy all the good things in life! All genuine calls answered. No males. Voicebox 0906 368 2074

FRENCH,
Bi sexual woman, 35, very feminine, half Asian, into culture, looking forward to meeting sensual, feminine, openminded women, for good, fun times. Ring Voicebox ***0906 368 0844***

- **Spanish** gay woman, 28, prof, slim, 5ft 4ins, interested in sport, cooking, clubbing, culture and cinema, romantic, caring and outgoing person, wltm similar feminine woman, 23-35 with gsoh. Ring Voicebox 0906 368 5970

...ARE ...OS

CONTACTS UK

...TACTS
...s & Photos of ...es/BI's/Gays
...411898
...O. BOX 1449, ...18 1BT
...E ACTION NOW? ...1 1610
67468

...EET PEOPLE ...IST SPA
...05
73716
...ON)

...cutives
...clusive events. ...s evenings. ...able for ...ful girls in ...quired · ...Bonnie ...3838 ...0.freeserve.co.uk
74239

★ NEW TO YOUR AREA? Want to make new friends? For drinks, dining out, theatre/cinema, walks, cycling, trips out of town, or just plain simple friendship! Answer an ad today in our Friendship UK Section 997 - or why not put one in yourself? To place a Voicebox ad, call 0541-566 666. For Mailbox ads, fill in the coupon on page 3. Start writing...

...! This sec- ...al and priva- ...Circulars or ...rature addre- ...Numbers will ...d. If you do ...ase let LOOT ...y by sending ...together with ...vas forwarded

LONELY LADIES AT HOME
LIVE
1-2-1 with bored lonely ladies

SPECIALS: 090-6960-6913
090-6960-6911
Ladies Chat, BCM 4673, London WC1N 3XX
£1 per min. Calls recorded

HOT NIGHTS
Brand New

0171 895 6969
Double the Fun!
09069 100 601

XTASY
THE HOTTEST LIVE CALL BACK
SEXY GIRLS
WAITING FOR YOUR CALLS NOW
STRICTLY ADULT CHAT
0374 705905
65p per minute for 10 mins
74791

XTC CLUB
New adult, Intimate Contact Club. Advertise **FREE** in our soon to be published Contact Newsletter for consenting adults looking for fun. Service includes **FREE** Box number. All tastes catered for.
Call 0171 511 6809 for details & year's free advertising
74477

The Paradise Club
The Club for liberated people for adult fun & friendship
0181 663 1744
Calls cost 50p per min
PO Box 493, London SE26 5DY
72355

CLUB EXCELSIOR
COUPLES & SINGLES PARTIES
STAG & HEN NIGHTS
Singles Parties 3 days weekly
BI & TV sessions monthly
0901 4700101
0956 109886
75066

Men seeking Men

- **Adult** fun and friendship offered to assertive bi male pal, 30-40, by divorced bi male, 39, discretion assured. Regular London visitor welcome. Ring Voicebox 0906 368 0726
- **Adventure,** fun, friendship, are back! If you are 18-26, call this fit, good looking, gay guy, 38, who's discreet and caring, for good times. Go for it and call me. Ring Voicebox 0906 368 3521
- **Adventurous,** gay, white male, 27, s/a, s/l, stocky, short blond hair, brown eyes, seeks good looking, slim guys, 18-30, for adult fun and friendship, possible one to one. Ring Voicebox 0906 368 3199
- **Adventurous** and broadminded, bi curious male, 45, average build, seeks couple, for exciting adult fun and frolics. Ring Voicebox 0906 368 5876
- **Aged** between 65 and 80, Living in the Earls Court/SW10 area and can accommodate during the daytime? Clean shaven man, 42, looking for fun, friendship and would like to hear from you. Ring Voicebox 0906 368 8436
- **Amersham,** bi male footie / rugger player, masculine, fit and friendly, seeks similar bi / gay lads 18-26 for adult fun and friendship, shy / bi curious welcome. Ring Voicebox 0906 368 5601

ARE
you a guy with long hair? Would you like to meet similar guy for mutual enjoyment, pleasure and friendship. You are between 18-35 & I'm 30, medium/athletic build, dark hair to my chin. Ring Voicebox ***0906 368 1502***

- **Are** you a black, Latin or Asian bi guy, 18-28, looking for fun and friendship? If so, call this bi guy now for details. South West London. Ring Voicebox 0906 368 5391
- **Are** you a discreet white/Mediterranean/Arab, bi or gay male, 18-35? I am a black, discreet guy looking for someone on a level. Ring Voicebox 0906 368 8572
- **Are** you a guy with long hair? Would you like to meet similar guy for mutual enjoyment and friendship. You are between 18-35 and I'm 30, medium/athletic build, dark hair to my chin. Ring Voicebox 0906 368 1502
- **Asian,** bi or gay guy, 18-30, wanted by white guy, ok looking, 38, for adult fun and friendship. East London/Essex Area. Ring Voicebox 0906 368 3311
- **Asian,** bi sexual male, 24, slim, smooth, good looking, fun loving, seeking Asian or white male, 18-26. Ring Voicebox 0906 368 4857
- **Asian,** gay male, 20, black hair, brown eyes, s/a, good looking, modest, seeking other Asian guys, 18-27, in the West London area. Ring Voicebox 0906 368 5796
- **Bi,** white male, 49, straight acting, gsoh, wltm Asian guy, under 30, for fun and friendship. Can accommodate. Acton area. Ring Voicebox 0906 368 4015
- **Bi,** Anglo Asian male, 60, smoker, gentle, quiet, easy going, placid nature, wltm similar males, 30-70, any status. Your needs are paramount. Can accommodate. Aca. Ring Voicebox 0906 368 8899
- **Bi,** Asian guy, 29, good looking, seeks well built, white, bi male, 30-45. London area. Can travel only. Ring Voicebox 0906 368 1429
- **Bi** black guy, 22, 6ft, slim build, s/a, s/a. very good looking, seeks mixed race or black guys, 18-25, for friendship, maybe more. Must be s/a, s/l. Ring Voicebox 0906 368 1566
- **Bi** black guy, 27, good looking, wltm masculine, attractive, black guys, preferably n/s, 27-35, discretion assured and expected. Ring Voicebox 0906 368 8965
- **Bi** builder, 42, 6ft, 15.5 stone, muscular, big build, wants stocky mates. Ring Voicebox 0906 368 2427
- **Bi** curious black guy, 29, 5ft 10ins, hairy, wltm white bi male, 21-40, for fun and friendship. Ring Voicebox 0906 368 4391
- **Bi** curious guy, married, 34, stocky build seeks similar guy, in same position for adult fun and friendship. Ring Voicebox 0906 368 4844
- **Bi** curious guy, 25, inexperienced, slim, 5ft 9in, bue eyes, brown hair, seeks similar males, 18-30, for possible first time experience. Ring Voicebox 0906 368 8497
- **Bi** curious guy, 35 seeks inexperienced bi male for adult fun and friendship. Aca. Ring Voicebox 0906 368 5945
- **Bi** curious guy, 42, good looks, fit, 6ft, fair haired, professional, clean shaven, gsoh but inexperienced, seeks likeminded guys, West Middlesex. Ring Voicebox 0906 368 3581
- **Bi** curious male, 30, slim, attractive, seeks assertive male, 25-45, for adult fun. Ring Voicebox 0906 368 5139
- **Bi** curious male, 6ft 1in, inexperienced seeks experienced, assertive men of any description for adult fun and friendship. Looks unimportant. Ring Voicebox 0906 368 3328
- **Bi** curious male, 23, slim build, seeks good looking, s/a, s/l, well build, experienced male. Must be discreet. Can travel but not accommodate. Ring Voicebox 0906 368 0766
- **Bi** curious male, active, assertive, seeks unassertive male, for fun times and excitement. Can accommodate. Ring Voicebox 0906 368 4571
- **Bi** curious male, 36, inexperienced, attractive, smooth, slim, Mediterranean looking, seeks good looking, slim-med build, smooth younger guys, 18-30, for fun and friendship. Middlesex area. Ring Voicebox 0906 368 8955
- **Bi** curious married male, 41, professional. white, non smoking, discreet, genuine, City area, seeks similar male, 18+ for adult fun and friendship. Ring Voicebox 0906 368 1565
- **Bi** curious, male, 32, seeks caring, bi male, for adult fun and friendship. All calls answered. Ring Voicebox 0906 368 5228
- **Bi** curoius guy, 33, tall, unassertive, attractive, seeks well built guy, 25-40, gsoh. Inexperienced welcome. North London. Ring Voicebox 0906 368 3873
- **Bi** guy amenable, easygoing, 52 seeks amiable relationship with assertive bi or gay guy, can accommodate, daytime or evening. Hounslow/W London. Ring Voicebox 0906 368 4714
- **Bi** guy, active, fit, 45, Mediterranean looks, seeks easygoing, down-to-earth bloke, 22-40, married/single, bi/gay, for discreet fun/friendship. Discretion assured. Can accommodate. N London. Voicebox 0906 368 1812
- **Bi** guy, distinguished looking, ex public school master, 51, 6ft 2in, good shape, seeks young guy, 18-30, attractive and fit for friendship and fun. Ring Voicebox 0906 368 2759
- **Bi** guy, masculine, straight acting, 23, good looking, black guy, wltm straight acting, white guy, ns, muscular, 18-35, for adult fun and friendship Ring Voicebox 0906 368 4701
- **Bi** guy, 18, good looking, straight acting, loves to laugh, looking for fun and friendship, seeks similar man 18-24. White or Asian. Ealing West London. Ring Voicebox 0906 368 8794
- **Bi** guy, 24, young looking, well built, seeking bi or gay males, for adult fun and friendship. Ring Voicebox 0906 368 0891
- **Bi** guy, 25, good looking, married, totally s/a, seeks good looking, young guys, 18-30, for no strings fun. N London area. Ring Voicebox 0906 368 8003
- **Bi** guy, 25, good looking, married, totally s/a, looking for good looking guys, 18-30, for no strings fun and friendship. N London, can accommodate and travel. Ring Voicebox 0906 368 8335
- **Bi** guy, 27, 5ft 11in, straight acting/looking, seeks similar, bi, married male, 20-35, straight acting/looking for fun and friendship. Discretion assured. Heathrow, Middx and Surrey area. Ring Voicebox 0906 368 3361
- **Bi** guy, 28, 5ft 10in, 15 stone, from SE London, seeks bi, married guys, 50+, for adult fun and friendship. Can travel or accommodate. Ring Voicebox 0906 368 3107
- **Bi** guy, 30, genuine good looks, 6ft 2in, average build, s/a wltm similar guys, 23-33, for adult fun and friendship. Discretion assured and expected. Ring Voicebox 0906 368 1622
- **Bi** guy, 30, 6ft 3in, green eyes, mousey hair, good body, good looking, down to earth, easy going, wltm other guys, 25-35, for good adult fun. Ring Voicebox 0906 368 3106

GAY CHAT ...NO STR...
Free!
AT STANDARD BT RATES FRO...
MrGAY chat &...
WOMEN CALL: 08701 25 26 00
08701 24 25...
Walk 34, Middleton Road, LS27 8BB

- **Bi** guy, 46, seeks younger guy, 18+, for adult fun and friendship. Can accommodate. Ashford, Kent area. Ring Voicebox 0906 368 4786
- **Bi** guy, 48, medium build, Asian, wltm similar guys, 22-40, for adult fun and friendship. Ring Voicebox 0906 368 4214
- **Bi** guy, 48, seeking bi/gay male, s/a, n/s, for possible one to one relationship. No time wasters, genuine callers only. Essex area. Ring Voicebox 0906 368 0720
- **Bi** guy, 49, 6ft 2in, St Albans area, wltm another bi guy, 18-30s, discretion assured, can accommodate. Ring Voicebox 0906 368 2082
- **Bi** guy, 50's, good looking, straight acting and caring, seeks bi guy for adult fun and friendship. Can accommodate. Ring Voicebox 0906 368 1944
- **Bi** guy, 50s, professional, seeks bi guy, for adult fun and friendship. Ring Voicebox 0906 368 0800
- **Bi** lad, 20, 5ft 8in, dark hair and eyes, good looking, fit, straight acting, inexperienced, looking for similar for adult fun and friendship. NW London area. Ring Voicebox 0906 368 4761
- **Bi** lad, 23, in Essex/E London, seeking other good looking bi lads, 18-24, for adult fun and friendship. Ring Voicebox 0906 368 2969
- **Bi** lad, 24, good looking, s/a, tall, dark haired, blue eyes, seeks inexperienced and enthusiastic guys, 18+, for fun and friendship. Ring Voicebox 0906 368 1291
- **Bi** lad, 26, sporty, attractive, straight acting, wltm similar guys, 18-30. Ring Voicebox 0906 368 3661
- **Bi** lad, 29, SE London, slim, s/a, s/l, wltm other, similar guys, 18-28, for adult fun and friendship. Ring Voicebox 0906 368 0949
- **Bi** ladidsh bodybuilder, 30, outgoing type, seeks bi, Asian/mixed race/Mediterranean laddish type, 20-35, for adult fun and maybe more. Ring Voicebox 0906 368 3591
- **Bi** male of Greek origin, hairy, open minded, looking for stocky, hairy male, 30-50, in the North/NW London area Ring Voicebox 0906 368 3963
- **Bi** male 52, into cross dressing, seeks bi male similar 20-35, for fun and friendship. Ring Voicebox 0906 368 2510
- **Bi** male, divorced, attractive, 54, seeks similar, 45+, for daytime or evening fun and friendship. SW London/Surrey. Can accommodate. Ring Voicebox 0906 368 8742
- **Bi** male, good looking, 6ft, short light brown hair, brown eyes, 28, wltm similar guys, for fun and friendship. Ring Voicebox 0906 368 8334
- **Bi** male, looking for other bi males, 65+, preferably married,. Ring Voicebox 0906 368 8254
- **Bi** male, 30, good looking, seeks guys, 20-35, for adult fun and friendship. Cannot accommodate, can travel. SE London. Ring Voicebox 0906 368 1157
- **Bi** male, 30, masculine, fit and good looking, seeks other bi, married man, well built. Ring Voicebox 0906 368 5418
- **Bi** male, 30, 5ft 11iins, bleached blond hair, s/a, medium build, seeks hairy, bossy, best mate, 18-27, up to 5ft 9ins, for drinking, smoking and fun nights in, Lewisham area. Ring Voicebox 0906 368 0705
- **Bi** male, 30, 6ft, clean shaven, 0 crop, slim, from Bethnal Green, good looking, wltm bi male, 18-35, for adult fun and friendship. Ring Voicebox 0906 368 3566
- **Bi** male, 31, tall, strong, solid, powerful build, straight acting, seeks hairy men only, tubby/chunky build preferred. Ring Voicebox 0906 368 2469
- **Bi** male, 36, attractive, sporty, seeks similar, in Canterbury area, for fun. Ring Voicebox 0906 368 0930
- **Bi** male, 39, seeks black or mixed race male, for fun and friendship. London/Essex/SE. Aca. Ring Voicebox 0906 368 0727
- **Bi** male, 39, slim, s/a, s/l, 5ft 10in, short dark hair, looking for bi or gay male, black/white/Asian or Oriental, slim, 18-25, looking for fun and friendship. can travel or accommodate. Ring Voicebox 0906 368 4438
- **Bi** male, 43, slim, 6ft 2in, clean shaven, seeks gay or bi males, 18-28, for fun and friendship, Medway Towns area. Ring Voicebox 0906 368 4199
- **Bi** male, 45, seeks similar, bi males, 18+, for fun and friendship, in the Southend/Essex area. Bi curious and first timers welcome. Ring Voicebox 0906 368 3452
- **Bi** male, 5ft 11in, slim-medium build, s/a, blue eyes, seeks other bi or gay males, for genuine fun and friendship. London SW6 area. Ring Voicebox 0906 368 8837
- **Bi** male,41, 6ft , medium build, wltm shorter stocky chubby male, 16-20 stone, hairy assertive for fun and friendship. Suit wearers especially welcome. Ring Voicebox 0906 368 5926
- **Bi** males, one black and one white, both 37, good looking, athletic, wltm similar, black guys, 25-35, for adult fun. Ring Voicebox 0906 368 8918
- **Bi** married male, late 40s, 6ft, big build, wltm young gay/bi guy, 18-35, for adult fun and
- **Black/Oriental** gay ... unimportant, easy goin... male, 26, chubby/fat b... hair, blue eyes, goaty be... Ring Voicebox 0906 368...

BLA...
gay, well sorted male, ... handsome, good phys... terests, seeks similar ... West Indian men, 27-... and friendship. Ring Voi...

- **Black,** bi curious guy ... black or mixed race guy, ... sible one-to-one. Ring V...
- **Black,** gay guy, 27, 5ft ... body, seeks similar m... friendship. Ring Voicebo...
- **Black,** gay guy, 22, 5ft ... unassertive, boyish looki... 18-25, for adult friends... Ring Voicebox 0906 368...
- **Black,** gay guy, 31, sli... looking, intelligent, carin... guy, 18-40, for friendship. ... Ring Voicebox 0906 368...
- **Black,** gay male, 32, me... 25-40, for adult fun and f... preferred. Ring Voicebox...
- **Black,** gay male, 24, ... muscular build, s/a, good... to: RnB, house and gara... Asian, well built male, 2... Voicebox 0906 368 1451
- **Black,** mixed race, or tan... by white, 29, male for fun a... or accommodate. Ring Voi...
- **Black,** streetwise guy, ... guy, 27, for adult fun and... Ring Voicebox 0906 368...
- **Black** bi guy, mid 30's, ... out going personality, wlt... 25+, for adult fun and frie... 0906 368 4976
- **Black** guy, 22, unasse... attractive, seeks bi or gay b... race assertive male, 20-3... looks unimportant, can ... Voicebox 0906 368 0748
- **Black** guy, 32, fit and m... black guy for adult fun and... cebox 0906 368 4069
- **Black** male, 33, fit, relaxe... sincere males, similar ag... friendship and genuine goo... ters please. Ring Voicebox...
- **Bored,** married males, ... guy, 34, for adult fun and... Absolute discretion assur... Ring Voicebox 0906 368 3...
- **Couple,** gay, 36 & 48, seek... gay guy in North Kent/SE L... lasting friendship & fun, can a... night stands. Ring Voicebox...
- **Cute,** half caste, s/a gu... unassertive seeks slim, ma... caste, gay or bi male. Ring Vo...
- **Cute** gay guy, 33, cropped ... physique, gentle, caring natu... tal or European male, student... Central London. Ring Voiceb...
- **David,** 6ft, black, bi, 27, lo... scene bi, black guy, for goo... box 0906 368 5012
- **Extreme** Deth Metal/Grin... natic, bi, cropped, bearded, ... likeminded guy for adult fun ... Voicebox 0906 368 3038
- **Friendly** guy, ok looks, gs... Redhill/Crawley area, seeks... guy, for fun, socialising and ... ship. Experienced/inexperien... Voicebox 0906 368 4863

FREE GAY CHAT!
• NO RIP OFFS!
• NO PREMIUM RATE CHARGES!
• NO CREDIT CARD NEEDED!

-40, shape/size ht by gay white assertive, blond fun & friendship.

ional, mid 30s, de range of in- uline, African/ adult pleasures 906 368 8229

king for similar, music, for pos- 0906 368 8010

ttractive, athletic adult fun and 368 1819

active, slim build, king white male, accommodate.

ium build, good wltm assertive possible 1-2-1.

uild, wltm males, p. London area 58 0924

, slim-medium/ , streetwise, in- m black/white/ ocky, s/a. Ring

ve male, wanted dship, can travel 906 368 4007

vanted by white ship, E London.

n athletic build, her black guy, Ring Voicebox

oyish, smooth, other, or mixed be, muscular, noadate. Ring

, seeks similar ship. Ring Voi-

yle, seeks other , s/l, for fun, . No time was- 368 4698

sought by s/a e relationship. don/Berkshire.

n/medium build age 20-35, for nodate, no one 368 3785

medium build, black or half 0906 368 3493

nooth muscular s Asian, Orien- 60 kilos, 18-25. 6 368 5832

for a s/a, non- s. Ring Voice-

rock music fa- lar, 30s, seeks endship. Ring

ature, living in 5, masculine going relation- welcome. Ring

• **Gay,** black lad, 23, 5ft 10in, good looking, s/a, sporty and fit body, wltm genuine, good looking, sport lads, 18-28, for fun and friendship, possibly leading to a one-to-one. Ring Voicebox 0906 368 2645

• **Gay,** professional male, 63, n/s, 6ft 2in, light build, wltm slim guy, 18-25, with gsoh, to enjoy the company of an older man. Ring Voicebox 0906 368 5016

• **Gay,** understanding school Teacher, 47, slim, non smoker, 5ft 10in, seeks slim-medium build, younger guys, 18-35, any colour, for adult fun. Inexperienced welcome. Ring Voicebox 0906 368 4261

• **Gay,** white guy, 5ft 11ins, 28, intelligent and sincere, seeks similar, ordinary black guy, any age, for fun and friendship, possible, 1-2-1. Ring Voicebox 0906 368 8448

• **Gay,** white male, 58, 5ft 2in, wltm, white male only, 40-60, for adult fun and friendship. Enfield area only. Cannot accommodate. Ring Voicebox 0906 368 4023

• **Gay,** Asian guy, 22, tall, seeks stocky and chunky guys, for fun at the weekends. Cannot accommodate. Ring Voicebox 0906 368 1532

• **Gay** black guy, SE London area, shy, likes jazz, gospel RnB, looking for honest, reliable, decent, male, n/s, if you want to get to know me please leave message, no time wasters. Ring Voicebox 0906 368 2201

• **Gay** black guy, 26, tall, sporty, good looking, wltm similar, tall, white guys, for adult fun and friendship. Ring Voicebox 0906 368 3823

• **Gay** black guy, 29, 6ft1in, 16 stone, large rugby player type build, s/a, s/l seeks similar lge build white males, 18-32 for adult fun & friendship. Can't accommodate but willing to travel, Ring Voicebox 0906 368 0777

• **Gay** businessman, Mediterranean, early 40's, medium build , ns, n/s, wltm ns mature male, over 55, for adult fun and friendship. Discretion assured and expected. Ring Voicebox 0906 368 1600

• **Gay** couple, 30 and 42, clean, discreet, adventurous seeking like minded guys, 25 plus, any nationality. Ring Voicebox 0906 368 4064

• **Gay** couple, 37 and 38, SE London, straight acting, not bad looks, seek inexperienced, younger guy for adult fun and friendship. Discretion assured. Can accommodate. Ring Voicebox 0906 368 4056

• **Gay** guy 40, assertive, looking for unassertive, guy 21-38, for friendship, possible 1-2-1. Herts/Essex. Aca. Ring Voicebox 0906 368 2387

• **Gay** guy, attractive, medium build, seeks assertive, attractive, mature guy, for mutual pleasure. West London. Can travel but not accommodate. Ring Voicebox 0906 368 8909

• **Gay** guy, discreet, slim to medium build, fit, 40, wltm a slim guy, 18-40, for fun and friendship, and maybe more. Ring Voicebox 0906 368 4202

• **Gay** guy, early 30s, black hair, brown eyes, wltm other bi/gay man for fun and friendship, possible 1-2-1. Ring Voicebox 0906 368 1756

• **Gay** guy, mid 30s, fair and slim, looking for assertive guys, over 30. Ring Voicebox 0906 368 0809

• **Gay** guy, mid 30s. fair and slim, looking for assertive guys, over 30. Ring Voicebox 0906 368 0809

• **Gay** guy, tall, 32, attractive, s/a, easy going, slim, seeks similar s/a guy, 25-39, for fun and friendship. Herts area. Ring Voicebox 0906 368 2626

• **Gay** guy, young 42, 6ft, slim, seeks guys 30+ for fun and hopefully more N Kent area. Ring Voicebox 0906 368 4241

• **Gay** guy, youthful, 55, s/a, seeks bi or married guys, discreet, for adult fun and friendship. Own flat, Kent area. Ring Voicebox 0906 368 2367

• **Gay** guy, Asian, 32, slim, attractive, wltm 35-50, professional, good looking, sincere, gay or bi guy, for adult fun and friendship, maybe more. Ring Voicebox 0906 368 2679

• **Gay** guy, London area, discreet, good looks, affectionate, wltm young guys, 18-30, for good times leading to 1-2-1. Ring Voicebox 0906 368 2667

• **Gay** guy, 21, 5ft 8in, blond fair hair, blue eyes, slim, tanned, good looking, wltm s/a, white guy or new friends, 20-26, for fun, friendship and possible one-to-one. SE London area. Ring Voicebox 0906 368 3007

• **Gay** guy, 24, 5ft 10in, slim, clean shaven, s/a, s/l. Seeks similar for adult fun and friendship. SE London area. Ring Voicebox 0906 368 5383

• **Gay** guy, 25, good looking, 5ft 9in, 10 stone, nice skin, seeks assertive, bi/gay guy, 35-45, medium/well built, for adult fun and friendship. Ring

• **Gay** guy, 35, 6ft, genuine guy, honest, fun, gsoh, really straight acting, non scene, seeks genuine, young, white or Asian guy, 18-20 for fun and friendship. Ring Voicebox 0906 368 2848

• **Gay** guy, 36, 6ft 2ins, well built, n/s, s/a, seeks genuine, good looking, fit, 18-26, bi or gay guy, for adult fun and friendship. Discretion assured. Ring Voicebox 0906 368 5625

• **Gay** guy, 37, good looking, 5ft 9in, medium build, s/a, s/l, wltm guy, 20-30, for adult fun and friendship. South Bucks area. Ring Voicebox 0906 368 3838

• **Gay** guy, 38, tall, chubby build, wltm genuine guys, for friendship and maybe more. North London/Herts. Ring Voicebox 0906 368 5484

• **Gay** guy, 38, tall, fit, good looking, friendly, seeks black or Asian guy, for fun and friendship, maybe 1-2-1. Ring Voicebox 0906 368 5027

• **Gay** guy, 39, seeks younger gu adult fun and friendship, discretion cated S London, Kent, Croydon, Sur Voicebox 0906 368 5021

• **Gay** guy, 40, 5rft 7in, medium b looks, masculine, working class, n/s, masculine guy for friendship and fu Sudbury area. Ring Voicebox 0906

• **Gay** guy, 44, 6ft, beared, chubby, s discreet, seeks gay or bi chubby cha fun and friendship. Can accommod Aca. Ring Voicebox 0906 368 8183

• **Gay** guy, 47, non scene, straight a guy, 18-30, for 121. Your place or m Finchley area. Ring Voicebox 0906 3

• **Gay** guy, 5ft 11ins, medium build, g new to London wltm guy, 18-30, fo eating out and all expenses shar breaks. Ring Voicebox 0906 368 36

• **Gay** guy, 50, 5ft 10in, 17 stone, liv West London, seeks guy, any nationa fun and friendship. Ring Voicebox 09

• **Gay** guy, 50s, 5ft 7in, slim, clean s assertive, well built muscular guy, 35- fun and friendship. London area. Ri 0906 368 5042

• **Gay** hunk, good body, from South W wltm similar n/s, s/a guys, for fun, frienc will see what else. Ring Voicebox 090

• **Gay** lad, ex forces, 28, straight act king, muscular, 5ft 8in, cropped hai meet similar, fit, black or white lads. box 0906 368 4019

• **Gay** lad, 18-25, interested in History, sought by mature gent, for weekends away and holidays. Students welcome. Can travel or accommodate. Ring Voicebox 0906 368 1169

• **Gay** lad, 26, good looking, s/a, 5ft 7in, slim fit build, into football and tennis seeks similar slim s/a lad, 18-28, for fun and friendship. Ring Voicebox 0906 368 5871

• **Gay** lad, 28, s/a, s/l, living in Central London, loves going out and enjoying life, looking for similar. Must be s/a and s/l. Ring Voicebox 0906 368 8514

• **Gay** lad, 31, genuinely good looking, smart, well adjusted and together, from West London, seeks smart, together, intelligent, good looking, younger lad, for fun leading to one-to-one. Ring Voicebox 0906 368 8001

• **Gay** lad, 5ft 10ins tall, alburn hair, s/a, s/l, good looking, living Central London, looking for similar, must be s/a, s/l. Ring Voicebox 0906 368 1070

• **Gay** male 30, tall, extra slim, smooth, vgl, s/a, s/l, non scene, seeks an interesting friend, around the same age for adult fun. Ring Voicebox 0906 368 4860

• **Gay** male, early 50s, 5ft 8in, wltm assertive guys, 55+ for adult fun and friendship, first time advert, genuine callers only, every call answered. Can accommodate. Ring Voicebox 0906 368 4296

• **Gay** male, ex-soldier, 24, seeks male, any age, for fun times and friendship. Cannot accommodate, but can travel. Croydon/London/Kent/Surrey borders please. Ring Voicebox 0906 368 2805

• **Gay** male, white, professional, 33, seeks hairy, Asian male, any age, for fun and friendship. Ring Voicebox 0906 368 5770

• **Gay** male, 22, 5ft 8ins, medium build, brown eyes, black hair, wltm gay male, with bubbly personality. Ring Voicebox 0906 368 8132

• **Gay** male, 24, slim, 5ft 8in, good looking wltm male, for fun and friendship and maybe more. Must be between 18-21, slim and good looking. North London. Ring Voicebox 0906 368 3313

• **Gay** male, 29, n/s, stocky build, 15.5 stone, 5ft 9in, blue eyes, fair hair, gsoh, wltm similar, who are not on the scene, for fun and friendship. Ring Voicebox 0906 368 5471

• **Gay** male, 33, straight lifestyle, medium build, good looking, sincere, honest, caring, with varied interests, wltm similar stocky muscular male, 30-40, for friendship possible 1-2-1. Ring Voicebox 0906 368 2194

• **Gay** male, 50, slim, s/a, gsoh, honest and caring, genuine, enjosy gardening, cooking and nights in and out. seeking s/a, genuine male, 30-45, for possible relationship/friendship. Ring Voicebox 0906 368 3398

• **Gay** man, 25, gsoh, good looking, blue eyes, long brown hair, seeks man, 18-24, for good times. Ring Voicebox 0906 368 8232

• **Gay** man, 40, chubby, cropped hair, beard, blue eyes, seeks slimmer guy, 35-45, for adult fun and friendship. Ring Voicebox 0906 368 3583

• **Gay** white guy, 32, attractive, slim, masculine, blue eyes, wltm slim, Asian, Oriental or South American guy, 18-27 for adult fun and friendship. East London. Ring

• **Italian,** gay guy, 26, 5ft 7in, Mediterranean looking, fit, attractive, easy going, seeks very masculine guy, 18-32, reliable, s/a, s/l, for adult fun and friendship. Discretion assured. Ring Voicebox 0906 368 3432

• **Male,** dark, muscular, short cropped hair, 38, 5ft 8in, 11.5 stone, handsome, masculine, looking for body builder, for adult fun and friendship. Can accommodate. Ring Voicebox 0906 368 1299

• **Male,** over 50, fit, good body, 6ft, 12.5 stone, clean shaven, n/s, seeking uninhibited men, for some clean adult fun. Daytimes or other times. Confidentiality guaranteed. I am s/a and s/l. Ring Voicebox 0906 368 5502

• **Male,** slim, fit, professional, East London, early 40's seeks fun and friendship, with stocky, assertive blokes, can accommodate. Ring Voicebox 0906 368 2032

• **To the Unknown Lover**

• **Horryfing,** the very thought of you,¶ whoever you are,¶ future knife to my scar,¶ stay where you are.

• **Be handsome,** beautiful, drop-dead¶ gorgeous, keep away.¶ Read my lips.¶ No way. OK?.

• **This** old heart of mine's¶ a battered purse.¶ These ears are closed.¶ Don't phone, want dinner,

• **make** things worse.¶ Your little quirks?¶ Your wee endearing ways?¶ What makes you you, all that?

• **Stuff it**, mount it, hang it¶ on the wall, sell tickets,¶ I won't come. Get back. Get lost.¶ Get real. Get a life. Keep shtum.

• **And just**, you must, remember this –¶ there'll be no kiss, no clinch,¶ no smoochy dance, no true romance.¶ You are *Anonymous*. You're *Who*?

• **Here's** not looking, kid, at you.

Carol Ann Duffy 0906 235 2786

Voicebox 0906 368 8060

• **Male** truck driver, 42, bi, lives rural Kent, tattoos, seeks similar male. Ring Voicebox 0906 368 8096

• **Married,** bi curious guy, 35, genuine 1st time ad, inexperienced and shy, wltm older male, 55-65, for adult fun and friendship. Must be bi. Discretion assured and expected. Ring Voicebox 0906 368 5857

• **Married,** bi curious, white male, attractive, 30, stocky/muscular build, into weights, masculine, seeks muscular or big build, bi curious, black guys, 25-45, married preferred. No timewasters. Voicebox 0906 368 1831

• **Married,** bi guy, 52, wltm younger bi lads, 18-28, for daytime adult fun and friendship, can travel or accommodate, Dagenham. Ring Voicebox 0906 368 5798

• **Married** bi curious male, early 40s, inexperienced, first time ad, wltm similar male, 18-35, cannot accommodate, genuine replies only. Ring Voicebox 0906 368 3961

• **Married** bi male, 31, good looking, professional, wltm good looking married guys for adult fun and friendship, Herts area. Ring Voicebox 0906 368 4179

• **Mature,** male couple, from North London, seeking other single males or male couple for friendship. We are slim, witty, adventurous, keen on the arts and can accommodate. Ring Voicebox 0906 368 8432

MEDITERRANEAN
male with good looks, 34, bi, fit, seeking other bi/gay guys, for discreet encounters. Athletic black guys welcome. Ring Voicebox ***0906 368 5749***

• **Mixed** race guy wanted by white bloke, 34, 5ft 11in, for fun and friendship. Can accommodate. Discretion guaranteed. Ring Voicebox 0906 368 0795

• **Muscular** and athletic black gay guy, 32, likes music, r & b, soul and jazz, seeks other similar guys, 25-35, race not important, for adult fun and friendship. No timewasters please. Ring Voicebox 0906 368 3137

• **My** name is Jay, from Basildon, bi, late 40s, looking for African or or any ethnic group bi males, 18-30, for friendship and occassional meetings. Ist time ad. Aca. Ring Voicebox 0906 368 1006

• **Nice,** English, gay guy, 40's, slim, I'm looking for an Asian mate. Ring Voicebox 0906 368 3544

• **Nice** looking, slim, gentle, well built, 25 year old man, seeks small, gentle, skinny, young guys, 18-21, for discreet friendship and maybe more. Ring Voicebox 0906 368 3243

• **Older retired,** teacher seeks friendship, fun and companionship, with male, 18-25, maybe student, any race or size welcome. Quiet, shy, distant lads please call. Chingford/Woodford/Layton. Ring Voicebox 0906 368 8283

• **Oriental/Asian,** gay or bi male, sought by tall, genuine, professional guy, 41. Ring Voicebox 0906 368 1722

• **Professional,** black guy, 32, East London,

• **Young** male, shy and inexperienced wltm understanding, older, mature male for adult fun and friendship. North West London. Ring Voicebox 0906 368 8727

• **Young** male, 25, wltm older guy, over 55, for adult fun and friendship. Ring Voicebox 0906 368 8895

• **2** guys, one Asian, 22, one white, 35, both attractive, slim, 5ft 7ins, looking for similar guys, Asian/black/mixed race, up to 26, for adult fun and nights in. Can accommodate. E London. Ring Voicebox 0906 368 5679

• **37** year old, bi guy, 14 stone, living in North London, looking to meet genuine, s/a male friends, for friendship and whatever else. Ring Voicebox 0906 368 4208

M... seeking Women

acrobats and ballerinas, need not ...er, if you are female and don't have a ...to my female relatives, then call this ...y. Ring Voicebox 0906 368 1677

...ourself into my arms, Anglo/Asian ...verseas, staying in London, seeks a ...ult fun and friendship. All calls dis...red. Ring Voicebox 0906 368 4017

...l boredom for a white male, 50ish, ...screet, friendly, caring, understan...oadminded female, any age/colour, ...nd friendship, days pref, aca Ring ...6 368 2908

... your worries, females, meet young ...dult fun and friendship, gsoh, a.c.a. ... 0906 368 8395

..., attached man, 38, tall, attractive, ...oving and passionate, seeks aban...ed lady for friendship and fun. Ring ...5 368 1999

...ur stress, for a attractive black male, ...and discreet, looking for white fema...dult fun and friendship, daytimes pre...vel. Ring Voicebox 0906 368 1447

...m, passion 6ft male, seeks female ...d friendship, please ring. Ring Voi...68 8192

...ess. 30-52, large, size 16-26, asser...ught by white, slim, unassertive, sol...n/s, for friendship, companionship ...s! Ring Voicebox 0906 368 8541

• **Able,** adventurous gentleman, assertive, 38, solvent, handsome, responsible and caring, exec home, wltm an attractive, unassertive lady who needs understanding, adult fun and friendship. Ring Voicebox 0906 368 0938

• **Able,** mature male, seeks full figured, cuddly female, any nationality, for adult fun and friendship. Daytime preferred. Can accommodate or travel. Ring Voicebox 0906 368 5815

• **Able** to please, my name is Mark, I'm 27, fit and attractive, I would like to meet similar female to partake in mutual enjoyment, pleasure and friendship. Ring Voicebox 0906 368 8382

• **About** me. 50 year old white male looking for an adult fun-loving lady, 40-55, from S.E. London. If this is you please call. Ring Voicebox 0906 368 2791

• **About** time, you gave me a call. White guy, 40, broadminded, wltm ladies, age/colour/size unimportant. Cleanliness and discretion assured and expected. Go on, call me now! Ring Voicebox 0906 368 0803

• **Above** average, tall, handsome, male, good physique, with friendly and pleasant personality, wltm white female, age unimportnat for adult fun. Daytimes preferred but not essential. Ring Voicebox 0906 368 8597

• **A** broadminded, unassertive, attractive, white male, mid 40s, seeks assertive woman, with alternative interests. Ring Voicebox 0906 368 1009

• **A** broadminded, unassertive male, early 40s, wltm assertive lady, for fun and friendship. Age, appearance and nationality unimportant. Ring Voicebox 0906 368 8846

• **Absent** is our mutual happiness until you meet this warm hearted male, 66, who seeks a slender woman, for a life enhancing relationship. Ring Voicebox 0906 368 1752

• **Absolute** discretion assured so be adventurous. Assertive but kind, understanding male, presentable, solvent, educated, 50s, seeks unassertive lady. Ring Voicebox 0906 368 2298

• **Absolutely** genuine, handsome, assertive Englishman, wltm unassertive lady for good times. Nice/genuine people preferred. Must be able to laugh. Ring Voicebox 0906 368 2986

• **Absolutely** genuine, married man, cross dresser, totally straight, seeks like minded female for adult fun and friendship. Age/looks unimportant. Ring Voicebox 0906 368 2700

• **Absolutely** genuine, caring guy, 45, Company Director, seeks mature lady with similar qualities for exciting adult fun, cuddles and tlc. Ring Voicebox 0906 368 3430

• **Absolutely** genuine, fun loving, fit, English male, 40, wltm an adventurous female, for fun times. Age/looks/nationality not important. Can travel. Ring Voicebox 0906 368 1855

• **Absolutely** gorgeous, young blond guy, with muscular, tanned body looking for fun and friendship. Very clean and discreet. Ring Voicebox 0906 368 2121

• **Accommodating,** over weight female, married or single with a fuller figure wanted by a mature male for daytime adult fun and friendship. Long term.

"what we call 'progress' is the exchange of one nuisance for
another nuisance."
henry havelock ellis

"men wiser and more learned than i have discerned in history a plot, a rhythm,
a predetermined pattern. these harmonies are concealed from me. i can see
only one emergency following upon another as wave follows upon wave."
h.a.l. fisher

living in the past:

ERIC HOBSBAWM

On the 28th of June 1992 President Mitterrand of France made a sudden, unannounced and unexpected appearance in Sarajevo, already the centre of the Balkan War that was to cost perhaps 150, 000 lives during the remainder of the year. His object was to remind the world opinion of the seriousness of the Bosnian crisis Indeed, the presence of a distinguished, elderly and visibly frail statesman under small--arms and artillery fire was much remarked on and admired. However, one aspect of M. Mitterrand's visit passed virtually without comment, even though it was plainly central to it: the date. Why had the President of France chosen to go to Sarajevo on that particular day? Because the 28th June was the anniversary of the assassination, in Sarajevo, in 1914, of the Archduke Franz Ferdinand of the Austria-Hungary, which led, within a matter of weeks, to the outbreak of the First World War. For any educated European of Mitterrand's age, the connection between date, place and the reminder of a historic catastrophe precipitated by political error and miscalculation leaped to the eye.

How better to dramatize the potential implications of the Bosnian crisis than by choosing so symbolic a date? But hardly anyone caught the allusion except for a few professional historians and very senior citizens. The historical memory was no longer alive.

SARAJEVO

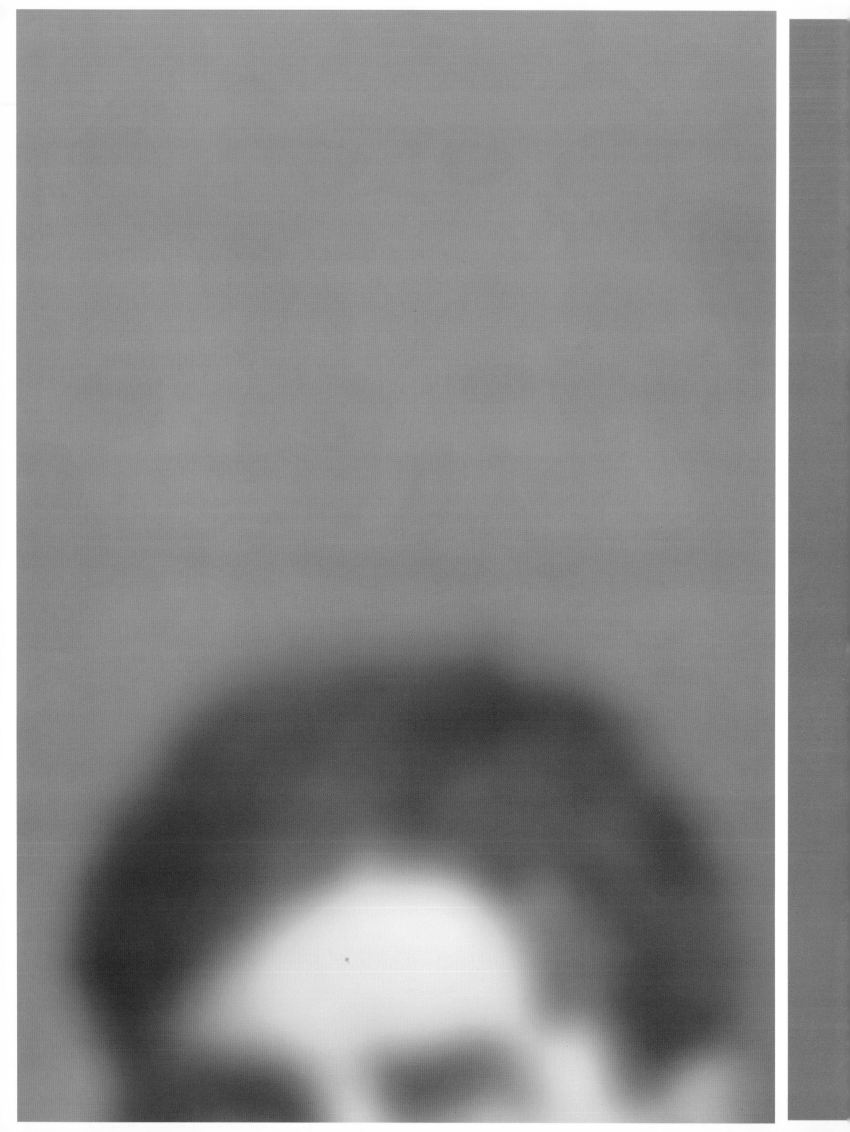

The destruction of the past, or rather of the the social mechanisms that link one's contemporary experience to that of earlier generations, is one of the most characteristic and eerie phenomena of the late twentieth century. Most young men and women at the century's end grow up in a sort of permanent present lacking any organic relation to the public past of the times they live in. This makes historians, whose business it is to ~~remember~~ remember what others **forget** more essential at the end of the second millennium than ever before. But for very that reason they must be more than simply chroniclers, **remembrancers** and compilers, though this is the historians' necessary function. In 1989 all governments, and especially all Foreign Ministries, in the world would have benefited from a seminar on the peace settlements after the two world wars, which most of them had appa apparently ~~forgotten~~ forgotten.

Sarajevo

Eric Hobsbawm

HERITAGE - BAITING

Raphael Samuel

eritage is a term which has been serviceable to the local authorities, who have used it to promote town improvement schemes and to extract government money for service sector jobs. It has been one of the flagships of nature conservancy and the environmentalist movements of our time. In cases like the campaign for Oxleas Wood, it is a rallying point for the opposition to the property developers and a challenge to the powers that be. Heritage is also popular with the general public, who seem untroubled by the philippics launched against it. 'Historic' towns (including newly historicized ones as Rochester-upon-Medway), ancient monuments (a category nowadays extended to industrial heritage sites), country parks, working farms and wildlife reserves, provide a natural focus for Sunday outings and weekend breaks — rather as the spectacle of the new, or the wonders of science and invention, used to do in the days when the promise of modernization was undimmed (on Whit-Monday, 1871, some seventy thousand visitors are said to have flocked to Liverpool to see the new warehouses). On summer holidays, nature 'mystery trails' and 'historic' walks minister to the romance of place; living history museums and theme parks offer a vivid encounter with the past — for some children it may be a first one; while steam railways offer a journey back in time — last year they carried some fifty million summer season passengers.

Intellectually, on the other hand, 'heritage' has had a very bad press, and it is widely accused of wanting to commodify the past and turn it into tourist kitsch. Aesthetes of both Right and Left, though especially perhaps the latter, have found it offensive, accusing it of packaging the past, and presenting a 'Disneyfied' version of history in place of the real thing. Purists have objected to the schemes promoted in its name, arguing that it blurs the line between entertainment and education and warning that, as with church restoration in the nineteenth century, it will replace real-life survivals with simulacra of an original that never was.

Heritage has also emerged as one of the principal whipping-boys of Cultural Studies, a prime example of those tutelary complexes which it is the vocation of critical inquiry to unmask. They cast it in the role of a 'project' designed at once to anaesthetize and 'sanitize' the record of the past while making it harmless and unthreatening in the present.

Heritage-baiting has become a favourite sport of the metropolitan intelligentsia, the literary end of it especially. Barely a week goes by without it being targeted for abuse in one or other of the 'quality' newspapers, and indeed *The Independent*, taking up arms against the restrictive covenants imposed on the owners of 'listed' buildings, has taken to calling conservation officers 'the heritage police'. The arts columns of the newspaper follow suit. For Tom Paulin, never at a loss for expletives where Ukanian matters are at issue, and flagging a recent *Independent*-sponsored conference on the subject, 'The British heritage industry is a loathsome collection of theme parks and dead values'. Even the television correspondent of *The Independent* weighs in: 'A medal to whichever TV critic it was who blew the whistle on Morse, saying, in effect, that he was a boring and pretentious middle-brow snob. The enormous, almost religious, following that John Thaw's detective amassed must have been something to do with the comforting "Brideshead-effect" of the series' timeless Oxford back-drop.'

Heritage is accused of wanting to turn the country into a gigantic museum, mummifying the present as well as the past, and preserving tradition in aspic. Exchequer grants to Environmentally Sensitive Areas — where farmers are subsidized to retain and enhance traditional features of the landscape and wildlife habitats — are currently under attack: according to the Whitehall correspondents they are potential targets for the next round of Treasury economies. In a kindred vein, though here the attack comes from the Left rather than the Right, the National Trust is accused of featherbedding the owners of historic properties, insulating them from the cost of maintaining their establishments, and allowing them, however impecunious, to continue in a life of pampered ease and upholstered luxury.

Local authority interventions in the field of heritage are routinely savaged, and treated with derision as though they were necessarily an exercise in bad taste (a recent article in *The Independent* lampooned the municipal authorities

in York for building a new-Georgian public lavatory; an earlier one ridiculed the City of Westminster for putting up 'heritage' traffic-lights in the West End). This is one of the very few spheres of municipal enterprise in which public sector employment, instead of contracting, has actually contrived to expand, and it may be that the critics, though coming from the Left, have taken on, as if by osmosis, the authentic accents of that New Right for whom the very idea of the public is suspect.

eritage, according to the critics, is the mark of a sick society, one which, despairing of the future, had become 'besotted' or 'obsessed' with an idealized version of the past. The historicist turn in British culture, which they date from 1975 — the year when the term 'heritage' began its inflationary career — corresponded to the onset of economic recession, the contraction of manufacturing industry and the return of mass unemployment. It testified to the collapse of British power. Heritage prepared the way for, or could be thought of as giving expression to, a recrudescence of 'Little Englandism' and the revival of nationalism as a force in political life. It anticipated and gave expression to the triumph of Thatcherism in the sphere of high politics. Heritage, in short, was a symbol of national decadence; a malignant growth which testified at once to the strength of this country's *ancien régime* and to the weakness of radical alternatives to it.

It was an admission, according to Robert Hewison in *The Heritage Industry* that history was 'over'. In Patrick Wright's *On Living in an Old Country* it was 'part of the self-fulfilling culture of national decline'.

Historians have been only too ready to join in this chorus of disdain, accusing heritage of travestying the past and counterposing its ersatz and kitsch to the allegedly objective inquiries pursued in the world of higher research. David Cannadine, who from his American fastness seems never to tire of deriding 'this heritage junk', charges it with encouraging a bunker mentality and attempting to imprison the country in a time-warp. He was already sounding a warning note in 1983, on the eve of his departure from these shores. 'Not since the 1890s or the 1930s has the worship of wistfulness been so widespread. And there in part lies the explanation; then, as now, depression is the begetter of nostalgia, disenchantment the handmaiden of escapism. As before, when the shopkeepers go out of business, we become a nation of ruminators.' Interestingly the History Working Party, drawing up their recommendations for the new core curriculum, and strongly committed to the study of both material culture and the built environment, nevertheless felt obliged to distance themselves from a word which had become contaminated, proposing to use instead – a distinction, surely, without a difference – 'inheritance':

> We have been careful to minimise the use of the word 'heritage' because it has various meanings and is in danger of becoming unhelpfully vague. For historical purposes the word 'inheritance' may be more precise in its meaning, implying 'that which the past has bequeathed to us'.... While all the people in Britain partake to a greater or lesser extent of shared 'inheritance' they also have their own individual, group, family, etc. 'inheritances' which are inter-related. The study of history should respect and make clear this pattern of inheritances.

or many radicals, 'heritage' is a sore on the body politic, reinforcing, or imposing, a reactionary version of the national past; feeding on fantasies of vanished supremacies;

ministering to nostalgia for a time that never was. Neal Ascherson gave eloquent voice to these doubts when, in an influential series of articles in the *Observer*, he characterized heritage as being 'right-wing' and accused it of pandering to what he was pleased to call – with fine disregard to the parallel developments taking place in relation to Historic Scotland – 'vulgar English nationalism'. Heritage, he argued, was a consolatory myth, entropy in holiday dress; it was the tourist industry's answer to secular economic decay:

> Where there were mines and mills, now there is Wigan Pier Heritage Centre, where you can pay to crawl through a model coal mine, watch dummies making nails, and be invited 'in' by actors and actresses dressed as 1900 proletarians. Britain, where these days a new museum opens every fortnight, is becoming a museum itself.

Ascherson's use of the word 'vulgar' when complaining of the effrontery, or 'vulgar arrogance', of living history's claim to have opened a hot-line to the past, is worth pausing on. It may seem a strange epithet to issue from the lips of one who is on public record as a socialist, a republican and a democrat, but it is not that strange. As moral aristocrats, waging war on the corruptions of capitalist society, socialists, like the radical nonconformists who preceded them, have often been at their fiercest when denouncing Vanity Fair, or what Aneurin Bevan called in his last great speech the 'vulgar materialism' of capitalist society. And from the time of William Morris onwards they have been apt to rebuke the masses for what another great Labour leader, Ernest Bevin, called the 'poverty' of their desires. In Ascherson's case, those attitudes are compounded by literary snobbery, an apparent belief that the only true knowledge is that which is to be found in books. Heritage is a fraud because it relies on surface appearance; like colour television, it takes the people's mind off higher (or deeper) things:

> The Total Museum, though it can entertain, is a lie. Pretending to open a window into the past is a technique which weakens the imagination much in the way that colour television weakens the intuition, whereas radio – by its incompleteness – so stongly stimulates it…. The claim to be able to 'recreate' history is a vulgar arrogance.

'Heritage', then, is accused of displaying the ignorance and brashness of the upstart. It is also by definition flashy, as meretricious as the baubles of Vanity Fair.

The heritage industry is a fraud. What happened to the people living in these islands can't be dug up, polished and sold. The past is not recoverable like some diamond brooch from the Titanic, partly because it is alive within us. It follows that the 'here is the past' display of heritage is not only a deception, but – more dangerously – a wall built across our awareness of history, and across the links between past and present.

iven an initial impetus, in this country, by Robert Hewison's 1987 squib *The Heritage Industry*, and a more substantial one by Patrick Wright's *On Living in an Old Country*, heritage-baiting rapidly established itself as a steady earner for TV documentarists, journalists on safari, and the writers of features in the quality press. Academics – radical academics – weighed in, proving, at least to their own satisfaction and that of Cultural Studies course-designers, that museums were a prison-house of artefacts, and souvenirs and gift shops a way of commodifying the past. By 1991, as a programme note suggests, exposures of heritage were competing with one another for prime time on the airwaves:

Chronicle: Past for Sale? (BBC 2, 8.10) and *Signals: Theme Park Britons* (Channel 4, 9.15). It's rotten luck on both parties that these two very respectable programmes on the same theme should be scheduled for the same night. Both are concerned about heritage, the country's largest growth industry, and with the way our past is packaged and dispensed like so much fast food in heritage centres and theme parks. Each highlights the concern that historical truth and local needs are sacrificed to profit as the entrepreneurs appropriate from the museums the role of informing us about our past.

One loving shot of a perfect Georgian window in *Chronicle* sums it up – the house is to go to make way for a Roman Heritage Centre flogging imitation antiquities, conceived by its designer as a 'Roman EastEnders'.

logging a Dead Horse, the recent exhibition at the Photographer's Gallery – sponsored by the Arts Concil and now reproduced as a coffee-table book with king-size colour reproductions and text by a presenter of *The Late Show* – might be described as anti-heritage's coming-of-age, a kind of *pot-pourri* of its clichés. The work of a colour documentarist, it takes in all the familiar targets, following a well-worn itinerary – a kind of anti-heritage trail – first marked out by Robert Hewison. Starting with The Northern Experience in County Durham, moving on to The Way We Were heritage centre at Wigan Pier (always good for a metropolitan sneer), it ends up with some softer Home Counties target – in this case 'Edward Elgar' country at Worcester.

Flogging a Dead Horse, a photographic commentary on 'hyper-history', cast as a critique 'not simply … of heritage' but also 'of the very notions of Englishness', is a sustained essay in disgust, in the manner of Wegee and Diane Arbus, though in colour rather than black-and-white, and with ordinary people – Northerners especially – as the grotesques rather than midgets and freaks. The Northern Experience at Beamish Hall, County Durham, is represented by a middle-aged man squinting uncomfortably through the eyepiece of a video camera; the Brontë museum at Haworth by a fat man and his even fatter wife standing by

the churchyard wall looking hot and bothered. Ironbridge – 'birthplace of the Industrial Revolution', now designated a World Heritage Site – is represented by, of all things, a white-haired man with a Rottweiler straining at the leash (just in case we miss the point, the text tells us that he looks 'like a gauleiter'). On an open-topped bus tour of Liverpool's Albert Dock, two elderly ladies gawp. At Eden Camp, the Second World War theme park at Malton, Yorkshire, an overweight grandad, shot from below in order to make him look sinister, bring out his double chin and exaggerate the size of his hands, stares sightlessly into space, while the little boy at his side clasps 'The Great War Play Set'. At Wigan Pier Heritage Centre a young boy with a Mickey Mouse tee-shirt watches a pit-brow girl pushing a coal-wagon. The Vintage Tram Museum at Crich, Derbyshire, is represented by the headless torso of a boy clad in lavender-coloured Bermuda shorts; Westminster Abbey by the rear view of a bald-headed man looking at nothing.

hough directed against the packaging of history, *Flogging a Dead Horse* is a slick production, using a series of stratagems to make its images repellent. Angles and frames are so manipulated as to make every picture out of joint; objects and viewers are juxtaposed so as to diminish the one and belittle the other. We are never once shown the objects themselves – they exist as a kind of mocking commentary on the sightseers. In the manner of 1980s avant-garde photography the people are pictured in a state of alienation, looking neither at each other nor at the objects they have ostensibly come to view. Even though most of the photography is in the open air it looks studio-lit, so that the people are unnaturally flushed; the interior scenes are cropped to look claustrophobic.

Behind the critique of heritage lie residues of that conspiracy theory according to which historical change is engineered by ruling elites, and popular taste is at the mercy of what 1960s and 1970s radicals took to calling the manipulations of 'the media'. In France this took the sophisticated form of countercultural high theory, developed by Michel Foucault in relation to the tutelary complexes of knowledge and power, and more specifically in relation to museum culture by Pierre Bourdieu and Philippe Hoyau. In the United States it was rather an extension of the 1960s radical critique of 'consumerism'. In Britain, where the rise of heritage was identified with the victory of New Right politics, a more traditional notion of the ruling class came to the fore and 'heritage' was said to represent a kind of return of the repressed, a victory of feudal reaction. It was a 'project' or 'strategy' (so radical critics alleged) undertaken on behalf of the wealthy, the privileged and the powerful, and actively promoted the ruling elites. It deployed a dominant form of 'Englishness', played with reactionary fantasies, and threatened to make the country-house version of the national past

(or even, as the Birmingham Centre for Contemporary Cultural Studies argued, the Warwick Castle one) hegemonic. For Neal Ascherson it heralded the advent of a permanent Conservative majority:

> The heritage industry, like the proposed 'core curriculum' of history for English schools, imposes one ruling group's version of history on everyone and declares that it cannot be changed. One of the marks of the feudal *ancien régime* was that the dead governed the living. A mark of a decrepit political system must surely be that a fictitious past of theme parks and costume dramas governs the present.

The denigration of 'heritage', though voiced in the name of radical politics, is pedagogically quite conservative and echoes some of the right-wing jeremiads directed against 'new history' in the schools. Like the videos, slide-shows or classroom exercises in 'empathy' it is accused of taking the mind out of history, offering a Cook's tour or package-holiday view of the past as a substitute for the real thing. It abolishes, or seems to abolish, the distinction between work and play, and turns potential learners into passive consumers. It invites spurious identifications, robbing the past of its terrors and turning it into an ideal home. Still worse — a kind of ultimate profanity in the eyes of the purists — is the use of the performing arts, as with the actors and actresses who dress up in period costumes and act as demonstrators, interpreters and guides. The 'hands-on', interactive 'living history' displays at the museums are almost equally suspect, offering a Pick-'n'-Mix approach to the past in place of coherent explanation or progressive narrative.

he charge of vulgarity could be said to be a leitmotiv of heritage criticism, and may account for the frequency with which heritage is bracketed with theme parks, toytowns and Disneyland. The association with the world of entertainment is clearly a cause of great offence, inviting the scorn of the high-minded, mingling as it does the sacred and the profane, high culture and low. Heritage is accused of trivializing the past, playing with history,

focusing on unworthy objects. Its predilection for dressing up is thought of as childish, while its association with the holiday trades is almost by definition demeaning. The scorn is no doubt spontaneous but it does not seem fanciful to point to the lineal descent from those ancient notions of the 'dignity' of history against which Lord Macaulay inveighed when calling for a recognition of the domestic and the demotic. Fact and fiction, the imaginary and the real, like the sacred and the profane, are supposed to be at war. In a context like this, the very idea of spectacle, with its undertones of the theatrical and its reliance on glitter, is offensive.

eritage is also discredited, in the eyes of its critics, by its association with what used to be called, in the heyday of aristocratic snobbery, 'trade'; but which in post-1960 critical theory, or Cultural Studies, is more apt to be labelled 'consumerism' and conceptualized as the Emperor's New Clothes. It is accused of making history a selling point; of trading on nostalgia; of commodifying the past. Here, as elsewhere, *Flogging a Dead Horse* has it off pat. A Brechtian slogan: 'THE PAST IS UP FOR SALE' — given a full-page spread — interrupts the flow of images, and serves as a kind of black-and-white equivalent to the voice-over. Constable's 'Hay Wain' is overprinted with a magenta-coloured price flash suggesting that, at 99p a time, the treasures of the past can come cheap. In another ironical juxtaposition, a studious-looking man is peering at a shelf-full of souvenirs in which regional types, such as the 'Geordie' and 'the Collier lass', are cased as mannequins and reduced to doll-like figures. The message is rammed home in the double-page spread which brings the book to a close. Taken from the 'Elgar Country', Worcester, it superimposes the 'M' of McDonald's American diner over the mustachioed elegance of an Edwardian tailor's dummy, and juxtaposes a group of denimed modern youths with the flannelled fools of a period cricket photograph (the modern youths, photographed from behind, are faceless clothes-horses, meaninglessly gesturing in the empty air; the Edwardian cricketers, highly

individuated, and no doubt among the first to volunteer in 1914, stare back at us with all the poignancy of the fallen dead).

Arguably it is not the traditionalism but the modernism and more specifically the postmodernism of heritage which offends. Aesthetes condemn it for being bogus: a travesty of the past, rather than a true likeness, let alone — the preservationist's dream — an original. In other words, in spite of the charge that heritage is imprisoning the country in a time-warp, and the accusation that it is sentimentalizing the past, heritage is being attacked not because it is too historical but because it is not historical enough. It lacks authenticity. It is a simulation pretending to be the real thing. It is not because heritage is too reverent about the past that it provokes outrage, but on the contrary the fact that, in the eyes of the critics at least, it seems quite untroubled when it is dealing with replicas and pastiche.

 iterary snobbery also comes into play: the belief that only books are serious; perhaps too a suspicion of the visual, rooted in a Puritan or Protestant distrust of graven images. Artefacts — whether they appear as images on the television screen, in costume drama, or as 'living history' displays in the museums and the theme parks — are not only inferior to the written word but, being by their nature concerned with surface appearance only, irredeemably shallow. Here Neal Ascherson's preference for wireless over television and his real hatred for open-air heritage displays is worth pausing on: reading a book is strenuous and demanding; spectacle — and here Ascherson is following a well-worn line in cultural criticism — is something which is passively consumed. The first is an intellectual activity; the second is mindless. The unspoken assumption is that people cannot be trusted with pictures; that images seduce where the printed word engages the full intelligence.

Some of the hostility aroused by the idea of heritage may be misogynist, and it is perhaps indicative of this that in the attacks on the 'commodification' of the past so much animus is directed against what is entirely a female gift culture — *pot-pourris* and toiletries, of the kind

on sale at the National Trust gift shops, earning particular derision. In the case of *Flogging a Dead Horse*, however, it is not the tea-shop ladies, those ancient targets of macho abuse, but the spectacle of the Northern working class — young and old, men and women — which excites sexual disgust. In the camera's eye they are no less repellent when smiling than when scowling, and it is difficult to imagine them doing anything which might make them appealing, or earn them a modicum of dignity and respect.

 omething might be said too about social condescension. The idea that the masses, if left to their own devices, are moronic; that their pleasures are unthinking; their tastes cheapo and nasty, is a favourite conceit of the aesthete — as it was of their predecessors, the moralists and philanthropists who, in the manner of Philip Stubbes' *Anatomie of Abuses*, took up arms against the meretricious attractions of Vanity Fair. Behind their radical rhetoric of such an exhibition as *Flogging a Dead Horse* it is not difficult to find echoes of the Arnoldian belief that anything connected with commerce was by definition 'vulgar', that provincials were necessarily Philistine, and the populace uncultured. Superimposed on this are the familiar Leavisite themes derived from the cultural criticism of the 1930s and 1940s, according to which mass civilization is by its very nature degraded, and popular tastes, as they succumb to it, debased.

Reas, in line with the film-school teaching of the 1970s and 1980s, wants to challenge the illusions of authenticity and to offer, in place of fixed images, a free-floating assembly of shapes which refuse any simple reading. And he seems to want to subvert those sentimentalized ideas of 'The Northern Experience', which *Coronation Street* and the 'new-wave' realism of the 1960s did so much to popularize. But his alienated figures conform to current film-school orthodoxy, and they also rejoin an older iconography, memorably represented in the Margate funfair of Lindsay Anderson's *O Dreamland* and the Piccadilly Circus of Alain Tanner's *Nice Time*, in which pleasure-going is represented as repulsive. It also echoes the age-old belief of the high-minded that the masses are being culturally debased. His 'heritage industry' is a kind of 1990s version of those 'mechanized' and 'Americanized' amusements, 'standardized' shows, and 'passive' audiences which J.B. Priestley in his 1934 portrait of holiday-making, and John Osborne in *The Entertainer*, contrasted to the 'old roaring Variety turns' of the Edwardian music hall.

heme parks — doubly offensive because they seem to come to us from America, and because they link history to the holiday industry — are a particular bugbear for the critics. As engines of corruption, or seducers of the innocent, they seem to occupy the symbolic space of those earlier folk-devils of the literary imagination, jukeboxes and transistor radios, or — the particular object of Richard Hoggart's spleen in *The Uses of Literacy* (1957) — candy-floss and milk-bars. In contemporary left-wing demonology they have become the latest in a long line of opiates of the masses, on a par with Butlin's holiday camps and bingo halls in the 1950s; 'canned entertainment' and 'Hollywood films' in the 1930s, or what J.B. Priestley feared was the 'Blackpooling' of English life and leisure. Their appeals are by definition meretricious and mechanical; their pleasures mindless, pandering to the lowest tastes. As the science-fiction writer E.L. Doctrow has put it, these simulated environments only offer 'shorthand culture for the masses … a mindless thrill like an electric shock, that insists at the same time on the recipient's rich psychic relation to his country's history and language and literature. In a forth-coming time of highly governed masses in an overpopulated world, this technique may be extremely useful as a substitute for education and, eventually, as a substitute for experience.'

or the aesthete, anyway for the alienated and the disaffected, heritage is a mechanism of cultural debasement. It leaves no space for the contemplative or the solitary. It forbids discrimination and the exercise of good taste. Its pleasures are cheap and nasty, confounding

high and low, originals and copies, the authentic and the pastiche. It brings 'crowd pollution', in the form of mass tourism, to sacred spots, surrounds art treasures with crocodiles of visitors, and turns ancient monuments into spectacles for the ignorant to gawp at.

The hostility of historians to heritage, though different in kind from that of aesthetes, is no less overdetermined. Our whole training predisposes us to give a privileged place to the written word, to hold the visual (and the verbal) in comparatively low esteem, and to regard imagery as a kind of trap. Books, from an early age, are our bosom companions; libraries rather than museums are our natural habitat. If we use graphics at all it will be for purposes of illustration, seldom as primary texts, and it may be indicative of this that, as with material artefacts, we do not even have footnote conventions for referencing them. The fetishization of archives – fundamental to the Rankean revolution in historical scholarship – reinforces these biases, giving a talismanic importance to manuscripts. Even when our point of address is material culture – as in, say, current preoccupations with consumerism or changes in the use of domestic space – our evidence is more likely to be drawn from manuscript remains: probate inventories or household budgets rather than museum exhibits or archaeological finds (a rare exception is Magaret Spufford's use of a cambric handkerchief to reconstruct the itinerary of a seventeenth-century pedlar).

odern conditions of research seem to dictate an almost complete detachment from the material environment – indeed, to follow the recommendations of some migrant scholars, it is a positive advantage to be writing English history from the other side of the Atlantic. We do not go out on archaeological walks, as our Victorian forebears did, or learn the lie of the land – as Marc Bloch and R.H. Tawney recommended – by putting on a pair of stout boots. We are unlikely to spend our summer vacations, as students, poring over the mysteries of numismatics, as the young Charles Oman did

in his apprentice days as a scholar, nor staking out positions on a battlefield, as Thomas Carlyle did when preparing his *Letters and Speeches of Oliver Cromwell*. The computer-literate, calling up a transatlantic or Antipodean printout, or downloading information from a terminal, may not even have to leave the study.

etrieval work is no part of our scholarly brief. We do not have to rescue our evidence from the teeth of the bulldozer, as archaeologists do, or call in the aid of the scuba-divers or the aerial photographers in search of an elusive quarry. Nor do we need a preservation order to protect our sources from the depredations of agribusiness, as is the case with those archaeologically sensitive landscapes protected under the Countryside Act of 1979. Blessed (or burdened) with a superabundance of records, we see no need to augment their number but are content to wait on the archivists and librarians, devoting our energies instead to record linkage or the exploitation of hitherto neglected files. With the exception of pre-Conquest scholars who, like classical historians, are heavily reliant on such fugitive remains as monumental inscriptions and burial mounds, we are very little interested in the evidence of material artefacts: we may initiate our students in the mysteries of the record office, but hardly of the cemetery or the dig.

The idea of 'living history' is even more remote from our scholarly routines – as well as being, in the eyes of the fastidious, offensive. We do not devote our sabbaticals to reconstituting a period street, nor spend our weekend breaks, or summer holidays, getting up steam on the footplate. Demographic historians, testing out their theories, do not dress up as Victorian mothers and fathers or pretend to be overseers of the poor. Economic historians, weighing the pros and cons of the machinery question, do not feel obliged to join in the steam ploughing match or crank a fairground engine into life; nor, studying the statistics of overseas trade, are they likely to feel moved to test out the speed of a tea-clipper by sailing one in a tall ships regatta or entering it for a North Sea and Baltic or cross-Channel race. Seventeenth-century scholars, preoccupied with their own internecine warfare, do not join in the annual re-enactments of the siege of Chepstow Castle or the Battle of Marston Moor.

The hostility of historians to heritage is possibly exacerbated by the fact that they are in some sort competing for the same terrain. Each, after its own fashion, claims to be representing the past 'as it was'. Each too could be said to be obsessed with the notion of 'period', though the one renders it through zeitgeist; the other in terms of icons. Interpretation, the privilege of the archive-based historian, and 're-creation', the ambition of heritage, also share a common conceit; the belief that scrupulous attention to detail will bring the dead to life.

 oes envy play some part? Heritage has a large public following, mass-membership organisations whose numbers run to hundreds of thousands, whereas our captive audiences in the lecture hall or the seminar room can sometimes be counted on the fingers of one hand. Heritage involves tens of thousands of volunteers. It can command substantial exchequer subsidies, and raise large sums by appealing to the historically minded public. It has royal patronage, and enjoys support from politicians of all stripes. It fuels popular campaigns and is at the very centre of current controversy about the shape of the built environment. It can mount festivals and pageants. It enlists corporate sponsorship and support for its retrieval projects. It is something which people care passionately about; where they are ready to enter the arena of public debate rather as, in the old days, they were ready to re-rehearse the rights and wrongs of the Norman Conquest or the English Civil War.

Whatever the reasons, history and heritage are typically placed in opposite camps. The first is assigned to the realm of critical inquiry, the second to a merely antiquarian preoccupation, the classification and hoarding of things. The first, so the argument runs, is dynamic and concerned with explanation, bringing a sceptical intelligence to bear on the complexities and contradictoriness of the record; the second sentimentalizes, and is content merely to celebrate.

 f the parable of the motes and beams were followed, as it should be, few of the historians' practices would emerge unscathed. Are we not guilty ourselves of turning knowledge into an object of desire? And is it not the effect, if not the intention, of our activity as historians to domesticate the past and rob it of its terrors by bringing it within the realm of the knowable? Historians are no less concerned than conservationists to make their subjects imaginatively appealing. We may not prettify the past in the manner of English Heritage or the National Trust, but we are no less adept than conservation officers and museum curators at tying up loose ends and removing unsightly excrescences. We use vivid detail and thick description to offer images far clearer than any reality could be. Do we not require of our readers, when facing them with one of our period reconstructions, as willing a suspension of disbelief as the 'living history' spectacle of the open-air museums or theme park? Is not the historical monograph, after its fashion, as much as packaging of the past as costume drama? And do we not call on our own *trompe-l'œil* devices to induce a hallucinatory sense of oneness with the past, using 'evocative' detail as a gauge of authenticity?

The perceived opposition between 'education' and 'entertainment', and the unspoken and unargued-for assumption that pleasure is almost by definition mindless, ought not to go unchallenged. There is no reason to think that people are more passive when looking at old photographs or film footage, handling a museum exhibit, following a local history trail, or even buying a historical souvenir, than when reading a book. People do not simply 'consume' images in the way in which, say, they buy a bar of chocolate. As in any reading, they assimilate them as best they can to pre-existing images and narratives. The pleasures of the gaze – scopophilia as it is disparagingly called – are different in kind from those of the written word but not necessarily less taxing on historical reflection and thought.

NICHOLAS CRANE

TOWPATHS AND GRAVE-ROBBERS

Huddersfield Narrow Canal

From Castleshaw by way of Dirty Lane and Bleak Hey Nook to Diggle: from Imperial Rome to the Industrial Revolution.

Diggle snuggled into the head of a valley near the highest point of the district of Saddleworth, a string of villages which follow the River Tame from the Pennines down towards the Manchester suburbs. The meridian was now grazing the western edge of the range and for the first time the softer forms of foothills met the moorland.

In Diggle, I found the western entrance to England's longest, highest canal tunnel, a day's work here in the full shadow of a building on...

The Standedge Tunnel was the crux of the Huddersfield Narrow Canal,

The Standedge Tunnel

an engineering feat that anticipated the financial and technical troubles experienced 200 years later by the builders of the railway between London and Paris. The canal had to burrow for an unprecedented 3¼ miles beneath the moor of Standedge.

Water poured from the millstone grit and flooded the workings; long sections of friable shale had to be shored with brickwork and then a surveyor discovered that the two ends of the tunnel were out of alignment, and were not going to meet in the middle. As the costs escalated, investors panicked and forced the committee to scrap plans for a towpath through the tunnel, a decision that was to affect future profitability.

Just as the Rochdale Canal had sought to shorten the route taken by the Leeds and Liverpool, so the Huddersfield Narrow Canal sought to cut the bends out of the Rochdale. Work began in 1794, the same year that the first clod was cut out of the Rochdale, but boats didn't pass through the summit tunnel until 1811, by which time the Rochdale had been operating for seven years. A crowd of 10,000 gathered at Diggle as boats carrying the company managers, local dignitaries and a band entered Standedge Tunnel to the ponderous chords of 'Rule Britannia'. The eventual cost of the canal was more than double the £178,748 projected by its engineer, Benjamin Outram, while the five years he'd allowed for boring the tunnel had stretched to seventeen.

With no towpath, and therefore no horses or mechanical devices available to haul the narrowboats through the tunnel, propulsion fell to 'leggers', pairs of men who laid back on the barges, pushing for up to four hours with their feet against the tunnel walls. The record for legging through Standedge Tunnel was set in 1914 by David Whitehead, who pushed his narrowboat through in eighty-five minutes. Six hundred feet above the leggers, the towing horses were walked over the moor by a company employee who would make four trips a day. One of these professional walkers, a Thomas Bourne of Marsden, reputedly clocked up 215,852 miles between 1811 and 1852, the equivalent of walking the Pennine Way twenty times a year for forty-one years.

I had the rare luxury of easy walking as the towpath stuck with the meridian for over three kilometres, falling in steps past locks that still bore their stonemasons' marks. Every turn produced ghostly whispers from that epoch of industrial purpose. Off on the right, stacks of new wooden pallets stood outside the old Dobcross Loom Works, which had once employed 500 and had its own branch line.

Downwind of Manchester, Salford and Rochdale, I was now in Lowry Country, the grimescape of smoking chimneys and faded white flake.

Saddleworth had landmarks that played allegorical roles in Lowry's oils: the stone obelisk to the fallen dominating the valley might have been 'The Landmark' (1936); the Loom Works must have known many a dawn when the incoming tide of coated workers funnelled through the factory gate as they do in 'Early Morning' (1955). The difference now is that Lowry's subjects have gone. The human minnows that swarm across his paintings travel in cars or not at all. There is little chance of seeing those Chaplinesque men in funny hats getting into fights, or being arrested. The children and gossiping adults, quaint invalid carriages and bikes, dogs and balls that Lowry employed to transform street scenes into fairgrounds have been cleared of human colour. Lowry's factory workers have gone the way of Breughel's animated peasants.

The towpath passed a milestone (12 to Huddersfield) and then toppled down a flight of locks to pass underneath the Saddleworth viaduct by way of a skew arch which gives the great spans a knock-kneed perspective from below. The viaduct was the scene of a ghastly accident on Christmas Eve 1866, when a passenger stepped out of his carriage unaware that the train had overshot Saddleworth station.

(AUTHOR'S ROUTE)

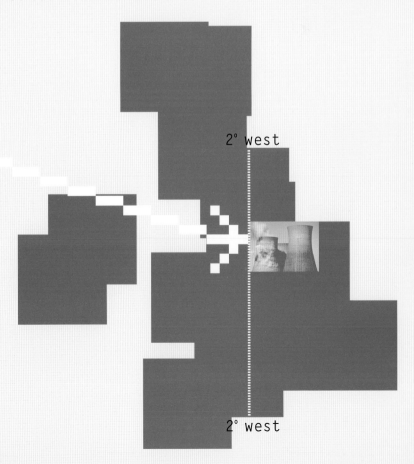

2° west

2° west

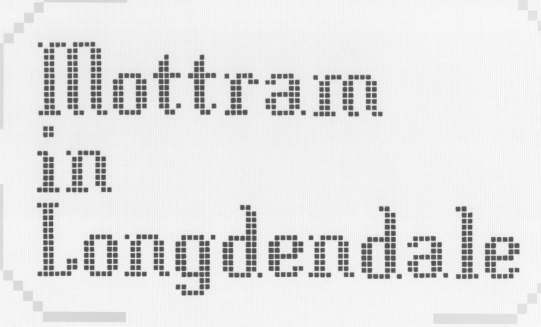

Mottram in Longdendale

The bins were being collected when I reached L. S. Lowry's home on Stalybridge Road.

Bless This House

Number 23 was a stone, semi-detached building in grey, slightly grander than its neighbours and disproportionately tall, as if Lowry himself had stretched its chimney and doorway.

It was not yet seven in the morning and the curtains were still closed. I stood on the far pavement, leaning on my umbrella ('Man Waiting', 1964, Oil on board), nonplussed by the ordinariness of The Elms. Yet in a backroom of this house had painted the man who symbolized the last days of the mill towns, whose work hangs in London and New York and whose life would soon be commemorated by the £64 million Lowry Centre under construction on Salford Quays, with a permanent collection, plaza, bars, cafés and restaurants (a good irony there, for a man who drank orange squash and favoured sausage, egg and chips) and a Hands-On Gallery.

Lowry had moved into the house in 1948, nine years after his mother died. He had no television, or phone or car; he didn't drink or smoke. He took his holidays in the Seaburn Hotel, Sunderland. Being alone sharpened his focus and placed him in a world of extremes, where there were not crowds, but multitudes, and where a lone individual became a solitary lamp-post. Detesting Rembrandt for his realism (his own living room was lined with Rossetti drawings), he was able to invent composite industrial landscapes and cartoon portraits, a magic reality that was funny and tragic. He lived in Gogol's 'world of visible laughter and invisible tears', and died in 1976, never having been abroad, or been in love.

Since Lowry's time the stub of a motorway had been extended to the edge of the village, precipitating deluges of heavy traffic into streets scaled for horses and carts. The air shuddered with noise and grime and despite the thousands of passers-by there was no café.

In search of breakfast, I found myself looking at a plaque to another Mottram man, Lawrence Earnshaw, a weaver's son whose seven-year apprenticeship to his father was followed by four years as a tailor and then a dramatic switch to mechanical invention. In 1753 he designed a machine that could spin and reel cotton, then destroyed it in the belief that it would deprive the poor of work. Later, he invented an astronomical clock that was sufficiently successful for him to win many orders, including a sale for 150 shillings to Lord Bute.

Lawrence Earnshaw died in May 1767, four years after his namesake Thomas Earnshaw completed his watch-makers' apprenticeship and embarked upon his race against Harrison, Arnold and others for a method of measuring longitude. Thomas Earnshaw invented the first economic chronometer and won an award of £3,000 from the Board of Longitude, dying famous and wealthy, at eighty, in Chelsea; Lawrence Earnshaw died poor, at sixty, in Mottram.

One hundred years after Lawrence Earnshaw's death, a series of articles in the *Cotton under Lyne Reporter* prompted a public subscription for a monument to be raised in Mottram's cemetery.

In the absence of a café, I walked up to the weathered Perpendicular church to find shelter from the wind while I ate the bread and cheese I'd carried from Uppermill. The church stood on the crown of the hill in the path of the westerlies that gust off the Irish Sea towards the Dark Peak. Virtually every gravestone lay flat on the ground, as if swiped by a giant hand.

'It's Captain Whittle's wind,' nodded a bearded man walking his dogs. 'When Captain Whittle's gravestone blew over, he gave his name to the winds that hit Mottram.'

'The other theory,' added Graham McCarg, 'is grave-robbers. There was this local man who'd wait for a burial then dig up the body and take it down and sell it to the anatomical school in Manchester.

Before he could do it, he'd go to the two pubs by the church to steal courage.' Eventually the body-snatcher got caught and thrown into a Manchester lime-pit.

Graham looked down at me huddled with my collar up in the lee of the tower (the church door had been locked). 'If you think this is bad, you should be here when there's a north-easterly down the Woodhead valley. I've been up here when it's been a typhoon.'

In 1891 the wind blew in the belfry window and stripped the village of chimney pots.

'This is called War Hill,' added Graham. 'There was a battle here in Anglo-Saxon times and after the dead were buried it became a Saxon shrine.'

My father's parents, Gedaliah and Malka Lichtenstein, escaped from Poland in the early Thirties and settled in East London. After the war they moved, with their three sons, to Westcliff in Essex. As my father and his brothers became successful businessmen they decided to anglicize their surname. I was born, in April 1969, Rachel Laurence.

Malka died of leukaemia when I was twelve years old. I remember her, head thrown back in laughter, revealing a mouth full of gold teeth that I would beg to be shown. I remember her bright auburn wig, which my sister and I would watch slowly sliding off her head during her afternoon nap. Through the crack of the door we would admire her majestic figure, wrapped in a red velvet cloak, draped over her pink **chaise longue**. I would stare in awe at the photograph that rested on the mantelpiece, showing her as a young woman, provocatively reclining in a V-necked silk dress.

In contrast, I have a memory of an anxious woman pacing outside the gate on our arrival, crying uncontrollably if we were five minutes late, 'My darlings, I thought you wouldn't come, I thought I'd never see you.' But most of the time she would be in the kitchen, cooking endless amounts of delicious food. My sister and I would sit at the table as our plates were piled up with fried chicken, gefilte fish and heaps of other delicacies. 'Eat, eat, think of all the starving children in Africa, eat and be well.' Guilt-ridden, knowing that as a girl she'd never had enough to fill her small belly, we would try to please her, stretching our skinny frames to bursting point.

The End
Rachel Lichtenstein

I remember the way my grandfather always ate. He would lower his head nearly into his food, wrap his right arm protectively around his plate and, using the other hand, shovel his meal with alarming speed, barely stopping for breath. He never lost this habit, always aware of potential hungry siblings. My grandparents were colourful characters in my childhood; they both fascinated and terrified me. They were different from other people around me, louder, bigger somehow.

When I was seventeen my grandfather died. He was over eighty and everyone agreed he'd had a good long life. After the funeral I remember entering his study, which was lined floor to ceiling with books. They were written in many different languages, none of which I could understand. I found a velvet bag in his bedside table, embroidered with Hebrew letters I could not read. Inside was a large piece of woven blue-and-white cloth and a small leather box with long leather ties. I did not know what they were for, but kept them anyway. I rescued his suitcase, full of old clock parts, certificates, photographs. In my room I examined them for hours.

When he died I panicked, realizing that with him was buried the key to my heritage. I became determined not to let it die with him. A week after his death I took the first step towards a reconnection between my past and my present and reclaimed by deed poll the surname Lichtenstein. That same summer, I left my parents' home to complete a degree in Fine Art, specializing in sculpture, at Sheffield University.

My desire to go to art school had been greatly influenced by my grandfather. When I was about eight years old, I asked him who had drawn the ink sketch of an old man that hung in a heavy gold frame in the hall of their house. He told me this story:

IT WAS ME.

As a young man I was very talented, although I did not dream too much about becoming an artist. I was poor, from a small village. I was not allowed to have such ambitions. But I had an uncle who lived in Łódź. He was very influential and grand, involved in politics I think. Well, one summer, he came to stay with us. My uncle saw my drawings and was greatly impressed. He had some influence at the art school and managed to secure a place for me there. After much persuading my mother let me go. My uncle was to pay the fee and I would live with him. I could not believe my good fortune and left the following week. The journey to Łódź was long and difficult then. We travelled by horse and cart and it took us nearly three days. The next morning I was to begin my studies. I cannot even describe to you my excitement that night. I could not eat or sleep. Eventually I must have drifted off, because I shall never forget what happened next. I awoke in a blind panic. The moon was still high in the sky but there was no possibility of me sleeping again that night. I had experienced the most terrifying and vivid dream and before even discussing the matter with my uncle I began to pack my bags to return home. I had dreamt that my brother was dying. The image and sensations were so real I had to check if he was all right. We did not have telephones in those days. The only way to know for sure would be to return to the village. By the time dawn had broken I was ready to leave. My uncle was understandably shocked and disappointed, but I would not change my mind. He arranged for my travel back and I began the long journey home, dreading my arrival with each mile that took us closer. Eventually we reached the outskirts of the village, and I ran home not stopping to greet anyone and found the house ominously empty. I stepped outside into the street to see my younger sister in floods of tears. She had just come from the cemetery where they were burying my brother. He had fallen into a fever the night I left and died the following day of cholera. I never returned to Łódź, but instead stayed and looked after the family, being now the eldest son. Soon after, things became difficult for us and the family left for England. I have not drawn anything since.

I took the opportunity my grandfather never had, and during my three years at art school nearly all my sculptural work was based on his life story.

The Kosher Luncheon Club became my ace card when conducting my own tours of the area in subsequent years. By then there was little left of the Jewish East End: crumbling buildings, derelict sites, rapidly fading signs.

'This used to be ----- now it is a car park.'

... 'If you look really hard you can just make out the mark of a **mezuzah** here.' After traipsing around the streets of Spitalfields, the crowds of tourists invariably were despondent by the end of the tour. Then I would take them to the Kosher Luncheon Club. That was alive and kicking. Crisp white tablecloths, the clink of glasses and the slurp of soup to a backdrop of Yiddish and laughter. It retained the warmth I've so often heard people talking about when they describe the Jewish world of East London.

In 1994 the luncheon club stopped trading, another victim in the story of the disappearing Jewish East End. Bloom's restaurant was to close less than a year later, and then Marks Deli in Wentworth Street. The luncheon club had certainly not had an easy time of it in recent years, and nearly closed down in 1992 after suffering a racist arson attack. The arsonists heaped up prayer-books from the synagogue next door before dousing them with white spirit and setting them on fire, causing ten thousand pounds' worth of damage. The attack came only nine months after vandals had broken into the club and daubed the walls with Nazi slogans and symbols. The fire started on the holiday of **Shavuot**, at the same time of year that I returned to the club in 1997, three years after it had closed down. I had been invited to an art event, organized by a gallery in Spitalfields Market that was being run from the former site of the old luncheon club. I was too curious not to take a last look, and walked from Whitechapel in the dank drizzle to Greatorex Street.

The once spotless blue-and-white hall now resembled a seedy nightclub. The tiles had been ripped from the floor and painted black. The old wooden table at the front of the hall that once housed an ancient till was littered with beer bottles and fag butts. The tables had disappeared and in their place stood black-clad artists shifting about uncomfortably. I moved through the crowd in a state of shock, reaching the end of the room, where a long trestle table covered in black velvet faced me. On the table were strewn flowers and open books. On closer inspection I realized the books were religious volumes belonging to the synagogue.

I passed the table and moved with the herd into the adjacent room. In all the times I had visited the luncheon club I had never been into the Great Garden Street synagogue before, even though I had known it was situated next door. A magnificent building: beautifully carved wooden **bimah** standing proudly in the centre, the pews still in place, with seat numbers carefully painted in white on their backs. The ark was surrounded with marble tablets commemorating various stages in the life of the synagogue and its members. All this was hard to focus on. I felt as if someone had dropped a tab of acid into my beer and I was not having a good trip. I moved slowly through the dark, smoky room, stopping behind the **bimah** to gain my balance. It was Friday night, Shabbat. Where the rabbi and cantor would have stood, a long-haired DJ with baseball cap secured by giant headphones was busily spinning nightmarish techno tunes while struggling to light a disintegrating cigarette protruding from his mouth.

Each corner of the **bimah** had a flame-throwing gas torch fixed to it, adding to the image of hell. Spaced-out ravers, with Technicolor trousers and dreadlocks, frantically waved their arms about in the pews. Others sat about, stubbing out cigarettes on the carpet. The ark had been shut off by a string of cheap flashing fairy lights, and from the women's gallery a smoke machine billowed obnoxious air to the revellers below.

My head began to spin, and, as I turned, attempting to make sense of the scene before me, I lost my footing and fell. The bouncer eyed me suspiciously: another raver who had popped one too many. Friends picked me up and ushered me out, suggesting we go and look at the art. In a daze, I re-entered the hall of the former luncheon club and moved towards the door where a gaggle had gathered to witness an 'art performance'. On a raised stage two women sat dressed in baby pink vinyl, garish make-up smeared on their blank faces. They sat behind a large desk piled knee-deep in old books arranged in a most aesthetic and appealing way. I pushed to the front of the zombified crowd. The young ladies were stamping the books with large rubber implements and then elegantly ripping pages out of them and tossing them onto the floor.

I approached the table and began to scrutinize the books. Ancient prayer-books were strewn around, broken spines balancing on top of old receipt books, registers and other archive material dating back to the beginning of the century.

My hand rested on a large faded album. I picked up the book and flicked through:

C10113, BURIAL SOCIETY OF THE FEDERATION OF SYNAGOGUES, 1 MARCH 1933,

Chaya Jablonsky, age 92 years, Hackney Hospital, Homerton ... exquisite handwriting filled every page with painstaking additional notes on each deceased person, their occupation described in detail, financial situation, next of kin, place of birth, Hebrew name, presence of watcher over each corpse.

'What the fuck do you think you're doing, this is a performance?' one of the pink plastic babes screeched.

'Excuse me, what exactly are you doing?' I howled back.

'We have been told to stamp these books and rip them up. You are in the way, put that fucking book down.'

A row ensued, and friends looked on in horror as I became part of the event; the crowd drawled greedily. In a quasi-hypnotic state I heaped books up in my arms and began walking towards the door. The pink girls screamed abuse and continued maniacally stamping and ripping books to shreds.

My friend Michelle managed to restrain me for a few moments and suggested it might be more constructive to try to locate the organizers of the show. Eventually, Marco from the Commercial Gallery arrived. I spoke quickly and urgently for ten minutes, pointing out that the performance was offensive and suggesting that maybe they might consider that the books were historically significant and would be better placed in a museum. At the end of that time the two men were apologizing profusely. 'We had no idea what they were, terribly sorry,' etcetera etcetera. The performance was stopped. The young women sulked on their chairs, then joined their friends in the synagogue. I told Marco that I would contact the appropriate parties and try to get the books housed or buried. He was willing to help, and then told me about all the other material that had been found in the synagogue: **tefillin**, prayer shawls, all manner of religious books. Thank God, they had had the sensitivity to store some of this material away. I also told Marco that I was taking the book I had picked up, the Register of Deaths. He did not argue with me.

I had seen insensitive events like this happen before on a number of occasions at the Princelet Street synagogue. Film crews would repaint the ark to create the right mood, artists would hang offensive work in the synagogue, and the stench of stale cigarettes and beer would often greet me when entering the building on a Monday morning. I accepted that buildings become abandoned, that synagogues are deconsecrated, and that new owners have every right to adapt them to suit their new purposes. But to destroy the books? Scenes of Nazi Germany came to mind. These books had not been ripped from the homes and synagogues of terrified Jews, they had been abandoned by the Federation of Synagogues, left scattered on the pews for new occupiers to play with.

Steve Aylett's novels and short-story collections include **The Crime Studio**, **Bigot Hall**, **Slaughtermatic**, shortlisted for the Philip K. Dick Award, and, most recently, **Toxicology**.

Paul Bailey lives in London. His first novel, **At the Jerusalem**, won the Somerset Maugham Award; later work includes **Gabriel's Lament**, shortlisted for the Booker Prize, **An Immaculate Mistake**, a memoir, and **An English Madam: The Life and Work of Cynthia Payne**.

J.G. Ballard was born in Shanghai; he was placed in a civilian prison camp after the Japanese attack on Pearl Harbour. He is the author of more than twenty books, including **Crash**, filmed by David Cronenberg, **The Atrocity Exhibition** and the semi-autobiographical **Empire of the Sun**, which won a clutch of literary prizes and was filmed by Steven Spielberg.

John Bayley, who was married to Iris Murdoch, is the author of numerous works of literary criticism, including **The Character of Love**, and the novels **In Another Country** and **The Red Hat**. He was Warton Professor of English at the University of Oxford.

Margaret Busby was born in Ghana and co-founded the publishing house Allison & Busby in 1968. Since 1987 she has worked as a writer, reviewer and broadcaster and compiled **Daughters of Africa**, an award-winning anthology of writing by women of African descent.

Simon Callow is an actor, theatre director and author. Amongst other works, he has staged the première of **Shirley Valentine** in both London and New York, **Die Fledermaus** for Scottish Opera and **Carmen Jones** at the Old Vic. He is the author of **Being An Actor** and **Orson Welles: The Road to Xanadu**.

Bruce Chatwin's award-winning first book, **In Patagonia**, redefined modern British travel writing. His work also includes **The Viceroy of Ouidah**, filmed as **Cobra Verde** by Werner Herzog, **Utz**, shortlisted for the Booker Prize, and **On The Black Hill**. He died in 1989.

Nik Cohn was brought up in Derry, Northern Ireland. His books include **Awopbopaloobop Alopbamboom** and **I Am Still the Greatest Says Johnny Angelo**. He also wrote the story that gave rise to **Saturday Night Fever**.

Nicholas Crane writes widely for newspapers and magazines. His critically acclaimed first book, **Clear Waters Rising: A Mountain Walk Across Europe** was recently followed by **Two Degrees West: A Walk Along England's Meridian**.

Michael Crawford is Director of the Institute of Brain Chemistry and Human Nutrition at the University of North London. He is also the author of **What We Eat Today** and **Conservation**.

Richard Dawkins is the first Charles Simonyi Professor of the Public Understanding of Science at the University of Oxford. His books include the ground-breaking **The Selfish Gene**, **The Blind Watchmaker** and **River Out of Eden**.

Norman Douglas worked briefly for the Foreign Office before being granted extended leave and settling in Italy. He was the author of three travel books, a novel, **South Wind**, and a recipe book, **Venus in the Kitchen**. He died on Capri in 1952.

Carol Ann Duffy was born in Glasgow. Winner of numerous literary prizes, her books include **Standing Female Nude**, **Selling Manhattan**, **The Other Country** and **Mean Time**.

Germaine Greer was born in Melbourne. Her books include **The Mad Woman's Underclothes**, and, most recently, **The Whole Woman**, as well as **The Female Eunuch**. She is Professor of English and Comparative Literary Studies at Warwick University.

Jane Grigson, award-winning translator of Italian literature, was one of the twentieth-century's most influential food writers. Her first book was **Charcuterie and French Pork Cookery**, her last **Fruit Book**. She died in 1990.

Robert Harris is best known for his bestselling novels, **Fatherland** and **Enigma**. He has worked as a journalist for the BBC, the Observer and Sunday Times and is also the author of **The Making of Neil Kinnock** and, most recently, **Archangel**, a novel.

Seamus Heaney, who won the Nobel Prize for Literature in 1995, was born on his family's farm in Northern Ireland in 1939. His poetry collections include **Death of A Naturalist**, **North**, **Field Work**, **Station Island** and **Seeing Things**. He was Professor of Poetry at the University of Oxford from 1989 to 1994.

NOTES ON CONTRIBUTORS

Eric Hobsbawm was born in Alexandria. Since retiring from Birkbeck College, University of London, he has taught at the New School for Social Research in New York. One of the most eminent British historians, he is the author of numerous books including the classic **The Age of Revolution** and **The Age of Empire** as well as a history of jazz.

Kazuo Ishiguro was born in Nagasaki in 1954 and moved to England at the age of five. He is the author of four novels, **A Pale View of the Hills**, **An Artist of the Floating World**, **The Remains of the Day**, winner of the Booker Prize, and **The Unconsoled**. He lives in London.

C.L.R. James was born in Trinidad and came to England in 1932. A central figure in the Pan-African Movement, his many writings include a study of the Haitian revolution, **The Black Jacobins**; Minty Alley, a novel; the play **Toussaint L'Ouverture**, in which he performed with Paul Robeson; and cricket journalism for the Manchester Guardian. He died in 1989.

Derek Jarman was a writer, painter, theatre designer and film-maker. His books include **Derek Jarman's Caravaggio** and the autobiographical **Modern Nature**, and his films **Jubilee**, **The Garden** and **Blue**. He died in 1994.

Victor Kiernan taught in India before becoming Professor of History at the University of Edinburgh. One of Britain's most distinguished historians, his many books include **The Lords of Human Kind** and **History, Classes and Nation States**. He is also the translator of two volumes of Urdu poetry.

Hanif Kureishi was Writer in Residence at London's Royal Court Theatre before his screenplay for **My Beautiful Launderette** was nominated for an Oscar. He was awarded the Whitbread Prize for the Best First Novel for **The Buddha of Suburbia**. He also directed his most recent film, **London Kills Me**.

Sarah LeFanu has edited seven anthologies of contemporary fiction, including **How Maxine Learned to Love her Legs and Other Tales of Growing Up**. The author of **In the Chinks of the World Machine: Feminism and Science Fiction**, she is also a broadcaster.

Rachel Lichtenstein is an artist who lives and works in East London. She is, with Iain Sinclair, the co-author of **Rodinsky's Room**. She also works as a tour guide and gives lectures on the history of the Jewish East End.

David Marsh is a writer and researcher on nutrition and other environmental matters. A contributor to a variety of magazines and journals, he is the author of **Magnetic and Energy Therapies: Science or Science Fiction?** and co-author, with Michael Crawford, of **Nutrition and Evolution**.

Peter Medawar was awarded the Nobel Prize for Medicine in 1960 for his work on tissue transplantation. He held professorships at Birmingham University and University College London. His books include **The Art of the Soluble: Creativity and Originality in Science**, **Advice to a Young Scientist** and **The Limits of Science**. He died in 1987.

Timothy Mo was born in Hong Kong and moved to England at the age of ten. His award-winning novels include **Sour Sweet**, **The Redundancy of Courage** and, most recently, **Renegade or Halo²**. He recently returned to live in Hong Kong.

George Orwell served as a policeman in colonial Burma and fought for the Republic in the Spanish Civil War. He is one of the twentieth century's most influential and widely read authors. A prolific journalist, his books include **Keep the Aspidistra Flying**, **Down and Out in Paris and London** and **Animal Farm**. He died of tuberculosis in 1950.

Anthony Powell is the author of the highly acclaimed twelve-novel sequence **A Dance to the Music of Time**, seven other novels, four volumes of memoirs as well as journals and two plays.

NOTES ON CONTRIBUTORS

Michèle Roberts, half-British and half-French, is the author of eight novels, including **Daughters of the House**, which won the W.H. Smith Literary Award; three poetry collections; a volume of short stories; and **Food, Sex & God**, a collection of essays.

Claudia Roden was born and raised in Cairo, educated in Paris and then moved to London. Her numerous books include **A Book of Middle Eastern Food** and **The Book of Jewish Food**.

Raphael Samuel was a founding editor of History Workshop Journal. He became Professor of History at the University of East London, where he had begun to establish a Centre for London History before his death in 1996. His many books include **East End Underworld** and **Island Stories**.

Matt Seaton is a freelance writer and journalist. A former racing cyclist, he was married to the late Ruth Picardie and lives in London with their four-year-old twins.

Lore Segal was born in Vienna and evacuated to England on a Kindertransport in late 1938. She lived with a series of English families for seven years before moving to the Dominican Republic. She and her mother were finally admitted to the United States, where she wrote **Other People's Houses** and **Her First American**, in 1951.

Colin Spencer has written a dozen recipe books and lobbied extensively on issues concerning food and the environment. His books include **The Heretic's Feast**, **Homosexuality: A History** and the autobiographical **Which of Us Two?** as well as nine novels and six plays.

Caroline Sullivan was the mistress of a large Jamaican household at the end of the nineteenth century and the author of the first ever book on Caribbean cuisine, **The Jamaica Cookery Book**.

Virginia Woolf, co-founder of the Hogarth Press, is widely recognised as one of the twentieth century's most important writers. Her major novels include **Mrs Dalloway**, **To the Lighthouse**, **The Waves** and **Orlando**. She also wrote two books of feminist polemic and **Flush**, a reconstruction of the life of Elizabeth Barrett Browning's spaniel. She died in 1941.

COPYRIGHT

First Published in 2000 by Booth-Clibborn Editions
12 Percy Street
London W1P 9FB
United Kingdom
info@booth-clibborn.com
www.booth-clibborn-editions.co.uk

New Millennium Experience Company (NMEC) logo © NMEC 1998

ISBN 186154 1457

The information in this book is based on material supplied to Booth-Clibborn Editions Limited. While every effort has been made to ensure its accuracy, Booth-Clibborn Editions Limited do not under any circumstances accept responsibility for any errors or omissions.

Printed and bound in Hong Kong

The publisher gratefully acknowledges permission to reproduce the following copyright works in this book.

Steve Aylett: 'Fiasco' copyright © Steve Aylett 2000.

Paul Bailey: 'A Curious Reader' from **An Immaculate Mistake: Scenes from Childhood and Beyond**, Penguin 1991. Copyright © Paul Bailey 1990. Reprinted in the UK by permission of the author c/o Rogers, Coleridge & White Ltd, 20 Powis Mews, London W11 1JN and in the USA by permission of Dutton, a division of Penguin Putnam Inc.

J. G. Ballard: 'Critical Mass' from **High Rise**, Jonathan Cape 1975. Copyright © J.G. Ballard 1975. All rights reserved. Reprinted by permission of the author c/o Margaret Hanbury, 27 Walcot Square, London SE11 4UB.

John Bayley: extracts from **Iris: A Memoir of Iris Murdoch**, Duckworth 1998. Copyright © John Bayley 1999. Reprinted in the UK by permission of Gerald Duckworth & Co. Ltd and in the USA by permission of St. Martin's Press LLC.

Margaret Busby: 'Memorial to a Migrant' copyright © Margaret Busby 2000.

Simon Callow: extract from **Love Is Where It Falls**, Nick Hern Books 1999. Copyright © Simon Callow 1999.

Bruce Chatwin: extract from **In Patagonia**, Jonathan Cape 1977. Copyright © Bruce Chatwin 1977. Reprinted in the USA and Canada by permission of Gillon Aitken Associates Ltd.

Nik Cohn: extract from **Yes We Have No**, Secker & Warburg 1999. Copyright © Nik Cohn 1999. Reprinted by permission of the author c/o Rogers, Coleridge & White Ltd, 20 Powis Mews, London W11 1JN .

Nicholas Crane: extract from **Two Degrees West: A Walk along England's Meridian**, Viking 1999. Copyright © Nicholas Crane 1999. Reprinted in the UK by permission of Penguin Books Ltd and in the USA by permission of A.P. Watt Ltd on behalf of Nicholas Crane.

Michael Crawford and David Marsh: extract from **The Driving Force: Food, Evolution and the Future**, William Heinemann 1989. Copyright © Michael Crawford and David Marsh 1989. Now published as **Nutrition and Evolution**, Keats 1995.

Richard Dawkins: extract from **Climbing Mount Improbable**, Viking 1996. Copyright © Richard Dawkins 1996.

Norman Douglas: 'Purée of Game' and 'Langouste à l'Americaine', from **Venus in the Kitchen**, William Heinemann, 1952. Reprinted by permission of The Society of Authors as the literary representative of the Estate of Norman Douglas.

Carol Ann Duffy: 'To the Unknown Lover' from **The Pamphlet**, Anvil Press Poetry 1998. Copyright © Carol Ann Duffy 1998.

Fat Les: lyrics from the song 'Vindaloo', written by Fat Les appear by kind permission, published by Peter Barnes @ Rock Music Ltd/EMI/Copyright Control. Copyright © Telstar Records Ltd 1998.

Germaine Greer: extract from **The Female Eunuch**. Copyright © Germaine Greer 1970. Reprinted by permission of Gillon Aitken Associates Ltd.

Jane Grigson: 'Carrots' from **Jane Grigson's Vegetable Book**, Penguin 1980. Copyright © Jane Grigson 1980.

Robert Harris: extracts from **Enigma**, Hutchinson 1995. Copyright © Robert Harris 1996. Reprinted in the USA by permission of Random House, Inc.

Seamus Heaney: 'Omphalos' from **Preoccupations: Selected Prose 1968-1978**, Faber and Faber 1980. Copyright © Seamus Heaney 1980. Reprinted in the USA by permission of Farrar, Strauss and Giroux, LLC.

Eric Hobsbawm: extract from **The Age of Empire 1875-1914**, Wiedenfeld & Nicolson 1987. Copyright © Eric Hobsbawm 1987.

Eric Hobsbawm: extract from **Age of Extremes: The Short Twentieth Century, 1914-1991**, Michael Joseph 1994. Copyright © Eric Hobsbawm 1994.

Kazuo Ishiguro: extract from **The Remains of the Day**, Faber and Faber 1989. Copyright © Kazuo Ishiguro 1989. Reprinted in the USA by permission of Alfred A. Knopf Inc.

C.L.R. James: **Beyond a Boundary**, Hutchinson 1963. Copyright © 1963 by the Executor to the Estate of C.L.R. James. All rights reserved. Reprinted in the USA by permission of Duke University Press.

ACKNOWLEDGEMENTS

Derek Jarman: extracts from **Derek Jarman's Garden**, Thames and Hudson 1995. Copyright © Derek Jarman 1995.

Victor Kiernan: 'A Coat of Many Colours' copyright © 2000 by Victor Kiernan.

Hanif Kureishi: 'My Son the Fanatic' from **Love in a Blue Time**, Faber and Faber 1997. Copyright © Hanif Kureishi 1997. Reprinted in the UK by permission of the author c/o Rogers, Coleridge & White Ltd, 20 Powis Mews, London W11 1JN and in the USA by permission of Scribner, a Division of Simon & Schuster, Inc.

Sarah LeFanu: 'Quail', first published in **New Writing 5**, edited by Christopher Hope and Peter Porter, Vintage 1996. Copyright © Sarah LeFanu 1996.

Rachel Lichtenstein: extracts from **Rodinsky's Room**, Granta 1999. Copyright © Rachel Lichtenstein 1999.

Peter Medawar: extract from 'Science and the Sanctity of Life' from **The Hope of Progress**, Methuen 1972. Copyright © Peter Medawar 1972.

Timothy Mo: 'Combinations', first published as part of 'Fighting for their Writing: The Unholy Lingo of RLS and Kung Fu Tse', in **New Writing 5**, edited by Christopher Hope and Peter Porter, Vintage 1996. Copyright © Timothy Mo 1996.

George Orwell: extract from 'The Lion and the Unicorn' 1996. Copyright © George Orwell 1941, from **The Complete Works of George Orwell**, Secker & Warburg 1998. Reprinted in the UK by permission of A. M. Heath & Co. Ltd on behalf of Mark Hamilton as the literary Executor of the Estate of the late Sonia Brownell Orwell and Martin Secker & Warburg Ltd and in the USA by permission of Brownell Orwell and renewed 1996 by Mark Hamilton.

Anthony Powell: extract fom **A Question of Upbringing**, William Heinemann 1951. Copyright © Anthony Powell 1951.

Michèle Roberts: 'The Earth Moves' copyright © Michele Roberts 2000.

Claudia Roden: extract from **The Book of Jewish Food: An Odyssey from Samarkand and Vilna to the Present Day**, Viking 1997. Copyright © Claudia Roden 1997.

Raphael Samuel: 'Heritage Baiting' from **Theatres of Memory**, London/New York: Verso 1994. Copyright © Raphael Samuel 1994.

Matt Seaton: **After Words**. First published in **The Observer**, October 1997, and republished in an extended version in Ruth Picardie, **Before I Say Goodbye**, Penguin 1998. Copyright © Matt Seaton 1997.

Lore Segal: extracts from **Other People's Houses**, The New Press 1994. Copyright © Lore Segal 1994. Reprinted by permission of the New Press.

Colin Spencer: extract from **The Heretic's Feast: A History of Vegetarianism**, Fourth Estate, 1993. Copyright © Colin Spencer 1993.

Caroline Sullivan: 'Salt Fish' from **Classic Jamaican Cooking: Traditional Recipes and Herbal Remedies** (first published as **The Jamaica Cookery Book**, 1893). Copyright © Serif 1996. Reprinted by permission of the publisher.

Virginia Woolf: extract from **A Room of One's Own**. Reprinted in the UK by permission of The Society of Authors as the literary representative of the Estate of Virginia Woolf and in the USA by permission of Harcourt, Inc. publisher. USA Copyright © 1929 by Harcourt, Inc and renewed 1957 by Leonard Woolf.

All quotations on pages 16, 66, 98, 118, 156, 204, 236 and 276 are taken from The Oxford Dictionary of Twentieth Century Quotations and The Penguin Dictionary of Twentieth Century Quotations.

The information contained within the maps on pages 281-289 copyright © 1999 National Geographic Society, Washington, D.C.

ACKNOWLEDGEMENTS

The publisher gratefully acknowledges permission to reproduce the following copyright illustrations.

pp 6-13 courtesy of PhotoDisc

pp 16-17 Tomoko Yoneda 2000

pp 20-21, 23-25 courtesy of PhotoDisc

p 28 Tomoko Yoneda 2000

p 29 courtesy of PhotoDisc

p 36 Jason Beard 2000

p 51 courtesy of PhotoDisc

pp 54-65 Six children's drawings from Terezin, from the collection of The Jewish Museum In Prague © by permission of the museum: No.129.400 by Edita Pollaková; No.131.996 by Rudolf Laub; No.133.502 by Josef Novák; No.129.181 by Jiří Metzl; No.121.976 by Erika Taussigová; No.124.736 by Ilona Weissová

pp 66-67 Tomoko Yoneda 2000

p 68 courtesy of PhotoDisc

pp 71-74 courtesy of PhotoDisc

p 76 courtesy of M. Plant 2000

pp 77-79 courtesy of PhotoDisc

p 81 Illustration by Jim Padgett, published in 'Bible Readings for the Home', by the Review and Herald Publishing Association 1914; illustrations copyright © 1963 by the Southern Publishing Association

pp 82-83, 85 Howard Sooley

pp 86-87 courtesy of PhotoDisc

pp 92-97 courtesy of PhotoDisc

pp 98-99 Tomoko Yoneda 2000

p 106 courtesy of PhotoDisc

pp 108-111 courtesy of PhotoDisc

pp 118-119 Tomoko Yoneda 2000

pp 120-121 courtesy of PhotoDisc

pp 122-137 courtesy of PhotoDisc

pp 139-142 Graphics from Handbook of Pictorial Symbols, © 1976 by Dover Publications, Inc.

p 144-152 courtesy of PhotoDisc

p 153 courtesy of PhotoDisc

pp 156-157 Tomoko Yoneda 2000

pp 168-170 Russell Wheelhouse 2000

pp 172-173, 175, 176, 182-6 First Aid Line Drawings by John Harold, © 1978 William Collins Sons and Co Ltd, published in 'HELP! First Aid for Everyday Living', William Collins Sons and Co Ltd

pp 173-175, 177, 181, 189 courtesy of PhotoDisc

pp 190-191 courtesy of PhotoDisk

pp 192-195 Stephen Gill 2000

pp 202-203 courtesy of Mark Gilmore 2000

pp 204-205 Tomoko Yoneda 2000

pp 206-211 courtesy of PhotoDisc

pp 212-213 Jason Beard 2000

pp 214, 223 Russell Wheelhouse 2000

pp 234-235 Loot, 24th August 1999

pp 236-237 Tomoko Yoneda 2000

pp 243-255 Tomoko Yoneda 2000

p 263 courtesy Rachel Lichenstein

p 264 courtesy of PhotoDisc

pp 274-275 Tomoko Yoneda 2000

pp 276-289 Maps © courtesy of RH Publications Ltd

p 288 courtesy of PhotoDisc

PHOTO CREDITS

"there is no terror in a bang, only in the anticipation of it."

alfred hitchcock

"time has too much credit…it is not a great healer. it is an indifferent and perfunctory one. sometimes it does not heal at all. and sometimes when it seems to, no healing has been necessary."

ivy compton-burnett

"if we could all live a thousand years… we would each, at least once during that period, be considered a genius. not because of our great age, but because one of our gifts or aptitudes, however slight in itself, would coincide with what people at that particular moment took to be a mark of genius."

john berger

this bloody tyrants

COUNTRIES WHICH HAVE McDONALD'S RESTAURANTS

A Coat of Many Colours
Victor Kiernan

Time can be counted as one of the things that make the whole world kin; there is no escaping from it for mortal men.

Immortality has been the grand privilege of their gods: Homer's dwellers on Olympus are *athanatoi*, deathless. They seem little conscious as a rule of the passage of time. Similarly their successor:

A thousand ages in Thy sight

Are like an evening gone,

the Christian sings to his deity. For men it was the coming of the clock that brought them face to face with Time, never before seen without disguise. An early seventeenth-century clock was flanked with images of Time as a crowned monarch, and the motto *Tempus Rerum Imperator* – Time, Lord of all Things.

A guide at the Ulster Folk Museum remarked to a visiting group that about 1900 American clocks were finding their way into local farmhouse and cottage and transforming their sense of time. Reactions have always been various. It is a surprise that Napoleon, with all his unbounded activities, did not carry a watch habitually, and when he had one might fling it on the floor in a rage. A more respectful attitude has been shown this year by the purchase of a choice 1939 watch for £1,400,000. Only laborious Europe took time seriously enough to invent the clock, and then the watch, a gain for the better-off private man, instead of for the public. These inventions gave Europe the lead, but in another sense enslaved it. The watch was a Protestant innovation, as its chronicler David Landes emphasises; it was part of the great economic advance of this millennium, and its individualism.

In spite of all conflicts, there must seem to have been from very early days a sense of humankind as a single, unique species, alone gifted with language, and therefore reason. Here sex, a great divider in many ways, could be an ally. Men might be trying to kill one another, as competitors, but seldom other women. Men and women somehow came together, even in lands like South Africa or the southern United States where races were furthest apart. Religion, once it reached the point of monotheism, could be another universaliser.

But whatever sense of solidarity men have felt, they have seldom found any but the crudest of ways to express it. Egyptian war-chariots rolled northward into Syria, southward into Nubia. But boundaries were fluid and changeable. Alexander's conquests soon broke up; if they did not vanish, it was because his army had carried with it Greek knowledge and culture, which the higher classes were eager to adopt. Brute force has not been the sole empire-builder. Eventually the fragments could be absorbed into the Roman empire, and helped to make it a Greek-and-Latin civilisation. It was within this shell or cradle, as St Augustine saw so clearly, that Christianity was able to grow, sometimes persecuted but more often tolerated, and eventually admitted to a sort of partnership. Finally it took the place of the old worn-out state religion. By contrast with its many rivals, it stood out by its unbounded aspiration to cast its fishing-net over all mankind, and bring it under a single heavenly throne.

For ordinary consciousness Time may be said to swirl about the mind, rather than to flow steadily through it. In India *kal* means yesterday or tomorrow, 24 hours in any direction from now. *Olim* in Latin might mean some indeterminate time in the past or the future, any time but now.

Hast-o-bud, the Persian 'is and was', means the whole past. In English 'I am going to London' may mean 'I intend to go there next week.' Meditating in Mexico on the 'extraordinary preoccupation with time' of the ancient Maya culture, Aldous Huxley felt that, 'The endless continuity of time is appalling,' and must have compelled men to seek ways of cutting up the flux into less frightening units. In some lands there was much making of calendars, for the benefit of farmers and also to impress people with the knowledge possessed by priests and rulers, their ability in China for instance to predict eclipses. Rome had a fictitious starting-date, 753 BC, for its own foundation. In 17 BC its first emperor Augustus revived the Etruscan festival said to have been held every 115 years, and employed the poet Horace to compose a choral song. The ode has survived, all else has vanished. But we still call one month by Augustus's name, another by that of his grand-uncle Julius Caesar. Like their effigies on coins, these titles in the calendar helped to keep their names in the public mind. A deified Sumerian ruler, Shulgi (2095-2048), had hit on the same device.

A date curiously close to that of Augustus's festival was chosen by the new Christian church as the official birthday of Christ, and was to become the world's most widely used milestone. Islam found a similar one. In the Christian scriptures could be found prophecies of a mysterious time when there would be a Second Coming of the Messiah, to establish a reign of righteousness for a thousand years – which meant simply a very long time. Among the believers were what we should call a 'left wing' of fanatics, wanting justice and equality for all without too much waiting. A prolonged struggle was needed to suppress these 'Montanists'. During the Reformation some of their ideas revived, and in England were championed by the Fifth Monarchy sect. Cromwell found it a nuisance; its rising in 1661, after the Restoration, brought its death-blow. Isaac Newton and Charles Wesley were later, more peaceable, sympathisers.

In the fifth century AD the Roman empire in the west collapsed, under both external and internal pressures. Yet somehow the Roman name and fame survived the Dark Ages, whereas Babylon and Assyria had disappeared, and the old Egypt was obliterated by Arab conquest; their grandeur was left to be dug out of the sands by wise men from the West. They had left no thoughts behind them in men's minds; strangely, their successor Alexander is still a folk-hero of the Muslim world and its poetry. Rome had bequeathed far more to later ages; one gift was the name 'Europe', borrowed from an improper Greek myth about a maiden seduced by Jupiter in the guise of a bull.

In Rome on Christmas Day, 800, the Frankish king and conqueror Charlemagne inaugurated what was to be the Holy Roman Empire, and to last for just a millennium before being put an end to by Napoleon. Though mainly Germanic, it was to be acknowledged as in some way representative of the western Europe where Latin Christianity was

we love:

eastern orthodox

sunni muslim

protestant

other christian

shia muslim

buddhist and shintoist

roman catholic

hindu

theravada buddhist

indigenous

sikh

jewish

mahayana buddhist, confucianist, taoist

distribution of religions worldwide

professed. To be elected as emperor was recognised as Europe's highest dignity; in 1519 the kings of Spain, France and England were in competition for it, with Charles of Spain the winner. Roman emperors had been in some sort divine, but now it was the empire, rather than a ruler, that claimed a heaven-sent mission.

Elsewhere national states were beginning to form and to fight. In 1000 AD, at the chaotic opening of our own millennium, Hungary – an irruption from Asia – became the 'Apostolic' kingdom of St Stephen. Emperor Otto III visited the tomb of Charlemagne at Aix, where two years later he himself was buried. Sylvester II was striving to reform the Church and strengthen the papacy. In France religious excitement, provoked by scaremongers predicting the end of the world, helped to lead to the Crusades. In Normandy the feudal nobility had just been crushing a revolt of their serfs; their grandsons were soon to reduce the peasantry of England to serfdom. But English freemen were already sinking in the social scale. In 991 there was a large-scale invasion by Swein the Dane. On St Brice's day in 1002, November 11, King Ethelred the Unready ordered a massacre of all Danes in the country.

This lugubrious record made a suitable send-off for the second millennium AD, destined to be a time of natural calamities as heavy as the Black Death, and incalculable crime and violence. But if we are to think of it, for convenience, as a long-drawn period with a character of its own, it can only be said that its really persistent feature has been change, increasingly fundamental and in some ways change for the better. In the middle there is a startling acceleration, dividing the millennium into two very distinct halves. In the first, plodding progress was lifting Europe out of near-barbarism. Its common medium, wherever writing was required, was Latin, of a debased but serviceable kind. (In Edinburgh chemistry lectures were still being given in Latin in the late eighteenth century.) With this lingua franca, a common Church and other institutions, Europe was in a way a single realm, or community of peoples, where Helen Waddell's wandering scholars could roam as they liked and drink as much wine as they could get with their ribald songs. In the arts there were beginnings of painting and music of the future, in architecture magnificent success, with skills partly developed by fortress-building. There was a scientific start in physics, to make up for a tediously long effort to twist Greek philosophy into Christian theology.

Underneath all this was a society thoroughly militarised, fighting all kinds of trumpery wars and laying foundations for many still to come. Discontents among the classes which had to bear the burden, and resentment among all classes at a Church growing in wealth and flagging in inspiration, provoked the grand upheaval of the sixteenth and seventeenth centuries, the greatest maybe ever known. From Italy the Renaissance fanned out northward, from Germany the Reformation spread out over northern Europe, to be answered by the Counter-Reformation. A new age was being inaugurated, at a fearful cost in bloodshed and tyranny and witch-burning, which left much of Europe in a protracted state of exhaustion. On the Catholic side there were some hopes, on the other side many fears, of what was talked of as a 'Universal Monarchy'. It would be headed by the two Hapsburg dynasties of Spain, with its vast overseas empire, and Austria. When Spain fell into decline there were fears of French dominance, and nearer to our time of German. One advocate was the Italian Dominican, Tommaso Campanella (1508-?). His reward was to be kept in prison by the Spanish government for 27 years. There he wrote his Utopian *City of the Sun*; he went on to discover a proof of the existence of God.

After the long mêlée there could take shape the often too self-flattering notion of Western (really north-western) Civilisation. Classes in the ascendant in many other corners of the world have cherished similar visions of themselves, like the Brahmins, those demigods in human form, or the Chinese mandarinate, or today the American plutocracy. They have always felt themselves fittest to enjoy the best of whatever the planet has to offer. In the West there was at the same time a stronger growth of nationalism. Britons and Frenchman might fight tooth and nail for possession of West Indian islands and their slave plantations, but nearer home, if properly educated, they could greet one another as gentlemen should.

A miniature picture of this society and its outlook can be found in the *Spectator*, the series of essays (1711-14) mostly by Addison and Steele, intended to show readers what true civilisation meant, and what blemishes were still disfiguring its progress in England. The picture may be compared with that of the cosy court circles of Heian Japan in the tenth century, as recorded in the memoirs of that mistress of taste and elegance Sei Shonagon, when every many of polish could read and write Chinese poems, while ladies wrote Japanese novels. This blossoming however was leading only towards social collapse, whereas the *Spectator* was, in its own fashion, pointing forward: its writers were reformers, holding up better standards of manners and morals. They saw much folly and vice around them, but were confident that Reason, the presiding spirit of the new age, was powerful enough to subdue all this and, as time went on, to carry its sway further and further afield.

Reason might have been laughing at them in its sleeve as it watched them burdening themselves with that silliest of fopperies, the wig, at its zenith in their time. Wigs have been found on some Egyptian mummies; they were helped to a new lease of life by that all-powerful sponsor Louis XIV, the 'Grand Monarch'. A small man in want of elevation, he wore the largest size, and also high heels. Men had to shave their heads to make room for them, and must have looked a fright in bed with blushing brides. Dr Johnson, who read all night in bed, kept his second-best wig on; it was always catching fire from his candle. Some well-off families sent their sons to school in wigs. Anything was worthwhile if it served to mark off the gentry from the lower orders. It took nothing less than the French Revolution to sweep wigs at last away.

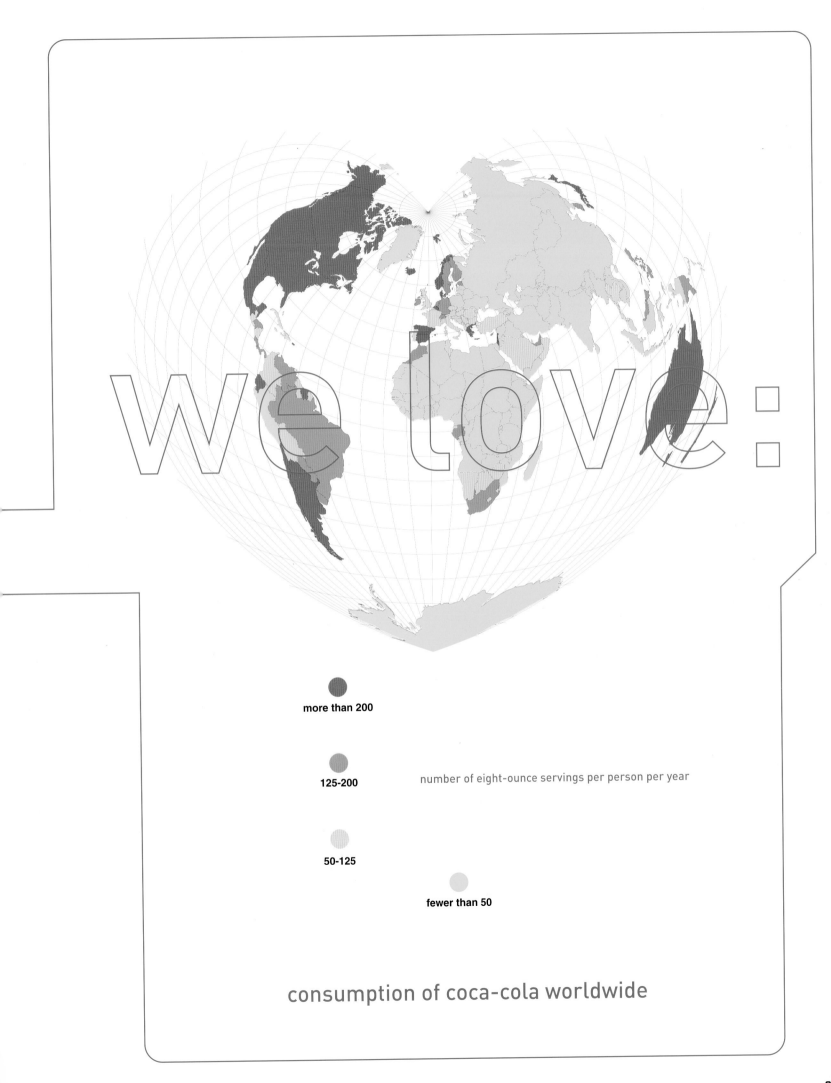

we love:

more than 200

125-200

number of eight-ounce servings per person per year

50-125

fewer than 50

consumption of coca-cola worldwide

1960s

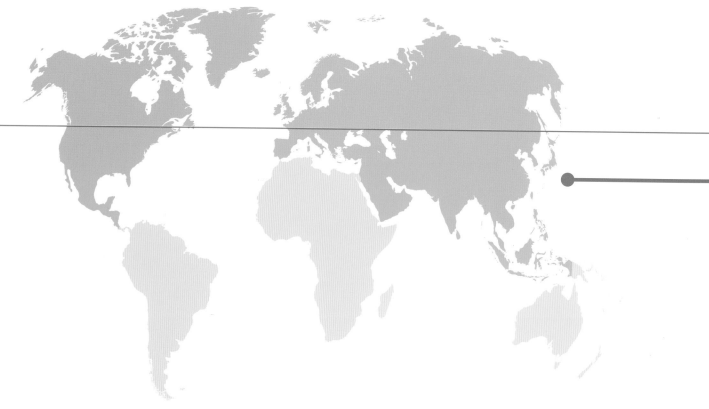

With all its high-principled claims, this born-again West kept exploding into wars, to say nothing of its chronic aggression against the world outside. In terms of factual knowledge and mechanical power, there has been an immeasurable advance. In moral, or even political terms, any improvement has been very uneven. Our own closing century has seen more savagery than any before it. We have earned no right to assume that man's vicious instincts have anywhere been or ever can be exorcised. National spirit has been hopelessly discredited by the two world wars. These have been the most dramatic display of how a whole world can be drawn into one arena. Europe's shuffling in the last few years towards a blend of military and economic combination has been very much less striking. Any great new departure must have some grand ideal to give it life, some hopeful plan for human betterment. After 1918 there was the vision of socialism, but the forces of obstruction banded together to smother it. There is a Green flag now in place of the Red flag; but most Europeans have scarcely got beyond a groping, uncertain half-trust in the continuing prosperity and supposed good will of capitalism.

Inventors and engineers have been putting more and more effort into improved communications; most of them unnecessary, for all one can see, except for the managers of war and its half-brother finance. Singapore has turned itself into a more than up-to-date state by making itself, or being made by an autocrat, a world centre of communications. All this seems to have reached the summit with the advent of the Web, or Cybernet, a synthetic substitute for human solidarity. Magically the Net will gather up together all mankind's roars or whispers. Life has been turned by the Westerners into a gambling-den, the great Indian poet Iqbal wrote half a century ago. A message received a hundredth of a second earlier may mean a large increment of profit, it appears. Lower down the ladder are budding talents like those of the student examinees who have been able this summer, we are told, to hand in identical essays on subjects they have not bothered to study.

Today our dictionaries enable us to talk – barbarously enough – of globalisation, conglomerates and so on, signifying a pushing and shoving of human beings, on the greatest possible scale. They all come from the Latin *globus*, a ball, and may remind us of Chaplin's floating globe in *The Great Dictator* or possibly of Dr Johnson's belief in the 'conglobulation of swallows' – the notion of swallows in autumn forming into a dense ball and throwing themselves into a river, to hibernate on its bed. We creatures may best be thought of as 'conglutinated', stuck together as if with glue: the word calls up a nightmare of earth's multiplying population, squeezed shoulder to shoulder, scarcely able to breathe, like passengers shoved by main force into a Japanese train – all the male sort wearing the same Western clothes.

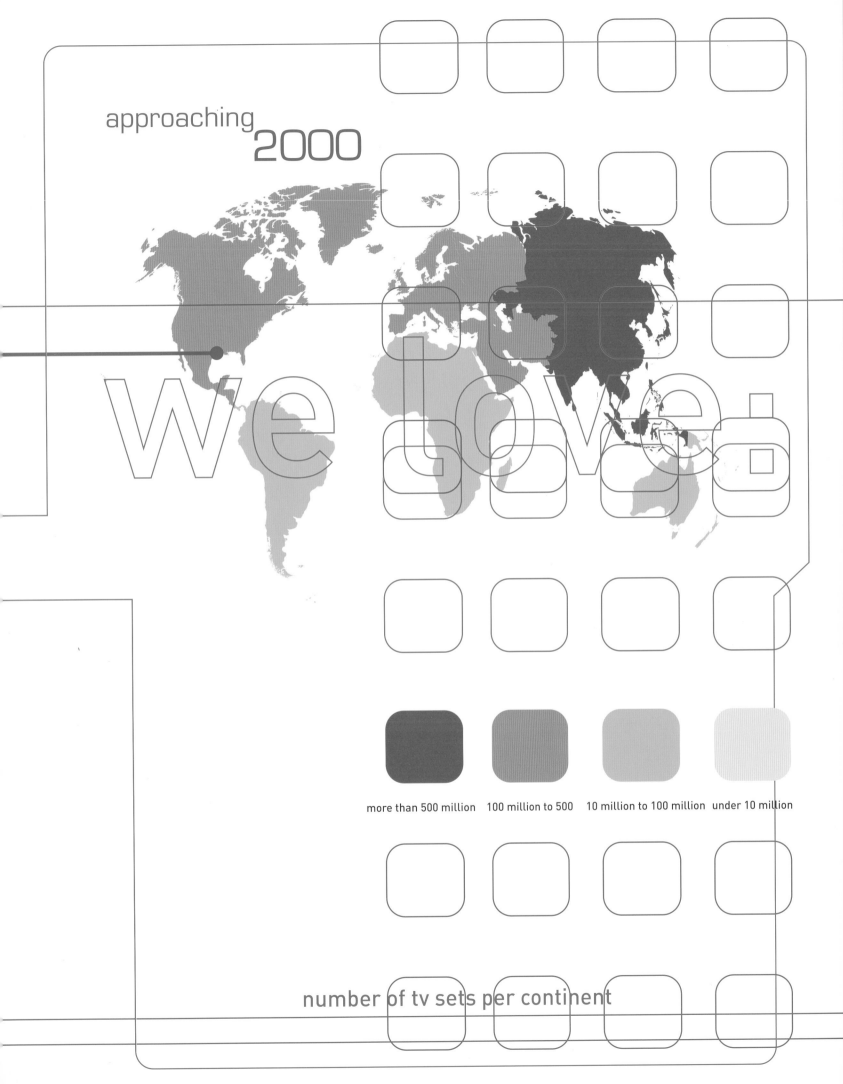

approaching
2000

we love a

more than 500 million   100 million to 500   10 million to 100 million   under 10 million

number of tv sets per continent

Lately there have been signs of a reviving admiration for Rome, as the grand dominator or pacifier, the law-maker and protector. There has even been some returning appreciation of Latin, partly as the key to all Rome's daughter languages, and an improved understanding of how Rome won its longevity. Besides a well organised standing army, there were some charities for the urban proletariat, and the baths, and above all the Arena, where prisoners, gladiators, and wild beasts were made to pour out one another's blood. Few countries have hit on any equivalents. Sir Thomas Wade, English minister at Peking in the later nineteenth century, commented on the government's nervousness about any 'conglomeration of multitudes, be it for work or play'. Today however the art of tactful soothing and amusing has come to be a chief part of political science. We have no arenas, except for Spanish bullfights, but we have films full of horrors, and novels about vices of every kind, far out-stripping the 'shilling shockers' of a generation or two ago. Games and tournaments play a better part than those of antiquity. Not much room is left for 'culture'. Painting has declined into the abstract, music into pop. Even in 'quality' newspapers and magazines a surprising number of column inches are devoted to sex, clothing or its removal, food and drink, and of course games. Life is being trivialised; serious things are getting too serious for us; astrologers and religious quacks multiply.

There is an O. Henry story of a century ago about an American father objecting to his daughter marrying a mere millionaire; his son-in-law must be a 'man of real substance'. Nowadays more and more billionaires are elbowing their way to the front, natural rulers or 'leaders' for coming times. In the West class incomes have been moving further apart, in Britain particularly. This may prove a hazardous starting point for our next millennium, especially with the menace of world population growth out of control. The Pope has been repeating his clarion-call to mankind to increase and multiply; even the British government has jibbed at this. There are rumours of a rapprochement between Rome and Mecca on this issue; the transparent motive of both is to swell the number of adherents, now that new converts are harder to find outside Africa.

From near the birth of our race men have been able to compel or persuade women, with the aid of religion, to submit to their rule. But the coercive strength of religion, in Europe at least, is no longer what it was, even in its old strongholds. Protestant Britain and Catholic France have been the countries longest exposed to the rude breath of secularism. Heinz Zahrnt's book on Karl Barth and Lutheranism since the wars shows official theology being dismantled brick by brick. Only 'liberation theology', directed towards social emancipation, has offered a valid substitute. How this situation will react in the long run on social psychology can only be guessed at. An incomprehensible world, left with no heavenly custodian, must be turning many to fix their eyes for relief on small things with little meaning, such as a football club's choice of a goalkeeper, or the American public's of a president. Others are turning inward in search of therapies like Freud's, or any of countless less reputable ones, all offering relief for the vertigo our millennium has been dropping into. Better advice can be heard from Shakespeare's doctor: 'Therein the patient must minister to himself.'

we love:

microsoft offices worldwide

In bygone days wise and foolish could join in the search for ways to foresee and forestall the future. Now when we know that all such conjuring-tricks are silly, interest has been turned to exploration of the past, partly as a base on which broad, rational conjectures about things to come can be framed. Historical searchings may have begun to expand comprehension. Still, however deep we dig, much of history will always be a Great Unknown, a counterpart to our mystery-shrouded future. Historians are beginning to take an interest in its 'might-have-beens', questions of a sort that examiners not long since were forbidden to ask. G.M. Trevelyan was a pioneer with his essay on how history would have gone if Napoleon had won at Waterloo.

Shakespeare with some prompting from Scripture could guess at an earth some day disintegrating and fading away. In a sense it, or its old familiar image, has already done so; science has reduced it in our century to a vortex of smaller and smaller particles. This is not altogether a novel way of perceiving it. Very widely in the East it has been thought of as illusion, unreality, dream, which the wise man should learn to see through, not mistake for a genuine dwelling-place. Scepticism like this dawned in India, and was scattered over much of further Asia by

Buddhism. Unlike some Greek philosophy, Christianity did not deny the solid substance of our earth, but did for long deny it any worth or meaning. It was something to be thrown off. Again parallels may be found in our own ranks. Our feeling for life, our loves and hates sprout too much from novelettes and shadow-plays on screens and superficial acquaintances, too little from real experience, to make up a firm edifice.

We may be able now to communicate with any corner of our globe, but by comparison it has been dwindling to a tiny globule, and enthusiastic communicators are groping for contact with worlds billions of miles away. Christians carried their message of salvation across the oceans, we have daydreams of astronauts carrying our gospel of interglobal friendship over the deeps of space. It has been disconcerting to learn that the universe is flying apart, running away from us. As a brake on this we can only hope to find invisible forms of matter able to reinforce the gravitational pull and hold things together. Just now all eyes are on the neutrino, a particle infinitesimally small but infinitely plentiful, which could, we have been told of late, pass through six trillion miles of solid lead without blinking. It may or may not be endowed with mass, or

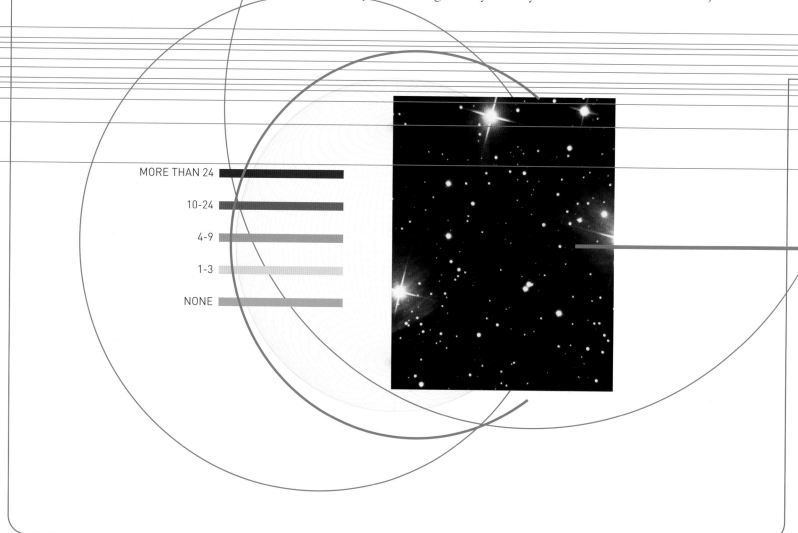

MORE THAN 24

10-24

4-9

1-3

NONE

weight: if it has any, the total addition may enable the universe to contract instead of expand.

To the plain man the advantage to us may not be obvious. Yet such recondite calculations can be curiously fascinating. They add to what our millennium can safely say for itself, that it has produced vastly more scientific discovery, and more artistic wonders, than any earlier epoch. Yet there has been enormous expenditure of energy and resources in many wasteful directions, including the mammoth futilities of war, and in our own concluding century above all. The human race may have been born too over-intelligent to be quite sane.

Twenty years ago my barber, a very serious man, was convinced that mankind had only five years left: it had grown so degenerate that youths were refusing to learn to sharpen scissors and razors, and God could not be expected to put up with this laziness much longer. There are many graver sins, and it is not unthinkable that Fate may take God's place and decide on summary punishment. At any rate, our millennium began with a plethora of saints and miracles, and is ending with a treasury of bombs in the custody of governments thirsty for yet more and 'smarter' weapons.

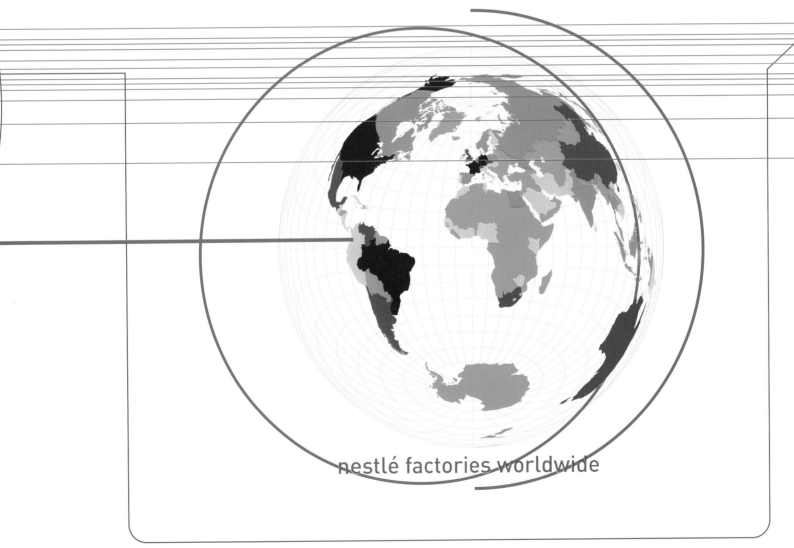

nestlé factories worldwide

00:01
00:02
00:03
00:04
00:05

"The men at work at the corner of the street had made a kind of camp for themselves,

00:06	where, marked out by tripods	00:40	the bright coals of the fire,
00:07		00:41	
00:08	hung with red hurricane-lamps,	00:42	causing flames to leap fiercely
00:09	an abyss in the road led down	00:43	upward, smoke curling about
00:10		00:44	
00:11	to a network of subterranean	00:45	in eddies of the north-east wind.
00:12	drain-pipes. Gathered round the	00:46	As the dark fumes floated above
00:13		00:47	
00:14	bucket of coke that burned in	00:48	the houses, snow began to fall
00:15	front of the shelter, several	00:49	gently from a dull sky, each
00:16		00:50	
00:17	figures were swinging arms	00:51	flake giving a small hiss as
00:18	against bodies and rubbing hands	00:52	it reached the bucket. The
00:19		00:53	
00:20	together with large, pantomimic	00:54	flames died down again; and
00:21	gestures: like comedians giving	00:55	the men, as if required
00:22		00:56	
00:23	formal expression to the concept	00:57	observances were for the
00:24	of extreme cold. One of them, a	00:58	moment at an end, all turned
00:25		00:59	
00:26	spare fellow in blue overalls,	01:00	away from the fire, lowering
00:27	taller than the rest, with a	01:01	themselves laboriously into
00:28		01:02	
00:29	jocular demeanour and long,	01:03	the pit, or withdrawing to
00:30	pointed nose like that of a	01:04	the shadows of their tarpaulin
00:31		01:05	
00:32	Shakespearian clown, suddenly	01:06	shelter. The grey, undecided
00:33	stepped forward, and as if	01:07	flakes continued to come down,
00:34		01:08	
00:35	performing a rite, cast some	01:09	though not heavily, while a harsh
00:36	substance – apparently the	01:10	odour, bitter and gaseous,
00:37	remains of two kippers, loosely	01:11	penetrated the air. The day
00:38		01:12	
00:39	wrapped in newspaper – on	01:13	was drawing in.

The Music of Time
Anthony Powell

01:13 For some reason, the sight of
01:14
01:15 snow descending on fire always
01:16 makes me think of the ancient
01:17
01:18 world – legionaries in sheepskin
01:19 warming themselves at a brazier:
01:20 mountain altars where offerings
01:21
01:22 glow between wintry pillars;
01:23 centaurs with torches cantering
01:24
01:25 beside a frozen sea – scattered,
01:26 unco-ordinated shapes from
01:27 a fabulous past, infinitely
01:28
01:29 removed from life; and yet

01:30 bringing with them memories
01:31
01:32 of things real and imagined.
01:33 These classical projections,
01:34
01:35 and something in the physical
01:36 attitudes of the men them-
01:37
01:38 selves as they turned from
01:39 the fire, suddenly suggested
01:40 Poussin's scene in which the
01:41
01:42 Seasons, hand in hand and facing
01:43 outward, tread in rhythm to the
01:44
01:45 notes of the lyre that the winged
01:46 and naked greybeard plays.

01:47 The image of Time brought
01:48
01:49 thoughts of mortality: of human
01:50 beings, facing outward like the
01:51 Seasons, moving hand in hand in
01:52
01:53 intricate measure: stepping slowly,
01:54 methodically, sometimes a trifle
01:55 awkwardly, in evolutions that
01:56
01:57 take recognisable shape:

01:58 or breaking into seemingly
01:59
02:00 meaningless gyrations, while
02:01 partners disappear only to
02:02
02:03 reappear again, once more giving
02:04 pattern to the spectacle:
02:05 unable to control the melody,
02:06
02:07 unable, perhaps, to control

02:08 the steps of the dance.
02:09
02:10 Classical associations made
02:11 me think, too, of days at
02:12
02:13 school, where so many
02:14 forces, hitherto unfamiliar,
02:15 had become in due course
02:16
02:17 uncompromisingly clear.